D0897696

Racism in U.S. Imperialism

Racism

in U.S. Imperialism

THE INFLUENCE OF RACIAL ASSUMPTIONS ON
AMERICAN FOREIGN POLICY, 1893–1946

Rubin Francis Weston

UNIVERSITY OF SOUTH CAROLINA PRESS *Columbia, South Carolina*

Contents

v

Foreword

When Dr. Rubin Weston asked me to write a foreword for his book, I felt both pleased and honored. To explain why, I beg the reader's indulgence for a bit of personal reminiscence.

Rubin Weston and Melvin Banks were the first black men whom I came to know really well. By origin I am a small-town New Englander. Like many other Yankees, I grew up generously endowed with an abstract belief in racial equality but almost devoid of personal relationships with black people. In the earlier years of my teaching I had a few Negro students, but only in large lecture courses. With Rubin and Melvin the situation was altogether different. By coincidence they appeared in the same graduate seminar that I was teaching at Syracuse University. What they learned from me I will not venture to say, but what I learned from them was extremely valuable. Fortunately for me, they were both friendly and articulate men, and in the give and take of discussion within a small group we exchanged ideas frankly and earnestly about the whole problem of race relations. I learned how black people felt about other black people and how they felt about white people. Not that they all felt alike on such matters. Indeed, I was soon warned against rash generalizations that ascribed to all Negroes the same characteristics and the same attitudes. Rubin and Melvin were both witty fellows, but even this delightful sense of humor, I soon learned, was not so much a racial endowment as a protective device that black people had developed to make their lives bearable.

Both men earned their doctorates and returned to their teaching posts in Negro colleges. Happily, however, we kept in touch with each other. What began as a teacher's relationship to his students continued as a set of cherished friendships. Indeed, Rubin still had a major contribution to make to my education. He invited me to lecture in his college, and for some twenty hours I learned what it was like to be the one visible white man in a black community. Rubin's fine wife and children, his students, and his fellow professors all treated me with great friendliness and courtesy. But once again there

ix

were no holds barred in the intellectual wrestling. Before the visit was over I had learned many things that helped me understand the deeper implications of the Negro freedom movement.

Not least among the things I have learned from Rubin Weston are the insights contained in this book. This is a revision of the doctoral dissertation that he wrote under my direction. He and I shared the familiar anguish of searching for a worthwhile topic for his doctoral research. For his master's thesis at North Carolina College of Durham he had written on the American intervention in Haiti, and he proposed enlarging upon this for his dissertation. I felt that this was not very promising because so much had already been written on the subject, at least in its diplomatic and military aspects. I was interested, however, in Rubin's discovery that the National Association for the Advancement of Colored People and W. E. B. Du Bois as an individual had vigorously opposed the intervention. This suggested that the black reaction to the Haiti business might be worth exploring in greater depth. But Rubin's preliminary research soon turned in quite a different direction. The intervention in Haiti was, after all, only one episode in a long cycle of events that saw the United States raise its flag over Hawaii, the Philippines, and Puerto Rico and send its armed forces, temporarily at least, into another half-dozen countries in the Caribbean and the Pacific. In each of these places the inhabitants were largely nonwhite, and the issue of race relations was somehow involved in the situation. What American politicians and publicists thought about race proved to be one of the critical factors in the whole controversy about whether the United States should acquire overseas territories. Rubin found a very challenging dissertation topic in the analysis of these arguments.

History always runs the risk of becoming too compartmentalized. The history of American imperialism has been the concern of diplomatic historians; the history of American race relations that of political and social historians. What tends to get lost is the close relationship between the two, and it is here that Dr. Weston makes his contribution. In the light of his findings, it becomes not a coincidence, but highly significant that the age of American imperialism overlapped what one historian called the nadir of black history. Ironically, most of the imperialists and most of the anti-imperialists shared identical assumptions about the superior intelligence and virtue of

Anglo-Saxons. To the imperialists, these racial assumptions inspired a pious commitment to "take up the White Man's burden"; yet the anti-imperialists used the same assumptions to argue that it was unwise to bring more black, brown, and yellow men under American rule. I learned a great deal from Dr. Weston's study and am very glad that the publication of this book will make his findings available to other historians and the general public.

One final comment should be made. In a narrow sense, this is not black history. It is, for the most part, a book about white people, written on the basis of white sources. Yet it seems to me a singularly appropriate study for a black scholar to make. From his own experience, the black man learns to penetrate the white man's hypocrisies —to see how his appeals to God, the flag, and the Constitution often serve as a cloak for racial prejudice and self-righteousness. Dr. Weston's study is, therefore, highly relevant to our present situation in which the nation must formulate appropriate policies toward Southeast Asia, toward the new nations of Africa, toward the restless countries of the Caribbean and South America, and toward the minorities in our own country.

I congratulate the University of South Carolina Press on its decision to publish this honest and dispassionate study in racial attitudes.

Syracuse University   NELSON M. BLAKE
May, 1970

Preface

The United States maintained imperial control over dependent peoples for a shorter time than any other imperialistic country. The lack of vigor of American imperialism was due in part to the opposition to the idea of expanding the Republic to noncontiguous territory, as expressed vigorously in the Congress and other organs of public opinion. Much of the opposition to expansion was related to the question, "Does the Constitution follow the flag?" Those who answered the question in the affirmative were generally opposed to territorial expansion to noncontiguous territory. Those who answered the question negatively were generally in favor of territorial expansion.

Racism created a dilemma for Americans in that expansion without making the Constitution coterminous with the new possessions compromised basic constitutional principles. Rather than compromise these basic principles, some individuals opposed imperialism altogether. But others wanted to avoid extending the Constitution to people supposedly unfit for self-government or to areas supposedly unfit for Anglo-Saxon settlement by creating special extraconstitutional provisions for governing the new possessions. Those who opposed expansion and those who supported expansion agreed that the peoples of the newly acquired territory were incapable of self-government. Race was the common denominator.

Historians agree that American imperialism lacked the tenacity exhibited by other imperialistic countries, but they are not in agreement as to the reasons for this lack of tenacity. Some have suggested that the loss of strategic value in the insular possessions negated the desirability of their retention by the United States. Others hold that these possessions did not contribute to the economic self-sufficiency of the United States. Still others view United States imperialism as a myth. Examination of documents on the relations of the United States to the Hawaiian Islands, the Philippines, Cuba, Puerto Rico, and Hispaniola supports the thesis that racism was high on the list of reasons for the lack of tenacity in American imperialism.

My investigation reveals that deep-rooted attitudes of racial superiority based on experiences with dissimilar peoples in the United States—particularly with Indians, Chinese, Japanese, and Negroes—contributed to the development of assumptions which prescribed a subordinate status for the insular possessions during a period of Americanization. When the insular possessions were deemed incapable of Americanization because of racial dissimilarity, they were released from United States control. The basic policy varied in accordance with prejudgments concerning the capacities and competencies of a possession's inhabitants to rule themselves and help rule Anglo-Saxons.

The United States today is aware of many problems whose origins are deeply rooted in the sociopolitical structure of her society. One problem with far-reaching implications has been the assignation of a role of inferiority to the non-Anglo-Saxon element in the United States. These beliefs, developed as a consequence of relations with these races, influenced America's relations with peoples in its insular possessions and also led to the asserted right of the United States to intervene in the affairs of Latin-American countries during the same period.

In this work I have used the views of white writers, teachers, politicians, statesmen, and publications to show attitudes concerning peoples of color at home and in the insular possessions. The study is based on the idea that Negroes and other minority groups in the United States have been studied in depth as bases for understanding the attitudes of whites toward these minority groups and the resulting problems, but that whites have been neglected as a subject for study. I have endeavored in these pages to show how American racial attitudes were exported to areas that came under the influence of the United States.

I am indebted to many people for aid in completing this book. I am deeply indebted to my advisor and friend Dr. Nelson M. Blake of Syracuse University who had the courage to work with me on a subject of this nature. I am also indebted to the Danforth Foundation for two teacher study grants which allowed me the necessary time to do research and writing.

I must express my appreciation to the library staffs of the following universities, without whose help this research could not have been possible: Syracuse University, Duke University, University of

North Carolina, North Carolina Central University, and also to the New York Public Library, 135th Street Branch, for use of the Schomburg Negro Collection.

To Mrs. Marcella A. Sampson, who was responsible for typing these pages, I owe my most sincere thanks.

Far from the least in importance is my obligation to my wife and children, who through many hours of sacrifice willingly submitted to many inconveniences, always giving encouragement to me so that I might pursue advanced study and research at Syracuse University.

Central State University   RUBIN FRANCIS WESTON
July 1, 1970

Racism in U.S. Imperialism

Introduction

American imperialism, while seemingly patterned on that of Europe, lacked the vigor and persistence exhibited by the European variety. Many arguments were advanced on the merits and demerits of imperialism. Some believed that the Republic should not be extended to areas not suitable for Anglo-Saxon settlement or to areas already inhabited by peoples of inferior races. Others argued that the United States should extend political control to these areas without extending the Constitution. The latter group claimed that the Anglo-Saxon nations had an obligation to civilize "inferior" peoples.

Expansion without making the Constitution coterminous with the new possessions tended to compromise basic constitutional principles. Rather than compromise these basic principles some Americans opposed imperialism completely. Others avoided extending the Constitution to people who were supposedly unfit for self-government by creating special extraconstitutional provisions for governing the new possessions. The following resolution is an example:

That the provisions of the Constitution do not, unaided by act of Congress, extend over Puerto Rico and the Philippine Islands.

That by the recent treaty with Spain the United States takes the sovereignty over Puerto Rico and over the Philippine Islands under the duty to use and exercise it for the general welfare and highest interest of the people of the United States and the inhabitants of the islands, unrestrained by the provisions of the Constitution, and over Cuba under the duty to exercise it for the pacification of the island.

That the successful discharge of this duty demands the establishment of a separate department of government to take charge of all outlying dependencies of the United States and the passage of a general law making appointments there nonpolitical.[1]

[1] *Congressional Record*, 56 Cong., 1 sess., XXXIII, pt. 1: 935 (January 18, 1900).

Both sides generally agreed that the peoples of newly acquired territories like Hawaii were not capable of self-government unless the controlling faction was Anglo-Saxon. This situation raised several questions: (1) Did racial assumptions influence the United States' imperialistic policies during the period 1893–1946? (2) How did racism affect Hawaiian annexation? (3) Did these assumptions affect the United States' Philippine policy? (4) To what extent did racial assumptions affect the intervention in Cuba, Haiti, and the Dominican Republic, as well as United States' relations with Puerto Rico? (5) To what extent did the policy of expansion and the concomitant policy of intervention derive motivation from American racism? (6) In the case of the Philippine Islands, for example, did this portion of a speech, and many another speech like it, delivered in Congress have any influence on subsequent policy?

We are asked to annex to the United States a witch's caldron. . . .

We are not only asked to annex the caldron and make it a part of our great, broad, Christian, Anglo-Saxon, American land, but we are asked also to annex the contents and take this brew—mixed races, Chinese, Japanese, Malay Negritos—anybody who has come along in three hundred years, in all of their concatenations and colors. . . .

This mess of Asiatic pottage, 7,000 miles from the United States, in a land that we can not colonize and can not inhabit, we are told to-day by the fortune of a righteous war waged for liberty, for the ascendancy of the Declaration of Independence, for the gift of freedom to an adjoining State, we must take up and annex and combine with our own blood and with our own people, and consecrate them with the oil of American citizenship.

. . . There has never been such condescension from a high ideal and from a noble and manifest destiny. Not only is it a degradation of this American land and of this American race, but the scholars and thinkers of this country . . . look upon our adoption of these people and our forcible annexation of them as giving the lie to the whole current of American history and repudiating all the great principles of constitutional freedom which we proclaimed at our beginning and which have tended to make us great.

. . . I am startled, I am thrown away from my ordinary bearings and conception of things to think that such gentlemen and such a body should contemplate the adoption of a treaty that utterly scorns and repudiates our position; that is essentially at war with our institutions; that embodies a country which is not part of the American continent and can not be made so, and that must inevitably take up and work into the destiny of the American people these alien races, or must make us get down from the throne of freedom. . . .[2]

(7) In the case of United States' intervention in Haiti, in the light that no foreigners had lost their lives, no Americans were in danger, and there was little threat to the Monroe Doctrine, was the intervention carried out on the assumption that so-called inferior peoples had no rights that Anglo-Saxons were bound to respect?[3]

Succinctly stated, the problems are (1) to what extent racism influenced the official policy in acquiring and governing noncontiguous territory in the Caribbean and the Pacific during this period, and (2) how did American racial assumptions based on domestic racial experience influence the relationship between the United States and its insular possessions?

[2] Speech of John W. Daniels of Virginia, *ibid*, 55 Cong., 3 sess., XXXII, pt. 2: 1430 (February 3, 1899).
[3] *Ibid.*, 71 Cong., 2 sess., LXXII, pt. 1: 286 (December 9, 1929).

Imperialism

T he spirit of colonialism in Europe was quiescent by the early
1870s. This spirit had been characterized by mercantilism—
a system designed to create a strong, self-sufficient economic state to be the natural partner of a strong political
state. The system was not rigidly fixed and had many adaptations
variously practiced by the European nations in their ascendancy.
Some of the basic tenets of mercantilism became the antecedents of
modern imperialism: economic self-sufficiency (the central theme),
colonies to supply raw materials and to serve as guaranteed markets
for finished goods, a favorable balance of trade, industrial and agricultural development, wealth (gold and silver), land and sea commerce, large population, large armies and navies, and absolute
government.[1]

Under the spirit of mercantilism Spain and Portugal wrested economic supremacy from the Hanseatic towns and the Italian city-
states, only to be superseded by France, Holland, and England as
commercial nations. England, by 1763, succeeded in establishing
her mastery over all contenders for commercial empire in North
America. With the close of the Seven Years' War, the vigorous colonialism which had been responsible for the expansion of Europe to
the remote areas of the world began to wane.[2]

Various reasons have been given for the demise of this vigorous
approach to the expansion of Europe, such as the expenses of standing armies and navies needed to protect the far-flung possessions,

[1] Shepard B. Clough and Charles W. Cole, *Economic History of Europe*, pp.
196–97.

[2] T. Walter Wallbank and Alastair M. Taylor, *Civilization Past and Present*,
p. 289.

the administrative expenses, and the inability to work out a system of political control satisfactory to the sponsoring government or to subjects in the far-off possessions.

Statesmen and philosophers found rational arguments to prove that colonies were a liability and not an asset. Turgot rationalized the loss of France's colonies in North America to England by implying that colonies were like fruit; when ripe they severed their connections with the tree. Adam Smith refined the concepts of laissez-faire and published the *Wealth of Nations* in the same year that the North American colonies declared their independence. Other writers showed that England's trade with her former colonies was greater after 1783 than before the independence of the colonies.

Early European colonialism was the pattern and the antecedent of modern imperialism, the consequences of imperialism resulted in wars and politics becoming global in nature. In the last quarter of the nineteenth century there was a resurgence of the spirit of colonialism, conditioned in many instances by the same factors that had previously led to European expansion. However, enough changes had taken place in the nature of government—economic and financial policy, transportation, and communications—to modify the old form into neocolonialism or imperialism.

The European nations reentered the struggle for colonies. They were motivated by nationalistic ambitions which espoused living room, commerce, and mission or destiny. These were some of the old tenets of mercantilism. Some European nations had retained from the previous colonial period remnants of colonial empires on which to build and thus became the chief beneficiaries of the new imperialism. Control of less developed areas was established by various means, but once established, the colonizing power held on tenaciously and erected barriers against interlopers in their spheres of influence reminiscent of the days of the earlier colonialism.[3]

ENTER THE UNITED STATES

Several new nations developed during this period. Japan was opened to Western influence and began to industrialize. Germany

---

[3] Moritz Julius Bonn, "Imperialism," *Encyclopedia of the Social Sciences*, IV (1937), 609–613. See also Louis L. Snyder, *The Imperial Reader*, p. 31. Parker T. Moon, *Imperialism and World Politics*, pp. 8–14.

and Italy became nations and followed the path to wealth and prestige—industrialization. Russia began to look westward for technological knowledge. The United States, as a consequence of the Civil War, became a nation. Each of these new powers began to practice old mercantilist concepts.

Whether these new nations were or were not imperialistic is a debatable question; that they were expansionist cannot be denied. For the most part, the expansion of these states took place through the acquisition of adjacent territory. The United States expanded into contiguous and sparsely settled areas peopled by non-Europeans—areas which were open to further European immigration. Bemis writes, "The continental Republic took shape in the empty spaces of North America without willful aggression against any civilized nation or people, and this is said with due cognizance to the circumstances of the War with Mexico of 1846–1848."[4]

By expanding into contiguous areas, the United States acquired territory at the expense of the indigenous people inhabiting the regions. These people stood between the settlers and the land they desired, a situation which had a far-reaching effect on the character and institutions of the United States. The struggle of the settlers with the Indian left the basic concept, held by the majority of Americans, that the Indian was to be pushed out of the way of progress. Progress was equated with white settlement. The disposal of the Indian was a continual problem for almost three hundred years. The "solution" resulted in the development of a race consciousness which made all Europeans forget their differences and unite against a common enemy, the Indian.

While the new colonialism developed in Europe, the United States rounded out its boundaries. The country was in the process of becoming a great industrial nation. The vast amount of natural resources, the great land mass, "a lack of surplus capital and surplus manufactures," left many of the classic causes for imperialism without foundation in the United States. Yet in the last decade of the nineteenth century America embarked on an imperial adventure.[5]

Motivated not primarily by the desire for territorial or economic gain, but by a sense of mission, the United States took up a share of

[4] Samuel Flagg Bemis, *Latin American Policy of the United States*, p. 385.
[5] Moon, *Imperialism and World Politics*, p. 56.

the "White Man's burden." In seventeen years, from 1898 to 1915, the nation acquired an empire which embraced colonies in the far reaches of the Pacific Ocean and the nearer Caribbean Sea. All of these possessions were acquired, with the exception of Haiti and the Dominican Republic, as a result of or at the time of the Spanish-American War. These possessions were located in the tropics and were inhabited by people whose cultural heritage differed from that of the United States. One author refers to the acquisitions as "America's Negro empire."[6]

Colonies gained in these years were given their independence or were held in such a way that independence or incorporation, conditionally, into the body politic was possible. The whole episode lasted less than fifty years.[7]

NATIONAL UNITY AT THE EXPENSE OF THE NEGRO

After Reconstruction the North and the South became united politically. The outcome of the election of 1876 was a compromise between the industrial capitalists of the North and the leaders of the South. The North took a "hands off" attitude as far as the South's treatment of the Negro was concerned. The South in return gave local and congressional encouragement and protection to Northern investments in the area. Congress then failed to reduce the representatives of states which deprived large numbers of Negro citizens of the franchise by adopting new constitutions.

It was in this atmosphere of national unity that imperialism was born; however, this unity had been achieved at the expense of Negro rights. The Southern point of view on proscription for the Negro was fast becoming the national point of view. It was not unusual in the latter part of the nineteenth century to find in the leading publications of the period "Northern liberals and former abolitionists mouthing the shibboleths of white supremacy regarding the Negro's innate inferiority, shiftlessness, and hopeless unfitness for full participation in the white man's civilization."[8]

In rendering its decision in the Slaughterhouse Cases, the Supreme Court failed to take advantage of the opportunity to nationalize civil

[6] John Hope Franklin, *From Slavery to Freedom*, p. 425.
[7] Bemis, *Latin American Policy*, p. 125.
[8] C. Vann Woodward, *The Strange Career of Jim Crow*, pp. 52–53.

liberty afforded by the North's victory.[9] In this case the "privileges
and immunities" clause was drastically curtailed. Following this
action, the Court rendered the *Plessy* v. *Ferguson* decision, a con-
firmation of the Court's suspected hostility to minority rights. Un-
fortunately the dissent of Justice Harlan was of little value at the
time.[10] The Court ruled that legislation was powerless to change racial
instincts. As a result, the American Negro was relegated to the status
of second-class citizen.[11]

Perhaps the Court was looking to the larger politics of nationalism,
and its action was a part of the reconciliation of the North and the
South at the expense of a dissimilar race. Sectionalism based on race
became a diminishing factor in politics, and all questions of a divisive
nature which could arise were being submerged in a new national
America. The unity which resulted, according to Robert Bingham,
made the country great. Bingham and others held that the country
would become "still greater and still stronger in the degree in which"
the American people "became more and more unitedly animated by
the spirit of national Americans."[12]

It is important to note the degree to which the new nationalism
extended to encompass the thinking and actions of Americans and
the manner in which minority rights were concomitantly compromised by the United States, in the atmosphere of the new nationalism,
as it annexed dissimilar peoples. Senator Warren G. Harding, alluding to the period, said, "The covenant of nationality led to the great
. . . Civil War. There is a strange significance to me in the fact that our
sovereignty in the Philippines was instituted by that . . . American
who first revealed the reconsecration of the South to the concord of
American union. . . ."[13]

In 1908 President-elect William Howard Taft in an address at the
dinner of the North Carolina Society of New York stated:

[9] John W. Burgess, *Reconstruction and the Constitution, 1866–1876*, pp.
vii–ix.
[10] Barton J. Bernstein, "Case Law in Plessy v. Ferguson," *The Journal of Negro
History*, XLVII (July 1962), 192–98.
[11] Woodward, *Strange Career of Jim Crow*, pp. 52–53.
[12] Robert Bingham, "Sectional Misunderstandings," *North American Review*,
CLXXIX (September 1904), 370.
[13] *Congressional Record*, 64 Cong., 1 sess., LIII, pt. 2: 1680 (January 28,
1916).

The fear that in some way or other a social equality between the races shall be enforced by law or brought about by political measures really has no foundation except in the imagination of those who fear such result. The Federal Government has nothing to do with social equality. The war amendments do not declare in favor of social equality. . . .

I come at once to the present conditions of things stated from a constitutional and political standpoint; and that is this: that in all the Southern States it is possible, by election laws prescribing proper qualifications for the suffrage, which square with the Fifteenth Amendment and which shall be equally administered as between black and white races, to prevent entirely the possibility of a domination of Southern state, county, or municipal governments by an ignorant electorate, white or black. . . .[14]

President-elect Taft made this statement despite the fact that the Supreme Court in the case of *Williams* v. *Mississippi* in 1898 opened the legal road to the compromising of Negro rights through proscription, segregation, and disfranchisement.[15] Other Southern states followed the course of Mississippi in disfranchising the Negro to the extent that he was no longer a political force in the country.

In 1898 some members of Congress became alarmed, fearing that the loss of republican government in many of the states might become a national pattern. Representative George White of North Carolina observed that the life blood of the Union was being sapped and that "one day or the other it would not be a Cuban question that confronts us; but a question as to whether or not the Federal Constitution in this great Republic of ours shall be perpetuated or not."[16]

Representative Marlin E. Olmsted of Pennsylvania introduced a privileged resolution designed to get Congress to enforce the provisions of the Fourteenth Amendment. Olmsted gave the following statistics from the Congressional Directories of the Fifty-second Congress and the Fifty-sixth Congress:

In the seven districts of Mississippi the total vote cast for all Congressional candidates in 1890 was 62,652; in 1898, 27,045. In the seven districts of South Carolina the total vote in 1890 was 73,522, and 28,831 in 1898. In the six districts of Louisiana 74,542 in 1890, and 33,161 in 1898.

[14] William Howard Taft, *The South and the National Government.*
[15] Woodward, *Strange Career of Jim Crow,* p. 54.
[16] *Congressional Record,* 55 Cong., 2 sess., XXXI, pt. 5: 4194 (April 22, 1898).

One member of the . . . House, representing ten counties in Mississippi, with a population in 1890 of 184,297, received only 2,068 votes. One member of the . . . House representing six counties in South Carolina, with a population in 1890 of 158,851, received only 1,765 votes, and one member representing thirteen counties in Louisiana, with a population of 208,802, received only 2,494 votes.

In the debate on the resolution no mention of race was made by the sponsor, yet the representative from Mississippi declared, "We all know what you meant."

Olmsted replied, "It is a matter of surprise to me that the learned and distinguished gentlemen who occupied so much time of the House . . . endeavoring to show that the Constitution follows into distant islands of the sea and wherever the flag goes, should be unwilling that the Constitution should have an opportunity to do business at home. . . ."[17]

A *Washington Post* editorial on a bill which proposed to reduce the representation of states that disfranchised Negro citizens, commented:

> . . . It appears that there will be both justice and common sense in voting down Representative Crumpacker's bill;[18] as the *Post* has stated in previous discussions of this question, this nation is not going into the new century with a revival of sectional animosity; the second McKinley Administration is not going to be a new era of ill feeling between the North and South. The South will not be further punished for the fateful mistake of the Fifteenth Amendment.[19]

That the McKinley administration was not interested in disturbing existing conditions regarding the disfranchisement of the Negro is shown by the editorial comment in *Outlook* which stated that "among other Republicans who showed themselves hostile to reducing the representation of states which disfranchised negroes* was Represen-

17 *Ibid.*, 56 Cong., 2 sess., XXXIV, pt. 1: 519–58 (January 3–4, 1901).
18 Representative from Indiana.
19 *Washington Post*, December 27, 1900.
* Editor's note: The spelling and capitalization of the original form of all quotations has been scrupulously followed. The reader is left to draw his own conclusions.

tative Grosvenor of Ohio, who has often been recognized as the spokesman of the Administration."[20]

Senator Morgan of Alabama observed:

> It was an auspicious day in the history of this grand Republic when the rules of constitutional restraint or mandate were so far relaxed as to allow the people to deal with this race question according to their just judgment concerning the safety of that race and the rightful supremacy of the white race. . . . . . In physical, mental, social, inventive, religious, and ruling power the African race holds the lowest place. . . . To force this lowest stratum into a position of political equality with the highest is only to clog the progress of all mankind in its march, ever strenuous and in proper order, toward the highest planes of human aspiration.[21]

The national unity achieved at the expense of the Negro at the close of the nineteenth century was continued into the twentieth century. Southern senators and representatives in their advocacy of white supremacy gave adequate argument to the imperialists for the proscription of the inhabitants of the new insular possessions. Many of the anti-imperialists used concepts of racial supremacy as the basis of their opposition to overseas expansion of the Republic. It was not necessary to give the "new-caught, sullen peoples" in the Philippines and elsewhere the right to vote, or to extend the Constitution to them.

If the right to vote could be denied "on the other side of the globe," asked the *Atlantic Monthly*, why not in Mississippi and South Carolina? The *Nation* very aptly showed the true conditions existing in America as regarded Negro rights and the influence of domestic conditions on the newly acquired, colored colonies in the Pacific Ocean and the Caribbean Sea. The people inhabiting these possessions were a varied assortment of inferior races which of course could not be allowed to vote.[22]

The imperialists, by their reluctance to extend the Constitution to the newly acquired territory, gave support to the view held by many

[20] "Shall Negro Disfranchisement Reduce Southern Representation?", *Outlook*, LXVII (January 12, 1901), 85.

[21] *Congressional Record*, 56 Cong., 1 sess., XXXIII, pt. 1: 673–74 (January 8, 1900).

[22] Woodward, *Strange Career of Jim Crow*, pp. 54–55.

Southerners that people of color were innately inferior. Representative Adolph Myer of Louisiana asked, "Why this unwillingness to accord self-government to Filipinos and suffrage to everybody in Cuba and Puerto Rico? Is it not the result of an idea that the inferior races cannot safely be invested with the ballot?"[23]

In the first decade of the twentieth century the lines of argument of the imperialist and anti-imperialist were clearly drawn. Republicans, for the most part, supported expansion into noncontiguous areas, whereas Democrats generally opposed such expansion. It is important to note that the Republicans were as intolerant and contemptuous of the rights of the colored people of the new possessions as the Democrats were of the Negro in the Southern states. The maltreatment of the Negro in the South was held up to the Democratic party to underscore the insincerity in that party's expressed opposition to the treatment of the inhabitants of the insular possessions. The *Nation* observed:

> . . . How hollow will ring Democratic protests against the oppression of the Filipinos while there is Democratic acquiescence in injustice to the negro. It would even appear that the great reason for making the Philippines independent is at least, if we hold them, we shall keep the brown men under our heel abroad as we mean to keep the black men at home. Self-government, the right of representation . . . are to be kept purely for use 7,000 miles away, while conveniently forgotten in this country. The campaign of the Democrats would be, in that respect, one of overflowing love for the brown brother whom they cannot see, but of callous disregard of the black brother whom they can see.[24]

Inconsistency on the question of imperialism and race was not confined to the Democrats, for the Republicans came under attack for advocating on one hand political rights for the Negro in the South while denying the same rights to colored people in the insular possessions. The Democrats argued that the description of the Filipinos' lack of capacity for self-government given by Senator Beveridge of Indiana fitted "exactly that of the negro in Louisiana." Why then, did some of the Republicans insist upon inflicting upon Louisiana and

[23] *Congressional Record*, 56 Cong., 2 sess., XXXIV, pt. 4: 52 (January 9, 1901).
[24] "The Caste Notion of Suffrage," *Nation*, LXXVII (September 3, 1903), 182.

North Carolina a government that they would not have tolerated in the newly acquired territories?[25]

Southerners were conscious of the changing attitude of the North in regard to minority rights. One Southerner found that though the Southern states had spent about $100,000,000 for the education of Negroes in the thirty years since 1870, as a race, they had become "less fitted for the duties of citizenship and more a menace to civilization and good government." This observer suggested that the true remedy for the problem was to be found in the repeal of the Fifteenth Amendment. Relating the national unity on proscription for less developed peoples at home and abroad to the possibility of gaining support for the repeal, he stated, "I know that this suggestion will be regarded by most persons as one the realization of which is beyond reasonable hope, but there can be little doubt that the mind of the country, North and South, especially since the acquisition of Hawaii, Porto Rico, and the Philippines, is in a more favorable condition to consider such a proposition than ever before."[26]

Many Southern senators supported the McKinley administration as though they were Republicans, and the Republicans generally supported the disfranchisement of the Negro. Two such cases of Democratic support of Republican policy were Senators John McLaurin of South Carolina and John Morgan of Alabama. The Nation observed that though Senator McLaurin of South Carolina was elected as a Democrat, he could not have had a better record had he been elected as a Republican, for he had "sustained the McKinley Administration on the Peace Treaty, the Porto Rico Bill, the Platt Amendment regarding Cuba and Philippine Legislation. . . ." In regard to Senator Morgan's avowed annexation policy for Cuba, the Nation saw this as the historic attitude of the South and stated that the South had always "cast greedy eyes on Cuba and made no hypocritical concealment of its purpose in desiring to annex the island. . . . Our new fangled notions of a protectorate, of exploiting island possessions without giving them a share in our government, did not enter

[25] Congressional Record, 56 Cong., 1 sess., XXXIII, pt. 2: 1064 (January 23, 1900).

[26] Ibid., 56 Cong., 2 sess., XXXIV, pt. 4: 73 (January 7, 1901). A. M Waddell at a conference held May, 1900, at Montgomery, Alabama. Quoted by Representative Edgar D. Crumpacker of Indiana.

the heads of the slave holders. It was left to the party of freedom to devise those little tricks for holding men in political and economic slavery."[27]

Thus, the *Nation* implied that a change had taken place in the basic philosophy of the Republican party. Both major parties held the same basic racial attitudes. Their beliefs denied political, social, and economic equality to so-called inferior peoples.

In compromising Republican principles abroad, the spokesman for the Republican party qualified Republican principles at home. This break of faith is pointed up in the questions raised by Thomas E. Miller, former Negro congressman from South Carolina.

Who is it that stands to-day in the United States Senate and warns negroes and white men of the South that right to vote is not a gift from the nation, but a matter left with each sovereign State to be regulated; that is, to be given or taken away? Why, it is a man from New England, the great Republican Senator PLATT. And why has this great change come over the North in relation to franchise? Why do they yield to this principle that has always been claimed by the South? This great New England Republican and august Senator from a sovereign State stands in the Senate Chamber and virtually admits that the fourteenth and fifteenth amendments are nugatory and of no effect.[28]

The view attributed to Senator Orville Platt was supported editorially by *Outlook*, which "regarded, the suffrage simply as a means to an end, the end being a just government. . . ." *Outlook* tried to define the position of those who agreed "that suffrage is an artificial, not a natural right. . . . The conditions on which it should be granted by those who have it to those who have it not are wholly to be determined by a consideration of the question: what conditions of suffrage will probably secure the more just, stable and free government?"[29]

By September, 1901, national unity was complete on the question of the Negro. An article appearing in *Forum* for the period summed up the situation. "An occasional politician and editor will rile in unrestrained fashion at the disfranchisement of the negro, and will

27 *Nation*, LXXII (May 2, 1901), 347.
28 *Congressional Record*, 55 Cong., 3 sess., XXXII, pt. 1: 639 (January 13, 1899). Thomas Miller, former congressman from South Carolina, quoted by Senator John L. McLaurin.
29 "The Right of Suffrage," *Outlook*, LXVIII (July 27, 1901), 711–12.

threaten the enforcement of the Fourteenth Amendment; but the best evidence that there is nothing behind such protests is the fact that the legal disfranchisement of the Negroes in several Southern States is an accepted fact. . . ."[30]

Seven years later the North was penitent in its attitude toward the South. Andrew Carnegie's glowing tribute to an address by President Taft stated that the speech had "found warm response in the hearts of the Northern people, who have not failed to sympathize deeply with their Southern fellow citizens during their long years of affliction." He concluded that President Taft had expressed Northern feelings "with rare felicity" and was so moved by the expressed sentiments that he "resolved to publish his address and send it to 'the fellow citizens of the South' as a messenger of peace and perfect reunion from their Northern countrymen."[31]

SOUTHERN ASSUMPTIONS BECOME NATIONAL POLICY

Those who advocated overseas expansion faced this dilemma: What kind of relationship would the new peoples have to the body politic? Was it to be the relationship of the Reconstruction period, an attempt at political equality for dissimilar races, or was it to be the Southern "counterrevolutionary" point of view which denied the basic American constitutional rights to people of color?[32] The actions of the federal government during the imperial period and the relegation of the Negro to a status of second-class citizenship indicated that the Southern point of view would prevail. The racism which caused the relegation of the Negro to a status of inferiority was to be applied to the overseas possessions of the United States.

Spokesmen with Southern views on race had access to the halls of Congress as well as to leading periodicals and the lecture halls of the North. One such spokesman was Senator Benjamin Tillman of South Carolina, the "Incendiary Senator." The *Independent* noted that Tillman earned $25,000 lecturing in one summer and, thinking it strange that the demand for his lectures came from the North, concluded

[30] George A. Thacker, "The Southern Problem," *Forum*, XXXII (September 1901), 116.
[31] *South and the National Government*, p. 7.
[32] George E. Simpson and J. Milton Yinger, *Racial and Cultural Minorities*, pp. 143–44.

that "Southern towns do not send for him and crowd halls for him. . . .
It is Michigan, Illinois—even New England—where he draws according to the intemperate radicalism he proclaims."[33]

Changes in attitude on the race question were not effected by
Southerners alone. While the Southern politicians were the most vo-
ciferous in their assumptions on racial superiority and inferiority, the
universities and churches aided, directly and indirectly, in creating a
unanimity of opinion.

John W. Burgess—whose influence was great on the minds and actions of many of the publicists, educators, jurists, and statesmen of
the country,[34] and indirectly on the masses—wrote that the United
States had embarked on imperial enterprise "under the direction of
the Republican Party, the great Northern party," that "the North is
learning every day by valuable experiences that there are vast differences in political capacity between the races, that it is the white
man's mission, his duty, and his right to hold the reins of political
power in his own hands for the civilization of the world and the welfare of mankind."[35]

Frank H. Hankins sums up Burgess' position:

So important is "the mission of conducting the political organization of
the world, with which Teutons have been commissioned, that they should
not entrust the balance of power in national or local affairs to any nationality; in fact, they should, in some cases, exclude other elements from participation in political power; though this should be done with justice and
moderation—it is these very qualities of the Teutonic character which
make it par excellence political." "The Teutonic nations can never regard
the exercise of political power as a right of man"; such right must be based
on political capacity of which the Teutonic nations are the only qualified
judges. Moreover, the Teutonic nations, as a world duty, "must have a
colonial policy." And in dealing with native peoples who resist the provi-
dential dominion of Teutonic nations, the latter "may righteously . . . clear
the territory of their presence and make it the abode of civilized man."

[33] "Men We Are Watching," *The Independent*, LXI (December 13, 1906),
1429–30.
[34] John W. Burgess, *Recent Changes in American Constitutional Theory*,
p. lx. Also Nelson M. Blake and Oscar T. Barck, *The United States in Its World
Relations*, pp. 355–56.
[35] John W. Burgess, *Reconstruction and the Constitution, 1866–1876*, pp.
vii–ix.

Tribal peoples have no rights which the Teutonic states are bound to respect. . . .[36]

Hankins concludes that Burgess' "views had unsurpassed influence and received reiteration from a thousand platforms and through hundreds of publications." That Burgess was not unaware of his influence is shown in the introduction to his book, *Recent Changes in American Constitutional Theory*, in which he writes, "Especially do I feel that I owe it to the more than ten thousand pupils whom I have been privileged to instruct in the evolution of political history and the principles of Political Science and Constitutional Law; in fact, it is to them especially, among whom are included many of the most distinguished publicists, educators, jurists and statesmen of our country, that I address this, maybe, final word from their old teacher. . . ."[37] Hankins alludes to the effectiveness of Burgess' teaching in saying, "It was not a matter of accident that Theodore Roosevelt, imbibing his political theory in Burgess's classroom, afterwards seized the Panama strip and justified this on the ground that it was unrighteous for backward nations to block the expansion of civilization."[38]

Josiah Strong influenced many through his writing for the American Home Missionary Society and especially the widely circulated *Our Country: Its Possible Future and Its Present Crisis*, in which he claimed that his ideas on the Anglo-Saxon and the world's future had been advanced some three years before the appearance of Professor Fiske's "Manifest Destiny," in *Harper's Magazine* of 1885.[39] He exalted the Anglo-Saxon race as "the representative . . . of the largest liberty, the purest Christianity, the highest civilization."[40]

Even the anti-imperialists seemed to contribute to the solidifying of the national sentiment on the treatment of inferior peoples. David Starr Jordan wrote, "Whenever we have inferior and dependent races within our borders today, we have a political problem," citing "the Negro problem, the Chinese problem, the Indian problem." Jordan

[36] Frank H. Hankins, *The Racial Basis of Civilization*, pp. 171–72.
[37] Burgess, *Recent Changes in American Constitutional Theory*, p. ix.
[38] Hankins, *Racial Basis of Civilization*, p. 172. Roosevelt studied political theory at Columbia under Burgess.
[39] Josiah Strong, *Our Country: Its Possible Future and Its Present Crisis*, p. 159n.
[40] Blake and Barck, *United States in Its World Relations*, pp. 355–56.

implied that it was possible by industrial training to make a man out of the Negro and even out of the Chinese, but there was no hope for the Indian who "disappears as our civilization touches him." Jordan concluded that since the peoples of the Philippines and Cuba were inferiors, they could never have self-government in the Anglo-Saxon sense.[41]

Jordan, however, played up an element that would have a conditioning effect on the American approach to imperialism. He pointed out the reciprocal nature of republican government, which implied that if the United States governed dissimilar peoples, then these people in turn had a right to participate in the governing of the people of the United States. Thus, the people of the Philippines, Cuba, Hawaii, Haiti, the Dominican Republic, or any other possessions acquired by the United States should have the same rights as any of the several states.[42]

William Graham Sumner in *Folkways* adopted a fatalistic attitude toward social change which was widely accepted by the nation. The ideas expressed in this work gave racists another weapon, in that Sumner said that laws were supposed to grow out of established custom.[43]

Albert Bushnell Hart, writing in 1899, linked America's imperial policy to its domestic policy.

. . . We may trust Puerto Ricans as far as we trust Peruvans and Guatemalans, but no further. Judging from the experience of other nations and ourselves, the Pacific Islands (except Hawaii) will not be allowed anything like our Territorial governments till the French let the Anamites govern themselves, and the English turn Bengal over to the natives; or the Sioux send a delegate to Congress, and the negroes are allowed to vote in the Southern States.

The only alternative is the rule of the few—and those few exercising power conferred by a distant administration: but the system means a change in American standards of government and human rights. We must give up our fine contempt for other nations which rule with an iron hand. . . .[44]

41 David Starr Jordan, *Imperial Democracy*, p. 32.
42 *Ibid.*, p. 102.
43 Simpson and Yinger, *Racial and Cultural Minorities*, p. 12.
44 Albert Bushnell Hart, "Brother Jonathan's Colonies," *Harper's*, XCVIII (December 1898–May 1899), 328.

The United States, Hart continued, would have to abandon the principle that "all just government depends on the consent of the governed." It would be necessary to look on the colonial status as permanent, not a stage towards statehood, and to compromise constitutional principles to the extent that difficult questions of religion and worship could only be settled by "orders from Washington." The United States would have to yield part of its protective policy or give up the principles fought for in the American Revolution, "that colonies exist for their own benefit, and not for the advantage of the mother country." The principle of free intercourse between the parts of the American empire would have to be changed or peoples heretofore excluded from the continental Republic would have to be admitted.

The most serious difficulty of all is that we are trying to apply a good system of Anglo-Saxon government to those who prefer a poor one. . . . In questions of human rights, the limited privileges which we can allow with safety will be freedom in comparison with the previous experience of our new colonists; and in the long run we must trust the American people who freed the negro slaves to deal justly with half-breeds—Kanakas and Malays—though justice no longer means political equality "even at home."[45]

Woodrow Wilson wrote in 1901 that to give indiscriminately the codes of Anglo-Saxon political morality or methods of political action to underdeveloped people would be a "curse," not a blessing, because these peoples were in the "childhood of their political growth" and needed the aid of the Anglo-Saxon character, not the "premature aid" of their institutions. Wilson was expressing in theory a philosophy which he subsequently carried into practice at home and in the Caribbean upon his election to the presidency.[46]

Advice from abroad was quickly and abundantly furnished by James Bryce and Gustave Le Bon of England and France respectively. Bryce's article, "The Policy of Annexation for America," contended that the energetic white population in the Southern states "which keeps the State government in its hands" was the saving factor for that section of the country. Bryce asked, "Supposing either Cuba or Hawaii or both of them to be annexed to the United States, how are

45 *Ibid.*
46 Quoted by Senator Borah in debate on Senate Bill 381, *Congressional Record,* 64 Cong., 1 sess., LIII, pt. 1: 607.

they to be governed? . . . The most obvious course would be to admit
each into the Union as a new State." But after looking at the quality
of the population in Cuba, consisting of many Creole Spaniard, but
many more Negroes and mulattoes, nobody "can think it desirable to
increase the black element in the American Union." He pointed out
that in Hawaii there was a large number of Asiatics in the population,
consisting of Chinese, Japanese, and Malays, which would preclude
its becoming a useful member of the Union and render this territory
"obviously unfit for free representative government."[47]

According to Bryce, tropical dominions cost more than they were
worth because they were occupied by races unfit to receive American
institutions. He observed, "One sometimes hears it said that [Ameri-
ca's] mission is to spread democratic principles. Polynesians, and Asiatics, Creole Spaniards and mulattoes are not fit to receive those principles. Neither are negroes fit, as the history of Hayti and most of the
South-American so-called 'republics' proves."[48]

The sense of mission was too strong to be suppressed by Bryce or
any other observer. The imperialists had no doubt that Americans
could cope with any future race problems, for in 1898 the nation was
united and the domestic problems of race were secondary. They did
not exist.

Gustave Le Bon observed:

. . . An empire, a people or a state is a more or less considerable number of
men united by political and geographical necessities, and subject to the
same institutions and laws. These men may belong to the same race, but
they may equally belong to different races. If the races are too dissimilar
no fusion is possible. They may . . . live side by side, like Hindus subject to Europeans, but we must not think of giving them common institutions. All great Empires uniting dissimilar peoples are created only
by force, and are condemned to perish by violence. Those only can endure which are formed slowly by the gradual mixture of races differing
but little, continually crossing with one another, living on the same soil,
subject to the action of the same climate. . . .[49]

[47] James Bryce, "The Policy of Annexation for America," *Forum*, XXIV (November 1897), 389–91.
[48] *Ibid.*, p. 394.
[49] Gustave Le Bon, "The Influences of Race in History," *Popular Science
Monthly*, XXXV (August 1889), 498.

Theodore Roosevelt, commenting on the writings of Le Bon, wrote to Henry Cabot Lodge, "What Le Bon says of race is very fine and true."[50]

Goldwin Smith wrote that no one of the British race would desire "union with a scattered empire embracing an indefinite number of people of inferior races, Negroes, Hawaiians, Chinese, and Malays" and that certain effects of imperialism on home principles and institutions were already evident. He pointed out that the "principle of universal suffrage hitherto deemed vital to the Republic," was being disparaged, if not openly discarded. "To wean the people from allegiance to it, attention was directed to the" inhabitants of the territories, who were not given the franchise. Attention was also called to the Southern legislation, which was practically subverting the Fifteenth Amendment and had taken the franchise from the Negro. He observed that these were two "precedents, of which the first is manifestly irrelevant, while the second is relevant indeed. . . ."

The treatment of the Indian by Americans was the pattern to be used in conquering the fierce tribes of the Philippines, for Smith commented that if some of the tribes were similar to the Apaches, "Uncle Sam will handle them in his accustomed style." Smith showed the effect of the Spanish-American War on domestic race relations in his observation that peace and good will between the North and South had been restored in a surprising degree prior to the Spanish-American War. However, after the war, the American newspapers almost daily recorded cases of lynching, "sometimes of such character as to evince the last extremity of hatred and contempt" for peoples of color. "Why should the American Commonwealth want more Negroes?" he asked.

Smith was most prophetic in his writing, anticipating the Wilson administration by seventeen years in concluding that "there is talk already . . . of an annexation of the West Indies by exchange with Great Britain for the Philippines. Hayti cannot be said to be less of a scandal or to afford less of a pretext for philanthropic conquest than Cuba. . . ."[51]

[50] Theodore Roosevelt to Henry Cabot Lodge, April 29, 1896, *Letters of Theodore Roosevelt and Henry Cabot Lodge*, ed. Henry Cabot Lodge, I, 218.
[51] Goldwin Smith, "The Moral of the Cuban War," *Forum*, XXVI (November 1898), 284–90.

The American people, as well as the American soldiers, were persuaded to believe in the innate unfitness of the less-developed peoples
to govern themselves, and the American racial experience was exploited for all it was worth. Most of the people in the new possessions
were compared to the Negroes or Indians living in the United States.
Illustrative of this type of persuasion is the excerpt from a letter to
Senator Hoar. "We had been taught (the devil only knows why)
that the Filipinos were savages no better than our Indians." The
writer implied that the individual soldier was not always willing to
subscribe to inhuman treatment, and that, after coming in contact
with the Filipinos, "neither the 'nigger' nor 'Indian' talk made them
enthusiastic soldiers."[52]

OTHER RACES

The "Indian problem" and the "Negro problem" in the United
States were both of long duration. The "Indian problem" began with
the inception of the country and the charters granted to John Cabot
and Sir Walter Raleigh, which carried provisos to respect only lands
held by Christian princes. Subsequent charters and patents, containing the provision to respect only lands held by those professing
the Christian faith, excluded the Indian from rights enjoyed by Europeans. The Indian became the object of injustices, ranging from the
seizure of his lands and loss of his liberty to the taking of his life.

The "Negro problem" was also of long duration, beginning in 1619.
By 1660 there had evolved a fixed status—slavery—for the servant of
African descent.[53] This status was given legal sanction under the
Constitution with the fugitive slave section, the three-fifths ratio,
which recognized the Negro as less than a person, and the compromise allowing the importation of Negroes for a period of twenty
years. The problem was further emphasized by the Dred Scott and
the *Plessy* v. *Ferguson* decisions.

The problem of Asiatics in the United States was the result, in part,
of the desire to exploit the land resources of the country. The era of

[52] *Congressional Record*, 56 Cong., 1 sess., XXXIII, pt. 1: 714 (January 9,
1900).
[53] Oscar Handlin, *Race and Nationality in American Life*, p. 7.

railroad building, designed to link the East Coast with the West Coast by rail, led to the recruitment of Chinese laborers. Another conditioning factor in the relationship between Americans and Asiatics was the development of intensive agriculture on the West Coast. Relations between Americans and Asiatics became acute in the 1870s due to the immigration of Chinese in large numbers into the Western states. The seriousness of this problem resulted in the Treaty of 1880 between the United States and China.

The treatment of the Chinese in the United States was similar in many ways to the treatment of the Negro and the Indian. In 1892 the Geary Act was supposed to solve the Chinese problem by restricting Chinese immigration.[54] The measure provided for the deportation of Chinese not legally in the country. In congressional debate on the bill, one advocate of restriction stated that at a general election held in California in 1879, the question was submitted to the people to vote "for" or "against" the policy of unrestricted Chinese immigration. Out of a total vote of 161,405 there were only 883 votes cast "for" the disputed policy. The speaker made the observation that "the Chinese do not, they cannot, they will not assimilate with us." He continued that they knew nothing about "our free government, our standard of civilization, or American citizenship. . . . They know nothing and care nothing about our institutions. . . ." The unprejudiced view of people who had had many years of experience among Chinese was that they were an undesirable class of people. Chinese labor was similar to slave labor in that it was debasing, degrading, and a curse to all who came in contact with it. It injured rather than elevated those who were associated with it. Chinese labor produced results, but "the results . . . are obtained at the sacrifice of American citizenship."[55]

In 1893 the Chinese minister, Tsui Kwo Yin, who was concerned about the safety of Chinese before the effective date of the deportation act of May 5, 1892, sent a note to the State Department, requesting protection from the government for Chinese subjects. In the same

[54] An act to prohibit the coming of Chinese into the United States, approved May 5, 1892. *Foreign Relations*, 1892, p. 107.

[55] *Congressional Record*, 53 Cong., 1 sess., XXV, pt. 3: 3046–48 (November 1, 1893).

note, Tsui called attention to the governor of Montana's approval of an unjust bill which forbade all citizens of that state to have commercial intercourse with the Chinese there. He believed that the anticipated ill treatment and outrage so much dreaded by the Chinese had started to show its effect.[56]

Under the Geary Act, the Chinese were denied the basic Anglo-Saxon right of bail in habeas corpus cases. Their cases were to come before a judge without jury, and at the discretion of the judge the Chinese could be sentenced to deportation. The only way he could be saved from deportation was for him to be able to "establish clearly to the satisfaction of the judge that by reason of accident, sickness or other unavoidable causes . . . he was unable to procure his certificate." The testimony of the Chinese had to be corroborated by the testimony of "at least one creditable white witness that he was a resident of the United States at the time of the passage of this act."[57] Under these conditions and contrary to Anglo-Saxon custom, the Chinese were considered guilty, and the burden of proof rested on them, not on the State. The magnitude of the injustice of the legislation against the Chinese as a race can be appreciated when one weighs the words of Senator John M. Palmer of Illinois against a background that includes the debauching of the Indian, the enslaving of the Negro, and the overall turbulence of the West.

Of course the bill allows a very large class of officers to make arrests . . . without warrant . . . "any United States customs official, collector of internal revenue or his deputies, United States marshal or his deputies," to make arrests without formal complaint made before some judicial officer. The consequence would be that the person is left without remedy and is at the mercy of a large class of officers all over the States, officers who are mere deputies, none of them elected, many of whom . . . are irresponsible persons. These officers are allowed to capture a Chinaman who may be engaged in some lawful industry; and yet at the will of one of these subordinates he may be taken by the neck and brought before a judge; . . . no one of his countrymen can speak; although he may be as truthful as the Apostle Paul, none shall be allowed to speak for him and a judgment of deportation is rendered. There may be errors of law and of fact in that judgment, because our judges are not infallible; and while that man is

56 *Foreign Relations,* 1893, pp. 247–48.
57 *Foreign Relations,* 1892, p. 107.

seeking a rehearing before the established tribunals of the country he remains in jail in the custody of the marshal until the question is tried.[58]

The Chinese ministers consistently called attention to the violation of the treaties existing between the United States and China as seen in the following note:

> In notes which my predecessor and I have some time ago sent to your Department we have shown how the Scott bill, passed by the Congress in 1888, was a clear violation of the treaty of 1880. Your own silence on the subject must be understood to be recognition that what we have charged is true. . . . Now, the Congress, in the bill which has just been voted, has a provision that this bad law shall be kept in force. . . .[59]

In commenting on the racial bias of the Geary Act, Congressman Davis from Minnesota said, "There is no nation on the continent of Europe, however feeble, that we would have enacted this legislation against, however undesirable their laboring people as immigrants. Our conscience would not have permitted it. . . . We have a general idea, unhappily too prevalent, that we need not deal with the Chinese upon the same footing of equal binding force and obligation, to say nothing of equality of rights, that we deal with other people."[60]

In a later note to the State Department requesting protection for Chinese after the effective date of the Geary Act, the Chinese minister observed that the Chinese residents throughout the United States and on the Pacific Coast were very apprehensive that personal injury would be inflicted on them and their property destroyed. They also feared that outrages similar to those committed at Rock Springs, Wyoming, and at Tacoma, Seattle, and Olympia, Washington, in previous years would recur. It was recalled that these outrages occurred despite the fact that Chinese were supposed to be enjoying the protection of the government. These violent attacks resulted in the loss of life, great destruction of property, and the forcible expulsion of the Chinese from some of the towns mentioned. The note

[58] *Congressional Record*, 53 Cong., 1 sess., XXV, pt. 3: 3043 (November 1, 1893).

[59] *Foreign Relations*, 1892, p. 149.

[60] *Congressional Record*, 53 Cong., 1 sess., XXV, pt. 3: 3085 (November 2, 1893).

concluded with an appeal to the "profound sense of fairness and justice" of the American people and the hope that "protection guaranteed by the treaty stipulations between our nations will be extended over the lives and property of the Chinese subjects who are now residing in the United States. . . ."[61]

Senator George F. Hoar of Massachusetts decried the passage of the Geary Act, saying, "These measures not only violate our treaty engagement with a friendly nation, but they violate the principle upon which the American Republic rests, striking not at crime, not . . . at pauperism but . . . at human beings because of their race. . . ."

Utterances reflecting an extension of the same mainland attitude toward Asiatics in the outlying possessions were voiced in Hawaii. The reason for the existence of a Chinese community in the Hawaiian Islands paralleled the reason for Chinese being in the United States; they were a source of cheap labor. The Chinese in Hawaii were accepted as a part of the community. Thus, at the time of annexation to the United States in 1898 some 20,000 Chinese resided in the Hawaiian Islands. These Chinese were in the islands in accordance with the laws of the Hawaiian government. Under the protection of that government, they had acquired various personal and property rights guaranteed by law.[62]

The Congress in 1898 proposed to extend the provisions of the act of May 5, 1892, over the Island of Hawaii, the adjacent islands, and waters of the islands acquired from Hawaii in the joint resolution of 1898. The act of May 5, 1892, required all Chinese laborers to take out certificates of residence or give up their right to remain in the United States. If the provisions of this act had been applied to Hawaii, it would have put the Chinese laborers in a very difficult position since they could not have taken out the certificates six years in advance of annexation. There were no provisions in the proposed extension of the laws to Hawaii to allow the Chinese to comply. This omission led the Chinese minister to write to Secretary of State John Hay:

By the terms of the joint resolution of the Congress of the United States, some of the most important . . . rights have been suddenly suspended; and,

[61] *Foreign Relations*, 1893, pp. 247–48.
[62] Gilbert Reid, "China's View of Chinese Expulsion," *Forum*, XV (June 1893), 407–15.

if the policy therein declared shall be adhered to, an uncalled-for discrimination and manifest injustice will result to this large body of the population of the annexed territory. . . .

The reason which brought about the immigration treaty of 1880 between China and the United States, the treaty of 1894, and legislation based on those treaties which exclude Chinese laborers from the United States, does not apply to the Hawaiian Islands. In this country, it is alleged that Chinese labor comes in competition with white labor to the detriment of the latter, and that it is contrary to its interest to admit the Chinese; but exactly the reverse is the case in the Hawaiian Islands, as they come into competition with neither white nor native labor, and have been and are regarded there as a desirable population.

The fact that the treaties between China and the United States regarding the immigration of Chinese to the United States were interpreted with unwarranted strictness by the attorney general and the secretary of the treasury, even to the exclusion of members of the higher classes of Chinese subjects, was called to the attention of the secretary of state by the Chinese minister.

I desire, further, to direct your attention to the fact that the line of policy indicated is an unnecessary discrimination against the Chinese race. They are not the only Asiatic people who do, or are likely to, come to the territories of the American Union. Does the Congress of the United States intend to declare that the Chinese are more objectionable than the Japanese, the Malays, the Siamese, or other of the Asiatic peoples?[63]

Minister Wu continued to plead for justice for the Chinese laborers, saying, "It seems unjust to make the enjoyment of the right to remain in those islands, to which the Chinese laborers now there are clearly entitled, dependent upon the fulfillment of a condition manifestly impossible." He suggested that the laws then in force pertaining to immigration and contract labor in the United States were stringent enough to keep out the undesirable elements of every foreign community. He felt that the extension of those laws to Hawaii without the enforcement of the Chinese exclusion acts would serve as an effective bar to the continued immigration of the objectionable class of Chinese as well as others. All that his government asked was that the

[63] *Foreign Relations*, 1899, pp. 202–204.

immigration of Chinese into American territories be placed on a common footing with that of other nations. "To single out the Chinese alone for exclusion from the islands is to lower the whole nation in the eyes of the world."[64] In spite of the minister's plea, laws excluding certain classes of Chinese were enacted by Congress.

After the events of 1898 the Chinese minister was apprehensive about the status of Chinese in the Philippine Islands, leading him to again point out to the Department of State that the treaties of 1880 and 1894 had as their object the exclusion of Chinese from United States territory on the continent of North America. He saw no possibility of the application of the treaties to the Philippine Islands since the causes which had occasioned them were not present in these islands. The policy of exclusion would not necessitate enforcement by congressional or military action. The minister suggested:

. . . If a policy of exclusion is adopted there, should the United States in its wisdom extend the practice of territorial expansion, for instance, to Siam and Annam, the Chinese might also be excluded from those countries. . . .
Trusting that the foregoing views will meet with the approval of your Government and that the Chinese residents of the Philippines will not be made to suffer any abridgment of their rights and privileges because of the extension of American sovereignty over them.[65]

Repeated inquiries from the Chinese legation to the secretary of state as to the status of Chinese in the Philippine Islands went unanswered throughout 1898. Finally, when an answer was forthcoming in August, 1899, it implied that the Department of State had to find out for itself what the status of Chinese was in the Philippine Islands.

Upon inquiry through the War Department, I learned by a telegram from Major-General Otis that the Chinese Exclusion Act is practically in force, except as to the methods for personal identification, for which other convenient methods, suitable to the special conditions in that quarter, have been adopted.
It is the opinion of the War and Treasury Departments that the enforcement of the Chinese Exclusion Act is incident to the Military adminis-

64 *Ibid.,* pp. 205–206.
65 *Ibid.,* pp. 207–208.

tration of the Philippine Islands during a state of hostilities therein, and therefore without prejudice to the future action of Congress in permanently extending the laws of the United States to such territory. . . .[66]

The order barring the Chinese from the Philippine Islands was issued by General Otis on September 26, 1898. A copy of the order was requested by the Chinese legation. The minister, upon receipt of the order, expressed surprise upon learning that the Chinese exclusion acts had been in force in the Philippine Islands more than a year without the official knowledge of the legation. Upon further inquiry Secretary Hay replied that the subject of Chinese status in the Philippines was being given consideration and that until American military control was extended, the matter would have to wait for further consideration. In conclusion he said, "I shall be unable to make definite response to your inquiry."[67]

Wu protested: first, because exclusion was not warranted as a military measure; second, because the President had announced that the status of the newly acquired possessions would remain unchanged; and finally, because it was a great injustice to a large body of Chinese subjects. On November 15, 1899, more than a month after the protest against the military exclusion of Chinese from the Philippine Islands, Wu wrote the Department of State:

I feel it my duty upon this occasion to renew the protest which I presented to you on this subject in my note of September 12 last, which remains unanswered by your department, and in the most solemn manner to enter the protest of my Government against this new act of the United States military commander, which I feel sure you will agree with me is in direct violation of treaty stipulations and unwarranted by any law of the United States.

I have to ask that instructions be sent to Major-General Otis to cease the violation of the treaty of 1894 by the exclusion of merchants and others of the exempt classes mentioned in Article 3 of said treaty.[68]

Before the United States established effective military control in the Philippine Islands and before the Treaty of Peace between the

[66] *Ibid.*, p. 209.
[67] *Ibid.*
[68] *Ibid.*, p. 215.

United States and Spain was concluded, the Chinese were excluded from the Philippine Islands by military orders.

The problem of Chinese in Cuba was handled differently. On April 14, 1899, the secretary of war, under the authority of the President, by Order No. 13, Division of Customs and Insular Affairs, declared that the laws and regulations of the United States governing immigration were to be effective in territories under government by United States military forces. According to that order, the laws and regulations relating to immigration in the United States were put into effect in Cuba. These laws and regulations, however, did not include those relating to the immigration and exclusion of Chinese persons, this notwithstanding Order No. 13. Chinese of all classes were admitted freely into Cuba during the entire period of military control of Cuba by the United States, as had been the practice under the government of Spain.

Until five days before the United States returned control of Cuba to the Cubans, Chinese were treated like all other immigrants in Cuba. At that time the United States' policy of Chinese exclusion was introduced into Cuba. On May 15, 1902, General Wood issued an order declaring the reenactment and continued enforcement, pending such action as the Congress of Cuba might take thereon, of laws relating to immigration. By this action, according to the Chinese ambassador, the United States put into operation against the Chinese, racial policies which had not been in force in Cuba and which were more severe and restrictive than the provisions of the Chinese exclusion laws of the United States.[69]

The Chinese were excluded from the United States, the Hawaiian Islands, the Philippine Islands, and Cuba as a consequence of the extension of American control. There was a strong correlation between the inclusion of the United States flag and the exclusion of the Chinese.

ENTER THE JAPANESE

The Japanese, in appreciable numbers, started coming to the United States after 1880. First they settled in the urban centers,

[69] *Foreign Relations*, 1902, pp. 263–64.

taking noncompetitive jobs. They then branched out into small businesses and shops. Once they became sufficient in number to offer competition to the local laborers, antagonisms developed.

As the opportunities in the cities became more scarce for them, the Japanese began an exodus to the country. First they became farm hands, for which many of them were excellently adapted because of their previous intensive farming in Japan. From farm laborers they gradually moved into the managerial and leasing aspects of farming. The very success of the Japanese at farm enterprise led to agitation for their exclusion.

The "gentleman's agreement" of 1907, worked out between the governments of the United States and Japan, was supposed to stop the trouble arising over the presence of large numbers of Japanese on the West Coast. However, the "gentleman's agreement" did not remove the real cause of the trouble, the Japanese already in the United States.

California and other Western states enacted legislation designed to exclude the Japanese from all economic activity, the ultimate objective being the complete exclusion of the Japanese as a factor in the Western states. The people of the Western states were determined to build their region on the basis of a white population "with its recognized social, political, and economic standards. If the Japanese had been coming in rapidly . . . when we established the rule of Chinese exclusion, the gates would have been barred against Japanese . . . as against Chinese. . . ."[70]

The legislation proposed by California and other Western states was designed to preserve the West for native-born, white Americans and to destroy "the Japanese holdings of farm interests, for they constitute a menace to the State, and to exclude completely and effectually Japanese immigrants on the ground that it is impossible to assimilate and amalgamate them with American people."[71]

In 1908, one writer, discussing the exclusion of the Asiatics despite their proved economic worth to the community, noted:

[70] "Japanese Feeling Against America," *Review of Reviews*, XXXVI (August 1907), 134.
[71] Dr. Troyokichi Iyenaga, "Japan and the Japanese California Problem," *Current History*, XIII (October 1920), 1.

They were excluded not for economic but for racial reasons. The Californians, having seen Magyars and other yellow-white mixtures, they either knew that the yellow mongrels were among the most worthless of mongrels, or their instincts told them the same truth. The desire of the West to keep people of the yellow race out of America has something instinctive about it. Racial, not economic reasons, cause the clamour against the admission of the Japanese.[72]

In the presidential campaign of 1912, Woodrow Wilson said on May 3, that in the matter of Chinese and Japanese coolie immigration:

I stand for the national policy of exclusion. The whole question is one of assimilation of diverse races. We cannot make a homogeneous population of a people who do not blend with the Caucasian race. . . .

The success of free democratic institutions demands of our people education, intelligence, and patriotism, and the State should protect them against unjust and impossible competition. . . . Democracy rests on equality of the citizen. . . . Oriental coolieism will give us another race problem to solve and surely we have had our lesson.[73]

The Japanese government opposed the California land laws and voiced its displeasure in a note to the United States government. According to this note, the framers and supporters of the bill contented that if the rightful claims of Japanese were disregarded, the aggrieved parties could use the courts to get redress. The operation of "due process of law" was very slow, and in the meantime the delay involved would cause great hardship for the parties. The disadvantages caused the Japanese would, it was observed, be wholly unknown to aliens who were eligible to become United States citizens. Thus the law would operate "in effect as a discrimination against" Japanese, whose rights "to become American citizens" had not definitely been established by the Supreme Court.

The Japanese government asserted that since Japanese subjects were "as a nation apparently denied the right to acquire American nationality," they would become the principal sufferers from the enactment of a law whose "avowed purpose . . . was to deprive" Japanese

[72] Alfred P. Schultz, *Race or Mongrel*, p. 230.
[73] Lothrop Stoddard, *The Rising Tide of Color*, pp. 286–87.

of the right "to acquire and to possess landed property in California. . . ." The Imperial government was "unable to escape the conclusion that the measure" was "unfair and intentionally racially discriminatory. . . ."[74]

In 1913 President Wilson was able to restrain temporarily by "moral suasion" laws racially discriminatory toward the Japanese. However, under renewed pressure of the anti-Japanese factions, the Alien Land Law was enacted by the State of California, forbidding the purchase and ownership of land by an alien ineligible to citizenship.

This law applied to Asiatics, for under the laws governing citizenship in the United States, "white men and Africans are eligible for citizenship but Mongolians are not mentioned."

The courts in 1907 decided that Mongolians were not eligible to become naturalized citizens of the United States. In California, following the First World War, the courts refused to allow Japanese who had served in the United States Army to gain citizenship under the statute providing that aliens serving in the army might become citizens. In Hawaii, where the Japanese population was far greater than in California, the Japanese were admitted to citizenship.[75]

Anti-Japanese feelings were again displayed in the debates on the League of Nations, when Senator Phelan of California said he was "very glad that our President at the Paris conference, standing with representatives of Australia and New Zealand, stemmed these insidious movements of the Japanese to establish a principle of race equality, under which they would have flooded this land. . . ." The senator alluded to the unassimilable nature of the Japanese people in saying that "our form of government rests upon the foundations of a prosperous and patriotic citizenry of assimilable people. To suffer its deterioration is to undermine democratic institutions and invite disaster." Not only would the Japanese destroy our institutions, but they were innately unpatriotic. The senator argued that President Wilson and Colonel House had voted against Japan's resolution for

---

[74] *Foreign Relations*, 1913, pp. 632–33.
[75] Clarence A. Locan, "The Japanese Problem in California: Past and Present Phases of a Situation that Threatens International Complications," *Current History*, XIII (October 1920), 7.

racial equality, and that Lloyd George had joined with them "because all the great tributary colonies of the British Commonwealth were of one mind on the question of denying equality to the Japanese on account of what it implied."

According to Senator Phelan, equality in practice and a resulting tide of Japanese immigration would destroy the standards of American civilization. This would result in "legal equality under which the Japanese would claim the right freely to come to the United States . . . just as do the nationals of any other country. . . ." The Japanese would then demand citizenship, the elective franchise, the right to hold land, and the right to intermarry.[76]

In 1920 the Japanese problem again threatened, and the *Nation* wrote that "the primary question was 'race antagonism'." On the subject of race, California still lived as did "some other sections of the country, in the dense and heated atmosphere of a bygone time." They assumed "without debate that the white race is superior and that all other races are inferior; that people of different races do not mix"; and that the presence of large numbers of peoples "with different, and hence presumably lower standards of living inevitably tends to pull down the standards of citizens whose plane of living is higher." Racial interbreeding was unthinkable according to this concept "because it is certain to produce a low quality of children." Thus, arose the war cry which reverberated from the anti-Chinese days of Denis Kearney and the San Francisco sandlots to the "anti-Japanese days of Senator Phelan, 'The Japanese must go'."

The article concluded that the American people "should make their position clear. The challenge which California is preparing to throw down should be met—as any other disloyal manifestation by a State should be met—by a firm assertion of Federal authority. . . . With that, however, should go also, the adoption of the only rational principle upon which a modern nation can safely stand; namely, the entire abolition of race discrimination."[77]

Americans, however, did not face the question of race squarely; and the Japanese, Chinese, and other Orientals played an important part in conditioning the American sense of mission in the Pacific.

[76] *Congressional Record*, 66 Cong., 2 sess., LIX, pt. 9: 9206 (February 20, 1920).
[77] "Editorial," *Nation*, CXI (August 7, 1920), 146.

THE IMPERIALIST CAMPAIGN

In the year 1899, Rudyard Kipling's poem, "White Man's Burden," was published in the United States in *McClure's Magazine*. Theodore Roosevelt received an advance copy which he sent to Henry Cabot Lodge saying that it "was very poor poetry but made good sense from the expansion point of view."[78] Most of the imperialists seemed to agree with Roosevelt, if their actions were indicative of their beliefs. For the sense of the poem was a powerful force in America, despite the hidden warnings therein. Nor did the imperialists heed the warnings of David Starr Jordan in the *Human Harvest*, in which he argued that wars over imperial possessions would result in the survival of the unfittest. America was prepared to take all the risks for imperial glory. It was the right, the duty, and the mission of the civilized nations to carry the blessings of civilization to the far reaches of the world, and America had to take up its share of the burden.

There was in the United States a climate of opinion, a *mystique* of white supremacy supported by the Darwinian concept of the survival of the fittest, which led racial theorists to be confident that the white man was superior.[79] The theories advanced were the work of such well-known racial propagandists as "Count de Gobineau, Huston Stewart Chamberlain, Lothrop Stoddard, and Madison Grant, whose type of analysis of [race relations] for two or three generations was circulated among the literate group and helped to reinforce the traditional views of millions who had never heard of these authors."[80]

Americans, however, needed little help from Darwin. Concepts of race or racism in America could be traced to the arguments used to counter those of the abolitionists. As Hofstadter once said, "As for the United States, a people familiar with Indian warfare on the frontier and the proslavery arguments of southern politicians and publicists had been thoroughly grounded in notions of racial superiority."

Of course, the American experiences with the Chinese and Japanese in the last quarter of the nineteenth century had an effect on American attitude concerning race. Hofstadter implied that the

[78] Lodge, *Roosevelt-Lodge Letters*, I, 384.
[79] Blake and Barck, *United States in Its World Relations*, p. 354.
[80] Simpson and Yinger, *Racial and Cultural Minorities*, p. 12.

"survival of the fittest" was a concept of American expansionism as early as 1849 and that Manifest Destiny carried the seeds of the idea that the nation as an organism must be expansive.[81]

Ideas of race superiority in the United States have been a clear and perceptible thread that runs through the warp and woof of the American fabric. Edward McNall Burns observed that the doctrine of racial superiority was ingrained in American life with "a tenacity almost unmatched by that of any other doctrine. From colonial times until well into the twentieth century there has never been a period when men of influence and prominence could not be found in substantial number arranged on the side of ethnological prejudice. And it is a melancholy fact that the ranks have included some of the most liberal and human thinkers in American history."[82]

[81] Richard Hofstadter, *Social Darwinism in American Thought*, p. 171.
[82] Edward McNall Burns, *The American Idea of Mission*, p. 187.

II

Racism and
The Imperialist Campaign

Take up the White Man's burden—
Ye dare not stoop to less—
Nor call too loud on Freedom
To cloke your weariness.
By all ye will or whisper,
By all ye leave or do,
The silent sullen peoples
Shall weigh your God and you.
—Kipling1

In 1893 Hawaii beckoned Americans with a promise of glorious adventure, presenting the opportunity for Americans to become involved in the mission of carrying Western civilization to the Pacific. Some Americans felt that the possession of Hawaii would be the first step toward empire. Others felt that the acquisition of Hawaii and other imperial possessions would be repugnant to republican institutions. The existence of the latter group necessitated a campaign to convert the majority of Americans to the glory of an imperial adventure.

The imperialist campaign enlisted a wide range of advocates. Among them were military experts, statesmen, publicists, politicians, and teachers. One such individual, Alfred T. Mahan, played the triple role of military expert, writer, and teacher. Historians are in agreement that some of his ideas became the basis of the imperialist argument.

Mahan was conscious of the rights of civilized nations. He respected the English, the French, and the Germans. In his blueprint for American expansion the rights of these Western powers were to be considered, but he failed even to mention the rights of natives in the path of empire. "This is no mere question of a particular act," he wrote, "for which possibly, just occasion may not yet have offered; but of a principle, a policy, fruitful of many future acts, to enter upon which, in the fullness of our national progress, the time has now arrived. The principle accepted to be conditioned only by a just and

1 The sixth verse of Rudyard Kipling's, "White Man's Burden," *McClure's Magazine*, XII (February 1899), 290–91.

candid regard for the rights and reasonable susceptibilities of other nations—none of which is contravened by the step here immediately under discussion. . . ."[2]

The step under discussion was the annexation of Hawaii. Since none of the European powers claimed Hawaii, the area was legally open for annexation by the United States. The policy, as envisioned by Mahan, was not new; it was the old colonial policy which respected only lands held by a Christian prince.[3] In the new departure, race rather than Christianity was the determining factor.

Another idea suggested by Mahan and subsequently by other American imperialists was the plebiscite. Various adaptations of the principle suggested by Mahan resulted in the annexation of Hawaii, the adoption of the Platt Amendment by Cuba, and the control of Haiti and the Dominican Republic. This device could be manipulated by the controlling Anglo-Saxon element, to the exclusion of natives, to effect union with the United States. The principle was suggested by Mahan when he wrote, "That the vaunted blessings of our economy are not to be forced upon the unwilling may be conceded; but the concession does not deny the right nor wisdom of gathering in those who wish to come."[4]

The prevailing political philosophy of the last decade of the nineteenth century was that inferior peoples were not capable of ruling over the advanced races. Since there were Americans in Hawaii who desired union with the United States, the foregoing principle could be applied. The desire of the Americans in Hawaii was the only one to be considered. The wishes of the majority of the inhabitants of Hawaii, made up of so-called inferior races, did not count in the consideration. Mahan predicted, "If this principle be adopted, there will be no hesitation about taking the positions—and they are many—upon the approaches to Panama."

Individuals such as Theodore Roosevelt accepted the teachings of Mahan as sound doctrine which should be put into practice by the United States. Roosevelt also played many important roles as a campaigner for an imperial adventure. John W. Burgess said of Roose-

[2] Alfred T. Mahan, "Hawaii and Our Future Sea Power," *Forum*, XV (March 1893), 8.
[3] Henry Steele Commager, *Documents of American History*, p. 6.
[4] Mahan, "Hawaii and Our Future Sea Power," *Forum*, XV, 8.

velt, "I regarded him from the first as a man of destiny, and felt sure that he would, sooner or later, lead the young men of the country into an adventure."[5] Burgess could have added "armed with political theories imbibed at Burgess' own feet."

In examining Roosevelt's writings and pronouncements, enough evidence is found to conclude that he believed that the Anglo-Saxon peoples had advanced to a position in the evolution of political societies not equaled by any other race. To this belief was added a strong nationalism, with all of its attributes and limitations. Against this background he expressed his dissatisfaction with the foreign policy of Cleveland in 1894, expressing the hope that the Republicans "would go in avowedly to annex Hawaii and build an oceanic canal with the money of Uncle Sam."[6]

There was a difference in the capacities of different people which produced different results under the influence of the same stimuli, according to Roosevelt. He took exception to Benjamin Kidd's view that ceremonial Christianity had its civilizing force in human societies, holding to the belief that Christianity had its civilizing influence only on the Western Europeans and Americans. He observed that "ceremonial Christianity in other races produced quite different results." The examples used by Roosevelt to illustrate his point were Abyssinia and Haiti, both Christian countries, but neither having advanced far along the paths of Western civilization.[7] He observed that "the negro, for instance, has been kept down by lack of intellectual development as by anything else. . . ." The cause of the decay of the Roman fiber was attributed to "the immense damage done to the Italian husbandman by the importation of Asiatic and African slaves."[8] This view found its practical application in Roosevelt's support of restrictive immigration legislation designed to exclude "especially, races which do not assimilate readily with our own."[9]

Roosevelt was thankful that democratic policy had "kept the temperate zone of the new and newest world a heritage for white

[5] Burgess, *Recent Changes in American Constitutional Theory*, p. 36.

[6] Roosevelt to Lodge, October 27, 1894, *Roosevelt-Lodge Letters*, I, 139.

[7] Theodore Roosevelt, "Review of Kidd, *Social Evolution*," *North American Review*, CLXI (July 1895), 107.

[8] Theodore Roosevelt, "Review of Brooks Adams, *The Law of Civilization and Decay*," *Forum*, XXII (February 1897), 581.

[9] Theodore Roosevelt, *The Works of Theodore Roosevelt*, XV, 27.

people." And for that policy the whole civilization of the future owed a debt of gratitude.[10] It was his belief that geography had a distinct influence on the development of the races. He agreed with Gustave Le Bon on race and thought the sense of the poem, "White Man's Burden," was good "from the expanionist point of view. . . ."[11] He did not take exception to the idea that the tropics were inhabited by peoples in the childhood of their development who had to be taught by the superior white race. Roosevelt believed in the superiority and inferiority of the races; the Negro he put in the latter group.[12] The people of the Caribbean area belonged also to the inferior group in the classification of the races. He observed that if a colony "is in a region where the colonizing race has to do its work by means of other inferior races . . . from the standpoint of the race nothing would be gained. The English conquest and colonization of Jamaica had been merely to turn Jamaica into a negro island with a future . . . much like Santo Domingo."[13]

These were some of the views which, with the vaunted blessings of Anglo-Saxon civilization, Roosevelt would advocate, assist, fight for, and sustain in regions inhabited by peoples he considered inferior in political capacity.

OTHER ADVOCATES OF IMPERIALISM

It is difficult to determine whether Roosevelt's early sympathy for the Cuban cause was genuine or whether he used it as an instrument of policy in his campaign for a larger imperialist foreign policy. His later actions point in the direction of the latter position. He supported Henry Cabot Lodge in his position on the Cuban resolution in 1896, which was in favor of recognizing the belligerency of the Cubans. Roosevelt advised Lodge that it should be made "clear that you will support any such resolution the moment there is hope of making it effective."[14]

[10] Roosevelt, "Review of *Social Evolution*," *North American Review*, CLXI, 107.
[11] Roosevelt to Lodge, January 12, 1899, *Roosevelt-Lodge Letters*, I, 218.
[12] Seth M. Scheiner, "President Roosevelt and the Negro, 1901–1908," *Journal of Negro History*, XLVII (July 1962), 182.
[13] Roosevelt, *Works*, XV, 230–31.
[14] Roosevelt to Lodge, January 2, 1896, *Roosevelt-Lodge Letters*, I, 205.

He praised Lodge, saying, "I thought your speech on Cuba excellent; one of the best things you have done."[15] In this speech, Lodge had said that Cuba in the hands of the United States or in the hands of its own people, who were friendly and attached to the United States by "ties of interest and gratitude," would be a bulwark of the United States.[16] In the same year Roosevelt expressed hope that President McKinley would "take a strong stand about Hawaii and Cuba."[17]

The campaign for territorial expansion continued into 1897 when Roosevelt wrote to Lodge, "My utterances are mild when compared to yours. Your speech about Cuba made me feel proud." In reference to his own contribution to the campaign of expansion he said, "I got the Southern Society literally standing on the table on Washington's Birthday when I talked about Crete and Cuba."[18] He felt that the United States should decide whether or not to annex the Hawaiian Islands regardless of the attitude of Japan. The annexation of Hawaii was an Anglo-Saxon prerogative.[19]

By 1898 Roosevelt had written about expansion, talked about expansion, and prepared the navy to be the instrument of expansion.[20] He was now ready to fight for the policy of expansion. He, therefore, offered his services at the beginning of the war with Spain.

From his camp, Roosevelt wrote Lodge not to make peace "until we get Porto Rico, while Cuba is made independent and the Philippines at any rate taken from the Spaniards."[21] Roosevelt would not concede that either the Cubans or the Puerto Ricans could be left free to develop their own governments.

After the war, the emphasis shifted to the duty of the United States to do its share of the world's work. As President of the United States, Roosevelt succinctly gave his views on the unequal development of the races:

---

[15] *Ibid.*, p. 214.
[16] *Congressional Record*, 54 Cong., 1 sess., XXVIII, pt. 2: 1971 (February 20, 1896).
[17] Roosevelt to Lodge, December 4, 1896, *Roosevelt-Lodge Letters*, I, 243.
[18] *Ibid.*, p. 252.
[19] Roosevelt to Lodge, August 3, 1897, *ibid.*, p. 268.
[20] Roosevelt to Lodge, September 21, 1897, *ibid.*, p. 278. Roosevelt had made plans showing the location of ships of the line in event of war with Spain.
[21] Roosevelt to Lodge, May 19, 1898, *ibid.*, p. 299.

It is no light task for a nation to achieve the temperamental qualities without which the institutions of free government are but an empty mockery. Our people are now successfully governing themselves, because for more than a thousand years they have been slowly fitting themselves, sometimes consciously, sometimes unconsciously, toward that end. What has taken us thirty generations to achieve, we cannot expect to see another race accomplish out of hand, especially when large portions of that race start very far behind the point which our ancestors had reached even thirty generations ago. In dealing with the Philippine people we must show both patience and strength, forbearance and steadfast resolution. Our aim is high. . . . We hope to do for them what has never before been done for any people of the tropics—to make them fit for self-government after the fashion of really free nations.[22]

Roosevelt did not believe in the technique of teaching inferior peoples by allowing them to learn by doing, as the Anglo-Saxons had learned. They were innately incapable of that kind of achievement. If the Filipinos were a little reluctant to accept the status of inferiority, they must be made to realize that the United States was their master.[23] The master-subordinate relationship should persist because "we ought in good faith to try to do our share of the world's work. . . . The problem presented to us in the Philippine Islands is akin to, but not exactly like, the problems presented to the other great civilized powers which have possessions in the Orient. There are points of resemblance in our work to the work which is being done by the British in India and Egypt, by the French in Algiers, by the Dutch in Java, by the Russians in Turkestan, [and] by the Japanese in Formosa. . . ."[24]

While the Japanese were included in the civilizing function, Roosevelt later showed that he was not adverse to compromising their rights in working out the "gentlemen's agreement." It was during his administration that the West Coast agitation against the Japanese reached alarming proportions. Roosevelt's solution to the problem was in keeping with the attitude of the people in the Western states, namely to work out a means for qualified exclusion. The Japanese government agreed not to issue any more passports to skilled or unskilled workers, except those who had previously resided in the

[22] *Foreign Relations,* 1901, p. xxxii.
[23] Roosevelt, *Works,* XVI, 476.
[24] *Foreign Relations,* 1904, p. xlvii.

United States or their wives or their children under twenty-one years of age.

The peoples of the tropics were to Roosevelt like children; they had not evolved to maturity in political matters. It was his belief that no one people "ever benefited another people more than we benefited the Filipinos by taking possession of their island." The Filipinos should remember, as should the Americans who had done so much damage in agitating for immediate independence for which the Filipinos were unfit, that self-government depended upon them. All the United States could do was to give them the "opportunity to develop the capacity for self-government. . . . We must be wise and generous; we must help the Filipinos to master the difficult art of self-control, which is simply another name for self government."[25]

Roosevelt implied that only the Anglo-Saxon was competent to measure the progress toward self-control. This required the dependent peoples to measure up to indefinite standards of civilization.

Roosevelt's nationalism was narrow in that it reserved to Anglo-Saxons the innate ability to govern themselves. Yet the same nationalism, colored by his racism, convinced him that the blessings of his kind of civilization should be exported to those who could not achieve them on their own and who had no rights in the matter. It was the duty of the United States to take up its share of the "White Man's burden."

No less ardent a campaigner for imperialistic adventure was Henry Cabot Lodge. Lodge was a writer, a senator from Massachusetts, and a good friend of Mahan and Roosevelt. He was also a nationalist, advocating the basic principles of preparedness held by Mahan and Roosevelt.

In his racial views Lodge had many of the basic preconceptions associated with the Anglo-Saxon *mystique*. He was willing to use the anti-Japanese, anti-Chinese agitation of laborers on the West Coast to help get more stringent immigration legislation through Congress.[26] Lodge's advocacy of Hawaiian annexation displayed his racism. To him, the Hawaiian queen was semibarbarous and corrupt. The Americans and Englishmen on the other hand represented all the

[25] *Foreign Relations,* 1908, pp. xlvi–xlvii.
[26] Lodge to Roosevelt, June 18, 1905, *Roosevelt-Lodge Letters,* II, 157–58.

wealth, intelligence, character, and civilization in Hawaiian society.[27]

In the Cuban matter, Lodge called some newspapers "alien" in order to discredit their accounts of conditions on the island. He sought to correct misconceptions gained "from headlines of one or two newspapers edited by aliens." Lodge was aware of the prevailing racial climate in the United States and used it in his campaign to intervene in Cuba. He ignored the importance of the Negro in the Cuban fight for freedom. In this respect he was in accord with other advocates of imperialism by first playing down the importance of the "inferior race" in the territory to be annexed, then playing up the importance of the "inferior race" to avoid just treatment under democratic procedures. Illustrative of the technique of playing down the importance of the Negro element in Cuba was Lodge's statement that "the officers of the provisional government are Cubans, white men. . . . Among the principal military officers there are only three of negro blood. . . ."[28]

On Rudyard Kipling's poem, "White Man's Burden," Lodge commented that the sense and the verse were both good.[29]

Writing to Roosevelt from Holland, Lodge had glowing praise for the Dutch people in racial terms:

What courage, fortitude and grim energy and pertinacity—a powerful race. I see in you some of the qualities which have made you great. . . . You ought to go to Holland. . . . After all you are one of the half dozen great men whom that little country or rather race has given to the world. . . . You ought to go to the home of your ancestors and your race. You owe them a great deal. . . .[30]

Lodge campaigned for a large navy to be the instrument by which conquest would be possible.[31] He pushed the annexation of Hawaii and supported a policy of American intervention in Cuba. During the war with Spain he became committed to the acquisition of Puerto Rico and wrote Roosevelt that he had had "a long talk with the Presi-

[27] Henry Cabot Lodge, "Our Blundering Foreign Policy," *Forum*, XIX (March 1895), 8.
[28] Henry Cabot Lodge, "Our Duty to Cuba," *Forum*, XXI (May 1896), 279–82.
[29] Lodge to Roosevelt, January 14, 1899, *Roosevelt-Lodge Letters*, I, 385.
[30] Lodge to Roosevelt, July 26, 1908, *ibid.*, II, 308–309.
[31] Lodge to Roosevelt, February 27, 1896, *ibid.*, I, 215.

dent . . . *and* he was very clear and strong about both Cuba and Porto Rico." Lodge was dejected that President McKinley had not given much consideration to the Philippines, but was elated that the President had done "everything to secure the annexation of Hawaii." It was a great satisfaction to him when the President spoke of the annexation of Hawaii "as a step in a policy."[32] In May, 1898, he wrote that "Porto Rico is not forgotten and we mean to have it. Unless I am utterly and profoundly mistaken the Administration is now fully committed to the large policy that we both desire."[33]

When, in 1899, Lodge was made chairman of the Committee on the Philippines, he wrote Roosevelt, "I have now got the Philippines in my especial charge, and I have been much gratified by the manner in which the committee insisted that I should take the place."[34] Lodge expressed pleasure at having Senator Albert J. Beveridge of Indiana as a member of the Philippine committee.[35]

Roosevelt and Lodge were almost methodical in their rise to positions of influence in the affairs of the nation. From these positions they could shape to a greater degree "the large policy" that they desired for the United States. This large policy encompassed acquisitions of land, naval bases, power, prestige, and commerce. The rights of the native inhabitants of the areas desired were only incidental in their thoughts.

If these two individuals built the fires of imperial adventure, they were aided immeasurably in keeping them burning by Senator Albert J. Beveridge of Indiana. Beveridge crusaded for the same cause, held the same views, and was eloquent in expressing them. Roosevelt expressed the desire that Lodge should meet Senator Beveridge, whose views on public matters were the same as theirs.[36]

Beveridge was a nationalist who read into the Hamiltonian doctrine of implied powers the right of the central government to do whatever it saw fit. In an address before the Middlesex Club on April 27, 1898, Beveridge said in support of the policy of expansion, "If this means the Stars and Stripes over an Isthmian canal . . . over Hawaii . . . over

[32] Lodge to Roosevelt, July 23, 1896, *ibid.*, pp. 329–30.
[33] Lodge to Roosevelt, May 24, 1898, *ibid.*, pp. 299–300.
[34] Lodge to Roosevelt, December 16, 1899, *ibid.*, p. 430.
[35] Lodge to Roosevelt, December 13, 1899, *ibid.*, p. 427.
[36] Roosevelt to Lodge, September 11, 1899, *ibid.*, p. 421.

Cuba and the southern seas . . . then let us meet that meaning with a mighty joy and make the meaning good, no matter what barbarism and all our foes may do or say." Before the first shot had been fired in Cuba, Claude Bowers quotes Beveridge as saying that he beheld, "as a part of the Almighty's infinite plan, the disappearance of debased civilizations and decaying races before the higher civilizations of the nobler and more virile types of men."

Beveridge was elected partly on his appeal to racial feeling. He asked in his campaign for the Senate: "Will you affirm by your vote that you are an infidel to American vigor and power and practical sense? Or that we are of the ruling race of the world; that ours is the blood of government; ours the heart of dominion; ours the brain and genius of administration?"[37] In this speech the march of the flag becomes the advance of the super-dreadnought, meting out, from Beveridge's point of view, liberty, self-government, and life. However, from the view of the peoples in the path of this super-dreadnought, there was a condition of slavery, qualified self-government, and foreign control.

Beveridge was an astute student of expansion and went to the Philippines to get firsthand information with which to sustain the arguments supporting the imperialist position. He went to reinforce the conviction he already had, that the only salvation for the inferior peoples was tutelage by the superior Anglo-Saxon. He pointed out that Congress dared not leave out of consideration the object lessons provided by the revolutions which had taken place in the various Latin-American republics. He attributed the frequency of these revolutions to the character of the population of those countries and observed that the people were the same in race and character as the people of Cuba. "Their racial origin is the same. If there is any element of difference, that element is the greater proportion of blacks in Cuba. But history and contemporaneous fact do not justify the belief that this element, left to itself, increases the Cuban capacity for self-government. . . ."

Haiti was an example of the Negro's inability to govern himself. British Guiana and British Honduras were examples of what could be done if administration was in the hands of those capable of govern-

[37] Claude G. Bowers, *Beveridge and the Progressives*, pp. 67–73.

ment. New Mexico, with a population racially similar to that of Spanish America, gave no trouble because it was administered by the United States. "In dealing with Cuba, Congress could not ignore all this. Congress was compelled to consider the character and inexperience of Cuba's population; the history of the attempts of similar populations to govern themselves; the present conditions of such experimental governments on one hand, and the situation of the same populations, guided and restrained by the protection of an administrative people on the other hand."[38]

Beveridge was committed to administration as the key to success in colonial policy. Administration was the principle upon which the American colonial policy should be based for a century to come. According to Beveridge, each time that a departure was made from the principle of administration, errors were made for which circumstances and natural conditions forced a correction.

Not self-government for peoples who have not yet learned the alphabet of liberty; nor territorial independence for islands whose ignorant, suspicious and primitive inhabitants, left to themselves, would prey upon one another . . . not the flimsy application of abstract governmental theories possible only to the most advanced races and which applied to underdeveloped peoples, work out grotesque and fatal results—not anything but the discharge of our great national trust and greater national duty to our wards by common-sense methods will achieve the welfare of our colonies and bring us success in the civilizing work to which we are called.

Truly, Beveridge felt that the underdeveloped peoples were unequal to the task of governing themselves and that it was a mistake to entrust them with self-government. The wards had to be trained in "continuous industry," in "orderly liberty," and in that reserve and steadiness of character through which self-government was possible. The period of colonial administration reached by the Americans was inevitable. The Spanish-American War afforded the opportunity. The rapidly increasing power of the United States "and, most of all, our duty to the world as one of its civilizing powers determined it." Beveridge saw as inevitable that American control would reach "over Cuba, San Domingo, and Porto Rico." It was also inevitable that

[38] Albert J. Beveridge, "Cuba and Congress," *North American Review*, CLXXII (April 1901), 548–49.

Hawaii, considered the halfway house in the Pacific Ocean, should belong to the United States. Further expansion into the Western Pacific would inevitably occur because it was the genius of the race not to stop halfway. People such as Anglo-Saxon Americans "never pause midway in the syllogism of events, but go on to its conclusion. . . ."

Only when the power of the United States began to wane and its decline had started, would any of the possessions be given up. "What we have we hold" was "the motto of our blood." Beveridge concluded, "If any one cherishes the delusion that the American government will ever be withdrawn from our possessions let him consult the religious convictions of the Christian people. Let him find what the American pulpit thinks of such surrender to non-Christian powers of our duty and opportunity. . . ."[39]

The duty of administering good government to weaker people would not be abandoned. To give self-government to the Philippines before the people were prepared for it would be a grave error. This should not be done at the very moment when suffrage was being restricted in certain sections of the United States.[40]

In Senate debate, Beveridge called on duty, commerce, opportunity, and race in support of the retention of the Philippines, making the mission one of divine ordinance. "We will not renounce our part in the mission of our race, trustee, under God, of the civilization of the world. And we will move forward to our work . . . with gratitude for a task worthy of our strength, and thanksgiving to Almighty God that He has marked us as His chosen people, henceforth to lead in the regeneration of the world."[41]

Beveridge observed that they were dealing not only with Orientals but with Malays. To compound the difficulty of administration, these people had been trained in Spanish methods. This made the people mistake good treatment for weakness, and forbearance for fear. The only way it could have been different with these people would have been to eliminate the centuries of savagery and orientalism, and also

[39] Albert J. Beveridge, "The Development of a Colonial Policy for the United States," *The Annals*, The American Academy of Political and Social Science, XXX (July 1907), 3–15.

[40] *Ibid.*, p. 7.

[41] *Congressional Record*, 56 Cong., 1 sess., XXXIII, pt. 1: 704 (January 9, 1900).

eliminate their Spanish character and custom. "What alchemy will change the oriental quality of their blood and set the self-governing currents of the Americans pouring through their Malay veins?" he wondered. "How shall they, in the twinkling of an eye, be exalted to the heights of self-governing peoples which required a thousand years for us to reach, Anglo-Saxon though we are? . . . Savage blood, oriental blood, Malay blood, Spanish example—are these the elements of self-government?"[42] The question was deeper than party politics, deeper than the question of isolation, even deeper than constitutional power. "It is racial. God has not been preparing the English speaking and Teutonic peoples for a thousand years for nothing but vain and idle self-contemplation and self-admiration. No! He has made us the master organizers of the world to establish system where chaos reigns. . . . He has made us adept in government that we may administer government among savage and senile peoples."

Were it not for such force in the world, Beveridge believed, barbarism and night would return. It was America's divine mission, promising profits, glory, and all the happiness due to man, to lead in the regeneration of the world. The United States of America was trustee of the progress of the world and custodian of its peace. "The judgment of the Master is upon us," Beveridge exclaimed. " 'Ye have been faithful over a few things; I will make you ruler over many things.' "

In his customary racist rhetoric, he appealed to nationalism and asked, "What shall history say of us? Shall it say that we renounced that holy trust, left the savage to his base condition, the wilderness to the reign of waste? . . . Shall it say that, called by events to captain and command the proudest, ablest, purest race of history in history's noblest work, we declined that great commission? . . ."[43]

Beveridge used such arguments as two-edged weapons, striking at those who refused to subscribe to the call of imperialism by appealing to race pride, while playing up to others the duty of the Anglo-Saxons and Teutons to be missionaries to the backward peoples of the world. For Beveridge it was a matter of the great and powerful United States, inhabited by superior people, taking up a share of the "White Man's burden."

[42] *Ibid.*, p. 708.
[43] *Ibid.*, p. 711.

Another outstanding imperialistic campaigner was Senator John T. Morgan of Alabama. Morgan, representing a state with one of the largest concentrations of Negroes, seemed not to worry about the problems associated with the control of dissimilar races. The problem had been solved in Alabama at the expense of the dissimilar race so why not in Cuba, Hawaii, and any other place the United States desired?

In 1896 Morgan advocated the annexation of Cuba to the United States. He suggested that if the island of Cuba had been as close to Great Britain as it is to the United States and if the same conditions had prevailed, Great Britain would have said, "You have a rich country that we need; you have people who are incapable of self-government, . . . and the best thing that Great Britain can do is to take you into the kingdom and govern you. . . ."[44]

It was the duty of the United States to annex Hawaii. Otherwise the silent invasion of the pagan races from Asia would inundate the islands. Morgan held that the monarchy would be reestablished through the combination of the lower classes of natives with the Japanese. "We shall be compelled, if we refuse annexation," Morgan concluded, "to stand by and witness the destruction of the people of our own blood, and our citizens, without being able to assist them. . . . If there is any way to prevent the submergence of Hawaii beneath this inflow of Asiatics, except by annexation to the United States, no one seems to have been wise or fortunate enough to point it out."[45]

The senator desired to extend America's influence over dissimilar peoples in order to prevent these same people from governing a small number of Americans in Hawaii. A similar view was held by Representative Sydney E. Mudd of Maryland, who saw the problem as a struggle between the races of Asia and those of the United States. He asserted that the question of the annexation of Hawaii was a question "between Asiatic and American control for the future; between the extension of Mongolian or American civilization; between the establishment of American institutions, American liberty, and

[44] *Congressional Record,* 54 Cong., 1 sess., XXVIII, pt. 2: 1975 (February 20, 1896).
[45] John T. Morgan, "The Duty of Annexing Hawaii," *Forum,* XXV (March 1898), 13–14.

American law, and Mongolian institutions . . . and law under Mongolian peoples and semblances of forms of government."[46]

These men were in many ways voicing ideas that were ingrained in the American mind, put there by tradition, custom, and association, then buried deep in the subconscious.

One of the many sources from which ideas of expansion were gathered was the magazine. A medium used in magazines for getting across to Americans the racial nature of her imperial adventure was the cartoon. If it is true that a picture is worth a thousand words, the cartoons of the period played a very influential role in the imperialist campaign. A typical cartoon for the period portrays a very stern and benevolent Uncle Sam, with four pickaninnies gathered around him in the comfort of his living room. Two of the four, Cuba and Puerto Rico, play happily together under the protection and care of the powerful uncle. A third member of the group, Hawaii, is seriously, but happily, studying her ABC's provided for her by Uncle Sam. The fourth, the Philippines, is off to the side making martial noises with horn and drum, refusing to take part in the happy relationship, distracting the benevolent uncle from his duty to his wards. The caption reads, "Uncle Sam to Aguinaldo, 'Now Aggy, stop your noise, and be a nice boy and play with your little sisters.'"[47]

Articles, however, were perhaps the most important molder of opinion, for they were disseminated throughout the nation and reached persons of power and influence. Therefore, it is pertinent to this study to examine some of the magazine articles in which inferences of race were made as justification for United States imperialist policies.

John R. Proctor wrote that it was in the interest of civilization and humanity for the United States to retain the Philippine Islands. He cautioned that the country should not make the "criminal blunder made in the past, when we bestowed with unthinking liberality the highest privilege of Anglo-Saxon freedom upon an illiterate alien race just emerging from bondage—a priceless privilege which our fathers attained only through centuries of patient self-development. . . ." Appealing to a new imperialism based on the blood of the Anglo-

[46] *Congressional Record,* 55 Cong., 2 sess., XXXI, pt. 8: 559 (June 15, 1898).
[47] "Current History Cartoons," *Review of Reviews,* XIX (February 1899), 160.

Saxon, Proctor prophesied, "From the blood of our heroes, shed at
Santiago and Manila, there shall arise a new imperialism replacing
the waning imperialism of old Rome; an imperialism destined to
carry world-wide the principles of Anglo-Saxon peace and justice,
liberty and law."[48]

The serious faults in the relationship between the Anglo-Saxon
Americans and other races which they considered inferior were duly
noted by Proctor. However, these faults did little to dissuade propagandists from the cause of imperialism. The deficiencies in equal application of law, justice, and suffrage were noted, but with blind
subjectivity these campaigners persuaded themselves and others
that the ends justified the means.

Francis Newton Thorpe noted that the Anglo-Saxon "has not easily
acted the part of the altruist among less civilized nations. Our treatment of the negro has not been so altruistic as to wholly persuade us
that we shall do better by tribes dwelling in the Philippines." Regardless of this fact, if the United States was going to establish a relationship with people to be treated as colonials, then it was obligatory
that the United States administer for them. Administration consisted
of doing things for people that they would not or could not do for
themselves.

Thorpe was of the opinion that Puerto Rico would not be able to
develop from the territorial form to statehood along the Anglo-
Saxon pattern because of race. "Race is the key to history," according
to Disraeli, and race was, according to Thorpe, also the key to
colonization.

Where subordinate races were concerned the Constitution did not
insure the principle of republican government. "Because our self-
confidence is so great, we as a people will not hesitate to adapt our
republicanism to monarchical methods whenever necessary. Our
written constitutions will not be suffered to stand in the way. Whatever civil service is demanded in ruling subordinate races within
our jurisdiction, that service will be construed as in harmony with
the republican form."[49] There were some observers who believed

48 John R. Proctor, "Isolation or Imperialism," *Forum*, XXVI (September
1898), 25–26.

49 Francis Newton Thorpe, "The Civil Service and Colonization," *Harper's*,
XCVIII (December 1898), 860.

that it was not necessary to compromise republican institutions in order to embrace dissimilar peoples. The most cosmopolitan population in the world already existed in the United States. Could "Americans listen with patience to any word that limits our great achievements as a people to a single race?" The United States had no choice but to accept the responsibility that she found thrust upon her as a result of the Spanish-American War. Since experience showed that subtropical regions were incapable of creating either self-government or public order, it was not the time for the United States to begin the practice of self-determination for all peoples.[50]

Proctor portrayed Hawaii as a derelict flying a distress flag in mid-ocean. "The government was representing a minority insignificant in numbers, liable to overthrow at any time . . . from dangerous complications growing out of the preponderance of aliens, the situation, . . . is such as to demand the immediate action of our government."

Proctor used the device of underplaying the importance of races considered unassimilable in Hawaii by saying that it did not matter "whether there are a few thousands more or less Orientals now in Hawaii. If this be an evil, with annexation it will prove a diminishing one; without annexation, it may become impossible. . . ."[51] If there were fears that annexation meant statehood, they were dispelled by showing that Hawaii would probably be consigned to the second state in territorial development for many years. Under that system laws could be enacted similar to laws already enacted in some Southern states prescribing a property qualification or educational qualification for voting, administered by the successors to the provisional government. This technique would "thereby greatly overcome one objection to annexation based upon the ill assortment of its Japanese, Chinese and other foreign-born population."

Charles J. Swith wrote that the American system of government had already been transplanted to the Hawaiian Islands by American people. He observed, "A government and a people whose system has subjugated the Indian tribes, which did not falter with the sword or in the forum to grapple with the great problem of negro slavery and

[50] Talcott Williams, "The Ethical and Political Principles of Expansion," *The Annals*, XVI (July 1900), 242.

[51] Proctor, "Hawaii and the Changing Front of the World," *Forum*, XXIV (September 1897), 41–42.

its emancipation . . . and with the Chinese problem by curtailing its worst tendencies—should not lack the faith or the courage to extend the profit of their experiences to their kindred on the Hawaiian Islands. . . ."[52]

The decisive factor was that the people in control were in complete sympathy with the American form of government and were in reality already a part of the United States. They were, according to one advocate of annexation, " 'bone of our bone and flesh of our flesh' and need no 'change of heart' to become thoroughly patriotic American citizens."[53]

The *Nation* reported that the feelings aroused by the struggle over the annexation of Hawaii were so bitter "as to color statistics" so that they misrepresented facts concerning race and the nativity of the inhabitants. Many of these misrepresentations had been exposed.[54]

The imperialists were unable to see the limitations caused by their own racial prejudices, but decried the use of the race issue by Spain. They charged that Spain was wrong in representing to the nations of the world that the independence of her colonies would result in another Negro republic and a relapse into barbarism. There was no danger of the supremacy of the Negro in Cuba because "there is no province in which the negroes have a majority and the census shows their number is diminishing. With Cuba free, the fertility of the island would attract thousands of people from the United States who would develop its resources and make a stable government. . . ."[55]

The dangers associated with the Negro in Cuba did not become real until after the transfer of power to the United States. Then conditions which the Americans charged as existing only in the Spanish imagination became arguments to justify American imperialism in Cuba.

Senator Orville H. Platt assured the doubters that the Negro in Cuba was not interested in participating in government.[56] This was a

[52] Charles J. Swith, "Practical and Legal Aspects of Annexation," *Overland Monthly*, XXV, 2d series (January–June 1895), 594.
[53] *Congressional Record*, 55 Cong., 2 sess., XXXI, pt. 8: 561 (June 11, 1898).
[54] *Nation*, LXVII (July 14, 1897), 21.
[55] T. Gold Alvord, Jr., "Is the Cuban Capable of Self-Government?" *Forum*, XXIV (September 1897), 123.
[56] Orville H. Platt, "Our Relations to the People of Cuba and Porto Rico," *The Annals*, XVIII (July 1901), 154.

part of the effort of the imperialists to play down the importance of the subordinate groups in the colonial possessions. Robert Hill used this method in pointing out that it was an error to indiscriminately consider together the Indian population of Mexico, the Negroes of Haiti, and the white Creoles of the West Indies. Hill was even willing to boost the Negro element ever so slightly.

"The conditions of the tropical countries in which the negro race prevails are better than is generally supposed," he stated. "The experiences of the Haitians cause us to overlook the fact that other negro populations such as those of Jamaica and Barbados,—where the blacks outnumber the whites in the proportion of 50 to 1,—under beneficent English colonial control, present most orderly examples."[57]

The Haitians had made more progress than was usually credited to them by Americans, according to this view. The immediate concern was for Cuba and Puerto Rico, where white men had become acclimated and were numerically dominant. The end result of the Spanish-American War was to end "our internecine quibbles, and arouse the American nation to the appreciation of its importance as one of the great factors in the Anglo-Saxon civilization of the world."[58]

[57] Robert T. Hill, "Cuba and Its Value as a Colony," Forum, XXV (June 1898), 404.
[58] Ibid.

III

United States-Hawaiian Relations

The only area of expansion open to the United States in the last decade of the nineteenth century was in the direction of the tropics. The tropics, according to the current opinion of the period, were inhabited by people in the childhood of their political development. Many Americans regarded the native inhabitants of Hawaii as incapable of self-government and saw in these islands an opportunity for the United States to take up the "White Man's burden."

The Hawaiian Islands are a group of tropical islands situated in the mid-Pacific south of the Tropic of Cancer. The most widely separated islands of the group are about four hundred statute miles apart.

Only a small proportion of the land area of the islands is capable of sustaining a dense population. The most habitable tracts are near the sea coast, and only a part of these are really fertile. The interior portions are mountainous and craggy, with a thin soil conducive in a few localities to pasturage but unfit for agriculture. Deep rich soils at altitudes adapted to the growth of sugar cane probably form less than the fortieth part of the entire area. Shallower soils are a little more extensive and yield other crops of tropical staples in abundance.

The climate of Hawaii is warm, the temperature equable, and the sky usually clear. There is little humidity in the air, and thus, it is rarely sweltering. In the months of January, February, and March, the wind blows strongly from the southwest, and the atmosphere is damp and unpleasant. There are varied climates upon the islands themselves. As a general rule, the windward sides are excessively rainy, and the leeward sides are generally arid. The climate of the Hawaiian Islands is in general that of a mild summer. The hottest months are July and August, when the thermometer sometimes rises to 90 degrees. Frost is unknown, rains are warm, and the days and nights are so nearly the same temperature that little daily change of clothing is necessary.[1]

RACIAL CHARACTERISTICS

The census of 1896 showed a total population in Hawaii of 109,020 inhabitants composed of 31,000 native Hawaiians; 24,400 Japanese; 15,100 Portuguese; 21,600 Chinese; 8,400 part Hawaiian and part foreign blood; 3,000 American; 2,200 British, 1,100 German; 479 Norwegian and French; and 1,055 of all other nationalities. Native Hawaiians made up 28 percent of the population; Japanese, 22 percent; Chinese 20 percent; Americans and Europeans, 22 percent; and mixed bloods, 8 percent.[2]

By 1946 Hawaii's population had increased nearly four times, from 109,000 to nearly 500,000. The growth was the result of improved economic opportunities afforded by the territory and consequent immigration from the mainland, the immigration of Asiatics, and natural increase.

The racial character of Hawaii's population was diversified greatly through immigration over the fifty-three year period. Three contrasting ethnic groups—Korean, Puerto Rican, and Filipino—were added to the earlier complicated racial pattern. There was also additional immigration of Japanese and Portuguese in these years. By 1920 there were eleven major ethnic or racial groups: Hawaiian, part Hawaiian, Spanish, Puerto Rican, Portuguese, haole[3] or other Caucasian, Chinese, Japanese, Korean, Filipino, and Negro.

In 1920, 57 percent of the population of Hawaii had been born outside of Hawaii or mainland United States. The movement of the population since 1920 has been in the direction of greater integration and interracial solidity. In 1940 nearly 80 percent of the Hawaiian

[1] Senate Report, No. 227, 53 Cong., 2 sess., pp. 48–51.
[2] Senate Report, No. 681, 55 Cong., 2 sess., p. 43.
[3] Mainland Americans.

population was native or mainland born, and by 1945 the ratio had increased to over 85 percent.

The tendency for the ethnic groups to intermarry resulted in a fused population—a single American-Hawaiian type—which made it necessary for the Census Bureau to combine certain of the previously enumerated ethnic groups showing Portuguese, Spanish, and *haole* as a single Caucasian group.

In the early 1920s, almost 70 percent of the children born were of Asiatic ancestry, with the Japanese alone constituting 48 percent of the total. Prior to the Second World War, the Asiatic births had declined to 53 percent, and the Japanese ratio was 34.8 percent.[4]

Such were the racial characteristics of the islands, characteristics that were to serve as the key to a policy of imperialism. It is to be noted that the tropical location, the basic Oriental culture, and the common practice of intermarriage between the races were all repugnant to the Anglo-Saxon.

The Japanese and other Orientals played an important part in conditioning the American sense of mission in the Pacific. A part of this mission was to "advance the twin stars of Christianity and constitutional liberty." The missionaries who had carried Christianity and constitutional liberty to Hawaii saw the Orientals as a threat to these ideals. The advocates of imperialism felt that the United States owed the missionaries a debt of gratitude, which could be paid by giving protection to their children in the enjoyment of the blessings "of free republican government."[5] It was the duty of the United States government to protect those Americans who had immigrated to Hawaii under the encouragement of the American government, as well as the native Hawaiians from "the silent but rapid invasion of the pagan races of Asia." American imperialists assumed that "if the white race was subject to the rule of the native Hawaiians, the islands would fall into speedy ruin." The only way to save the Hawaiian race from extermination, or "while they exist, from being driven from their homes by the Asiatics," was to annex Hawaii to the United States.[6]

[4] *Hearings,* 79 Cong., 2 sess., H. R. 236, Subcommittee of the Committee on Territories.
[5] *Senate Report,* No. 681, 55 Cong., 2 sess., pp. 6–7.
[6] *Ibid.,* p. 12.

A RÉSUMÉ OF CONDITIONS BEFORE 1898

At the beginning of his administration in 1893, President Cleveland showed such strong opposition to the annexation of Hawaii that the proponents of annexation "both in Hawaii and in the United States, abandoned all hope of attaining their ends while he was chief executive."[7]

Shortly after his inauguration, President McKinley submitted to the Senate a treaty of annexation, which could not command the two-thirds vote to assure passage. Even after war had broken out between the United States and Spain, there was not enough support in the Senate to insure ratification. Bailey shows that a glimmer of consideration for the rights of the Hawaiians was evidenced by the oldest pro-annexation newspaper in the Hawaiian Islands when it wondered editorially how far "we the annexationists and dominant power here, numbering a small percentage of the inhabitants have the right to push men, women, and children, who largely outnumber and do not agree with us, into the risk of war."[8]

Bailey, speaking of the fear of inundation of Hawaii by Japanese, observed that "the situation . . . became so desperate that the Hawaiian officials . . . refused admittance to 1,174 Japanese immigrants during March, 1897, and sent them back to Japan. . . . In some quarters the impending dangers were thought to be so serious that annexation to the United States was urged as the only alternative."[9] Regulations and laws based upon those of the United States preceded annexation, and the proposed treaty of annexation excluded the Chinese and Japanese.

The laws of Hawaii were modeled upon the laws of the United States, and many of them were copies. "The two statutes . . . which Japan was objecting to as limiting Japanese immigration, were almost exact copies of the United States immigration laws" restricting the immigration of contract laborers and undesirable persons.[10] The

[7] Thomas A. Bailey, "The United States and Hawaii During the Spanish-American War," *The American Historical Review*, XXXVI (July 1931), 552.

[8] *Ibid.*, pp. 554–55.

[9] Thomas A. Bailey, "Japan's Protest Against the Annexation of Hawaii," *Journal of Modern History*, III (March 1931), 46.

[10] *Senate Report*, No. 681, 55 Cong., 2 sess., pp. 48–49.

Chinese and Japanese were the undesirable population because they were not, according to some Americans, able to understand American governmental principles.[11] Orientals were sometimes described as less than human, without souls, and were therefore subjected to injustices. It was alleged by Frank M. Pixley, editor of the *Argonaut*, "that where one Chinese soul has been saved, a hundred white souls have been lost by contamination of their presence. . . . The Chinese are inferior to any race God ever made; they have got the perfection of crimes of 4,000 years; they have no souls to save, and if they have, they are not worth the saving."[12]

RACE—A CONDITIONER

Many of the advocates of annexation believed that Hawaii would sustain a population many times the size of the population of 109,000 that inhabited the islands in 1898. They argued that the native race was dying out, that the Chinese and Japanese could be controlled, and that, in fact, the laws of the islands were patterned on the laws of the United States as far as coolie labor was concerned. A combination of these trends would make Hawaii a white man's country in the future.[13]

The arguments of those who opposed annexation were related to: (1) the dissimilar characteristics of the population; (2) the need for exclusion or drastic control of dissimilar peoples; (3) the idea that the tropics could never be the habitat of peoples of Anglo-Saxon and Teutonic ancestry; (4) the belief that tropical peoples were innately inferior to Anglo-Saxons and unable to assimilate; and (5) the belief that the United States had already experimented with dissimilar races and in each instance the results had been unsatisfactory.

From this viewpoint, Benjamin Kidd's *Control of the Tropics*, published in 1898, seemed to furnish the greatest support for the anti-imperialists. Kidd's arguments convinced many that the only reason for Anglo-Saxons to go into the tropics was to develop the area in the capacity of trustee in the name of civilization.[14] There were serious

11 *Ibid.*
12 See symposium in *The Pacific Review*, I (December 1920), 377.
13 *Senate Report*, No. 681, 55 Cong., 2 sess., pp. 48–49.
14 Benjamin Kidd, *The Control of the Tropics*, pp. 50–51.

doubts as to the wisdom of a policy, however humanitarian, that would lead to "inferior peoples" eventually being incorporated into the body politic of the United States and participating in the governing of Anglo-Saxons. Some believed that universal experience had taught that in countries with a tropical climate, such as Hawaii's, the great mass of the population would never consist of the Anglo-Saxon or, more broadly speaking, of the Germanic race. The Anglo-Saxon, it was said, could "be the strongest in intelligence, wealth and directing power," but would always be the weakest in numbers.[15] If Hawaii were annexed, the United States would continue to annex countries with equally heterogeneous populations.

In discussing the obstacles to Hawaiian annexation, Thomas M. Cooley alluded to both the racial preconceptions that prevented the annexation of the Dominican Republic and the limiting influence of the Constitution.

. . . When brought face to face with the question whether it was ever contemplated that the Constitution of the United States should have capacity for expansion that might extend it over independent states of colored people located upon an island in the Atlantic Ocean, there was an instinctive feeling among American people that protested against the thought. . . . The Union was to be of "United States of America," and if it could reach out into the sea for the bringing-in of a people so different from our own as were those then occupying San Domingo, or for the founding of states of colored races, it might so far as the constitutional question was concerned . . . be extended to cover colonies in Arabia or in Zululand which would eventually become states and send representatives to Washington to assist in governing us. . . .[16]

It was his belief that racial considerations were responsible for the rejection of the treaty proposing the annexation of the Dominican Republic during the Grant administration and that these should be the basic consideration in the rejection of the proposed Hawaiian annexation treaty.

The fear that Anglo-Saxons would be subject to government by

[15] *Harper's Weekly*, XLI (January 2, 1897), 2.
[16] Thomas M. Cooley, "Grave Obstacles to Hawaiian Annexation," *Forum*, XV (June 1893), 406.

inferior peoples was strengthened when it was pointed out that cru-
cial decisions in the legislature of the United States and the electoral
college, in many instances, hung on a few votes. The idea that a Hawaiian delegation elected to represent Orientals would control deciding votes affecting the lives of the Anglo-Saxon population in the
United States was more than many people were ready to accept. In
debating the question of annexation, Congressman Henry V. Johnson of Indiana asked:

> . . . Shall great public issues affecting the vital interest of all our people
> be submitted for determination to the Senators and Representatives from
> Hawaii? . . . Shall they by holding the balance of power and casting the
> decisive votes where the questions are close, shape thereby the civil policy
> and direct the destiny of 70,000,000 of free people?
> You cannot break the force of this objection . . . by admitting these
> islands as States in the Union and yet depriving the masses of the right to
> vote by the imposition of restricted ballot. Such a policy . . . would impose
> upon Hawaii . . . by the force of positive law the same deprivation of suf-
> frage claimed to exist in the Southern States now, in defiance of law. . . .[17]

The objectors pointed out that immigration laws were designed to
exclude persons and classes which endangered the standards of
American citizenship. Yet these new imperialistic schemes would
bring into the Union populations far more undesirable not merely by
the thousands but ultimately by the millions.[18]

In a Senate report on conditions in Hawaii leading to the revolution
of 1893, it was reported by Senator John T. Morgan, chairman of the
investigating committee, that the revolution was a result of a racial
struggle. He reported that the "queen and her party had determined
to grasp absolute power and destroy the Constitution [of Hawaii]
and the rights of the white people." This report showed that the
queen's action was based on racial distinction and prejudice entirely.
If her program had been allowed to go into effect, it would have
resulted in the destruction of the rights of the missionaries. It was,
according to the report, an effort to exclude all white persons from
participation in the government of Hawaii and to return the govern-

---

[17] *Congressional Record*, 55 Cong., 2 sess., XXXI, pt. 7: 5998 (June 15, 1898).
[18] *Harper's Weekly*, XLI (January 2, 1897), 2.

ment to "that condition of debasement from which those very people and their fathers had relieved it."[19] The overthrow of the monarchy was occasioned by the efforts of a majority racial group to submerge and control the influence of a minority dissimilar group. It was clear that the native Hawaiians were trying to practice the kind of control over a dissimilar people that was being practiced in the United States.

The annexationists believed that the Hawaiians were incapable of administering their government and had to be led by the superior white element in Hawaii. This element created, through the Hawaiian Constitution of 1894, a republican government in which it was difficult for the native Hawaiians and other Asiatics to participate. It was reported that "the electorate consisted of all male adult citizens who took an oath of renunciation of the monarchy" and gave allegiance to the Republic. Under this constitution, Asiatics were not eligible to become citizens or to vote. The Americans in Hawaii, from their positions in control of the legislature, were able to effect a bloodless revolution with the avowed purpose of annexation to the United States.[20]

Because of the opposition of Cleveland, the advocates of annexation had to wait until the imperialists had sufficiently publicized their cause. The opponents of annexation were not idle in the public debate on the question. They implied collusion on the part of the United States in the Hawaiian revolt and charged that the revolt was undemocratic. In the words of Representative John Fitzgerald of Massachusetts, it was a fundamental principle of democratic government that government should rest on the consent of the governed. Yet "in Hawaii but 2,700 persons—out of a population of 100,000—have been consulted in regard to the annexation of that country to the United States. There are nearly 40,000 of native Hawaiians in these Islands. . . . They were not given an opportunity to express their views on the annexation question."[21] Americans, with their homegrown racial prejudices, had denied the majority of the native population the right to participate in their government through a successful revolt. Champ Clark of Missouri asked earlier why not submit the question of annexation to a vote of the Hawaiian people? President

[19] Senate Report, No. 227, 53 Cong., 2 sess., p. 9.
[20] Bemis, A Diplomatic History of the United States, pp. 459–62.
[21] Congressional Record, 55 Cong., 2 sess., XXXI, pt. 7: 5967 (June 15, 1898).

Dole dared not because he knew he held office through usurpation and that the vast majority of the Hawaiians were opposed to him and all of his works. Under the monarchy more than 14,000 persons voted, but under the oligarchy only 2,800 were given the elective franchise, many of whom worked for the Dole Pineapple Company.[22]

Representative Richard P. Bland of Missouri observed that no one could vote in Hawaii without swearing to support a constitution which provided for annexing the island to the United States. The constitution had been forced upon the people of the island by a handful of Americans and had "disfranchised all the inhabitants of the island who will not swear that they will vote to surrender their native land and to another government before they are permitted to vote."[23] The American people were horrified, according to Representative Fitzgerald, when the news of the "attack of Jameson and his English mercenaries upon the Transvaal country was made known; yet we submit to the spectacle of so-called American citizens deliberately overthrowing and capturing this Hawaiian territory, and then ask that it be annexed to the United States."[24] Here was the principle espoused by Mahan, that those who wanted to join the United States should be accepted and all native opposition discounted.

Questions were raised as to the status of the children born of Chinese or Japanese parentage in territory belonging to the United States. Would they not be United States citizens? Under the Constitution would not the native inferior races be given the franchise as soon as annexation took place? Would not this place the government in the hands of inferior races beyond redemption? What benefits would be derived from such a population? Would the security of our institutions be increased? Representative Bland wanted to know whether or not the superior race would not find some pretext to disfranchise the inferiors after they were admitted to the Union, much as the Dole government had disfranchised the native Hawaiians in order to form a treaty proposing annexation to the United States. He alluded to the effects the domestic racial experiences would have on relations to Hawaii in asking, "Have we not enough of race prejudice and race conflict in this country? This race question is not settled

[22] *Ibid.,* pt. 6: 5793–94 (June 11, 1898).
[23] *Ibid.,* p. 5841 (June 13, 1898).
[24] *Ibid.,* pt. 7: 5967 (June 15, 1898).

here. . . . It is one of the most perplexing problems in the future of this Government to settle, and the more perplexities you add to it the more difficult it becomes."[25]

According to Representative Robert F. Broussard of Louisiana, problems would be created by annexation that were similar to problems already existing in the Southern states. It was hoped that some of the Southern states had made some progress toward solving the vexing problem of race. South Carolina, Mississippi, and Louisiana set the pattern of camping outside the Fourteenth and Fifteenth Amendments to the Constitution. In this connection, Broussard considered it advantageous to the white men of Hawaii to allow them to run their government without the interference of the Fourteenth Amendment. He entreated, "In the name of the white men of America, let us not enlarge the scope of this race question."[26]

John F. Shafroth of Colorado stated that the Constitution declared that "no person shall be deprived of the right of citizenship on account of race, color, or previous condition of servitude. . . . When territory is added to this nation, we are bound to give the inhabitants there all of the rights of citizenship or overturn the guaranty of the Constitution."[27]

Local government in Hawaii or admission to statehood, Shafroth said, meant a race problem. One race problem, in some states where the dissimilar races were almost equally divided, had almost destroyed republican institutions. How much more difficult would be the problem where the proportion against the white race was more than fifteen to one? Was it possible that it was a wise policy to add to the United States "the same Asiatic inhabitants against whom the people of the Pacific Coast once rose in their wrath and compelled the enactment of laws excluding them from our shores?"[28]

Questions were raised about the legality of the procedure used to annex Hawaii to the United States. The advocates of annexation argued that Texas was the precedent; however, the opponents observed that there was a difference in method. Texas was required to form a state government with a republican constitution and under those

[25] *Ibid.*, pt. 6: 5842 (June 13, 1898).
[26] *Ibid.*, pt. 7: 5938 (June 14, 1898).
[27] *Ibid.*, p. 634.
[28] *Ibid.*

conditions was admitted to the Union. Every man in the State of Texas was given the rights of citizenship.[29] Only a select group was given the rights of citizenship under the proposed joint resolution for the annexation of Hawaii. Race obviously played a part in delineating the citizenship of Hawaiians and in defining the status of the territory.

Carl Becker found that the Supreme Court had, with possibly minor exceptions, interpreted the United States as "all of the territory under the jurisdiction of the Federal Government."[30] The Court had always maintained that the Constitution extends to the territories and that the Congress is not absolute there, but has plenary legislative power modified by the positive and absolute limitations found in the Constitution.[31] The Constitution had traditionally followed the flag according to this view. If this was true, then race would have no adverse effect on the acquisition of Hawaii, for the Constitution was color blind.

Americans committed to the imperial idea persuaded themselves to play down the race issue in Hawaii in arguments favoring annexation. The important thing was to annex the islands. They reasoned that Hawaii could support 1,000,000 people rather than the 100,000 already there. The 21,000 Chinese would not be a problem, for within ten years after the source of supply was effectively cut off, as in the United States, Orientals in Hawaii would be found infrequently, "and only washing the dirty linen of the superior and more prosperous people."[32] These expansionists minimized the close relationship between the economy of Hawaii and the labor of so-called inferior peoples.

Many Americans were not willing to take the chance suggested by the proponents of annexation, who argued that the Hawaiian race was dying out, that the Chinese could be effectively controlled, and that there would be an influx of Anglo-Saxons to Hawaii from the mainland. Champ Clark of Missouri was one of the doubters and voiced his doubts in Congress. A Chinaman never could be fit for

[29] *Ibid.*, pt. 6: 5777–78 (June 11, 1898).
[30] Carl Becker, "Law and Practice of the United States in the Acquisition and Government of Territory," *The Annals,* XVI (July 1900), 407.
[31] *Ibid.*, pp. 407–408.
[32] *Congressional Record,* 55 Cong., 2 sess., XXXI, pt. 6: 5787 (June 11, 1898).

American citizenship. According to Clark, "His color, his diet, his mental conformation, his habits of thought, his methods of conduct, his style of living, his ideas of government, his theory of domestic relations, his code of morals, his religion, his passiveness in servitude, . . . his manners, his amusements, the very fashion of his dress, are radically un-American." He asked, why not learn something from the facts of history and science? "For fact it is, though it may be amazing —that Tuetonic civilization and representative government are co-extensive with the wheat belt." In an effort to ridicule the Republican supporters of the joint resolution, he asked, "How can we endure our shame when a Chinese Senator from Hawaii, with his pigtail hanging down his back, with his pagan joss in his hand, shall from his curule chair and in pigeon English proceed to chop logic with George Frisbie Hoar or Henry Cabot Lodge? O Tempora! O Mores!"

Senator Justin S. Morrill of Vermont thought the character of the greater part of the ill-gathered races of the population of Hawaii was most undesirable. He said these races were "gathered by contract to long years of semi-slavery by sugar employers." This did not warrant and never could entitle them to an equal representation in the Senate with any other state.[33]

Former President Benjamin Harrison found that the United States had departed from its traditional form of expansion; that is, expanding into regions that were either unpeopled or very sparsely peopled by civilized man at the time of annexation. Further, by their situation, climate, and soil they were adapted to the use of an increasing American population. The departure was to acquire people rather than land and these chiefly of other races who would not "homologate." Out of the attempted solution, an effort was made to wrest the "government from its constitutional basis; by introduction of wholly new views of the status of the people of the territories, and of some startling new methods of dealing with them."[34]

The minority members of the House Committee on Foreign Affairs reported adversely on the proposed joint resolution for the annexation of Hawaii. Some of their stated reasons implied racial bases.

[33] *Ibid.*, pp. 5790–92, 6141.
[34] Benjamin Harrison, "The Status of Annexed Territory and Its Free Civilized Inhabitants," *North American Review*, CLXXII (January 1901), 1–2.

First, "the people of Hawaii have not been consulted about the proposed annexation." As previously pointed out, a small group of whites controlled the government in Hawaii. The minority of the committee was sure that under democratic procedures the native Hawaiians would have rejected the treaty. Second, "the people of the United States have not been consulted about the proposed annexation." The minority charged that "the only hope for Hawaiian annexation, and therefore the desire of the annexationists, is to consummate their scheme under the cry of 'war emergency' before the American people could be consulted. . . ." The view held here was that the American people would not knowingly incorporate dissimilar peoples into the Union with the possibility of creating another race problem. Third, "the annexation in the manner proposed is unconstitutional. . . ." It was the opinion of the minority that the House of Representatives was brought into the question because the administration lacked enough votes in the Senate to approve the treaty, due to the racial composition of Hawaii's population. Fourth, "the population is not racially nor religiously nor otherwise homogeneous with our own."[35]

There were many persons in the United States who agreed with the minority report. Daniel Agnew observed that the lawful Hawaiian government had been overthrown by Americans who, "with the connivance of abettors in the United States, had secretly imported arms and ammunition, expelling the lawful native government," and held it by force of arms. Subsequently, they put down the attempts of the natives to regain their "God-given rights." The small revolutionary body of Americans was the government with which President McKinley made the treaty to incorporate the islands and their people into the Union. The people of Hawaii did not have a voice in making the treaty. "This mixed . . . brown, yellow, and dusky people, partly pagan, cannot be absorbed by assimilation, for they cannot marry with American whites." President McKinley had warned the people "against a citizen too ignorant to understand, or too vicious to appreciate, the great value and beneficence of our institutions and our laws." At that moment Hawaii was below his horizon.[36]

[35] *House Report*, No. 1355, 55 Cong., 2 sess., II, Views of the Minority.
[36] Daniel Agnew, "Unconstitutionality of Hawaiian Treaty," *Forum*, XXIV (December 1897), 467–70.

After Congress had finally passed the joint resolution, Rear Admiral L. A. Beardslee, U.S.N. (Retired), wrote an account of the annexation ceremony showing that the United States had not received the consent of the Hawaiian people for annexation. Protest against annexation had been filed with both the Hawaiian government and the American government. Of the three divisions into which the Hawaiian people were classed, the only one that showed up in numbers at the annexation ceremonies was that affiliated with the government. The native Hawaiians, half-whites, and Royalists were conspicuous by their absence. The Hawaiian girls who were supposed to lower for the last time the flag of Hawaii, as the band played for the last time the official Hawaiian anthem, did not lower the flag. The band did not play as instructed, and the only music was the loud weeping contributed by the natives.[37]

Another account of the subordination of the Hawaiian nation to American imperialism stated that the raising of the United States flag over the Hawaiian Islands was not the happy occasion that many in the United States imagined. The natives were not to be seen, for they were unable to witness their flag taken down and the life of their nation snuffed out. "It was but another roll of the Juggernaut car in which the lordly Anglo-Saxon rides to his dream of universal empire." The account of the annexation was one in which the *Independent* and other religious papers could take no pride, for in reality their missionary zeal for humanity had only aided the United States to roll over a helpless race.[38] Here was the principle suggested by Mahan executed with precision: the United States was taking in those who wished to come—but along with them a host of dissimilar races.

After passage of the joint resolution, Congress proceeded to provide a government for the Territory of Hawaii. The government provided for the extension of racially biased laws, as illustrated in the following provision of the joint resolution:

There shall be no further immigration of Chinese into the Hawaiian Islands, except upon such conditions as are now or may hereafter be al-

---

[37] L. A. Beardslee, "Pilekias," *North American Review*, CLXII (October 1898), 475. (*Pilekias* means *trouble* in Hawaiian.)
[38] "Hawaii," *Nation*, LXVII (August 25, 1898), 139.

lowed by the laws of the United States; and no Chinese, by reason of anything herein contained, shall be allowed to enter the United States from the Hawaiian Islands.[39]

Continuing the pattern laid down in the joint resolution, the bill to provide a government for the Territory of Hawaii delineated on the basis of race the citizenship of the island. Section 4 stated:

All white persons, including Portuguese, and persons of African descent, and all persons descended from the Hawaiian race on either the paternal or maternal side who were citizens of the Republic of Hawaii immediately prior to the transfer of the sovereignty thereof to the United States, are hereby declared to be citizens of the United States.

Section 5 stated that "the Constitution and all the laws of the United States locally applicable . . . shall have the same force and effect within the said teritory as elsewhere in the United States"[40] and extended to Hawaii the contract labor laws and Chinese exclusion laws in force on the mainland.[41]

The advocates of annexation, who argued that the Asiatics would cease to be a factor after annexation, failed to realize that the economy of Hawaii was dependent on coolie labor—an economic, and racial, factor that would have far-reaching effects on Hawaii's efforts to gain statehood. This economic factor was responsible for the increase in the number of Asiatics in the population of Hawaii. By 1901 out of a population of 154,000 in Hawaii, 89,000 were Chinese and Japanese. There were 27,000 of the former and 62,000 of the latter. The increase resulted from the planters' anticipatory demand for and importation of plantation labor before annexation to the United States became an accomplished fact. The *Nation* recognized the conflict between racism on one hand and economic necessity on the other—a conflict which was complicated by extension of exclusion laws to Hawaii—and commented that "in this case it would have been highly inconvenient to have the Constitution follow the flag, except at a very respectful distance."[42]

[39] The provision went into effect on July 7, 1898.
[40] *Senate Document*, No. 16, 55 Cong., 3 sess., Hawaiian Commission Report, p. 5.
[41] "A Satisfactory Solution," *Review of Reviews*, XXI (April 1900), 388.
[42] *Nation*, LXXII (February 21, 1901), 146.

CIVIL GOVERNMENT IN THE TERRITORY OF HAWAII

In the House report on the bill to provide a government for Hawaii, the majority urged the necessity for speedy passage in order to forestall the importation of large numbers of alien contract laborers. The majority thought that the labor and immigration laws of the United States should have "early force in Hawaii that its citizenship, like its government, may be always and in truth American."[43]

The Senate saw to it that the proposed bill was so constructed as to make sure that the government was in the hands of the whites who owned the property of the islands. In order to qualify for senator in the Hawaiian legislature, one had to be thirty years of age and a male citizen of the United States. He must have resided in the territory a minimum of three years and be the owner in his own right of property worth $2,000, or have during the preceding year earned $1,000. The qualifications for the Hawaiian house of representatives required a candidate to be twenty-five years of age, a male citizen of the United States, to have resided in the territory three years, and to have owned property in the territory worth $500 or to have received a money income of not less than $250 during the preceding year.

Voters had to qualify to vote for both the senate and the house of representatives, the criteria being different for each house. To vote for representatives, the voter had to be a male citizen of the United States, twenty-one years of age who had resided in the territory one year preceding the election and six months in the district prior to his registration. He had to register in a prescribed period of time on a register for representative for his district. A report of all taxes due by him to the government had to be filed. Taxes had to be paid before March 31, preceding the date of registration. He had to be able to speak, read, and write either the English or Hawaiian language.

In order to vote for a member of the Hawaiian senate, a body which had veto power over the legislation coming from the house, the potential voter had to meet the above qualifications and in addition had to own in his own right real property worth $1,000 upon which taxes had been paid for the year preceding that in which he wished to register, or must have earned not less than $600 during the year ending April 1 of the year before the proposed registration.

[43] *House Report*, No. 1808, 55 Cong., 3 sess., p. 6.

In order to make sure that the undesirable class of people did not vote, each applicant for registration to vote for either senator or representative was to be examined by a board of registration as to each one of the required qualifications. Even if he had successfully passed the reading examination, it was left to the discretion of the board to examine him further concerning such qualification. The board had the power to examine and summon witnesses, and to maintain order, including the power to punish for contempt. Individuals who had, under oath, knowingly made a false statement before the board were guilty of perjury.

To further control the elective process it was possible for any lawful voter to challenge the right of any person claiming to be eligible to register as a voter and to cross-examine the applicant and witnesses produced by him. He could even call witnesses against the eligibility of the applicant. The law was very positive in stating that "no board of registration shall enter the name of any person upon the register of voters until satisfied that such person possesses the requisite qualifications."[44]

These laws were approved by the Congress and the President for the government of Hawaii. This was an undisguised adaptation of the methods used by many Southern states for control of a dissimilar race. The enactment of these laws led William Kitchin of North Carolina to remark that the laws were "very like ours—yet Republicans will praise them and denounce ours! Great consistency for statesmen."[45]

The minority on the Hawaiian Commission submitted a report which stated that they could not agree with the majority because their recommendations indicated "an intention on their part to make a new departure from our well-established custom of governing territories," a departure which "recognizes by law the right of wealth to govern."[46]

These implications are readily understood when viewed against the background of the commission's report that the Americans "although in such a small minority, practically dominate the governmental affairs of the country. . . ." According to this report, other

[44] *Senate Document*, No. 16, 55 Cong., 3 sess., pp. 557–58.
[45] *Congressional Record*, 56 Cong., 1 sess., XXXIII, pt. 7: 300 (May 3, 1900).
[46] *House Report*, No. 1808, 55 Cong., 3 sess., pp. 7–8.

whites—British and German—combined with Americans and Hawaiians of part-American ancestry to control the business of the country. Alluding to the effective elimination of the Asiatic element under the proposed legislation, the commission reported that the Chinese and Japanese element lacked political power and that the entire population of 110,000 was dominated "politically, financially, and commercially, by the American element."[47] This statement gave substance to the minority charge that the legislation recognized the right of wealth to govern. By the same token it pointed out the fact that the whites controlled the property and under this legislation would also control the government. The majority of the Hawaiian Commission, however, deemed the measure one that would best "promote the interest of the Hawaiian people and "at the same time . . . the interest and . . . sovereignty of the people of the United States."[48]

EFFORTS TO ACHIEVE STATEHOOD

The large percentage of Orientals in the population of Hawaii during the first fifteen years of the twentieth century precluded statehood, though petitions from the island were presented in 1903, 1911, 1913, and 1915. It was inconceivable that the United States would incorporate into the body politic thousands of Asiatics at the same time that the "gentlemen's agreement" was being worked out and tightened up.[49]

During the years of World War I the Immigration Act of 1917 was debated and passed. This act had the specific purpose of excluding undesirable classes of people from the United States. The bulk of the population of Hawaii was considered by most Americans as undesirable for citizenship.

Following the war the Japanese government pursued a policy at the Paris Peace Conference that caused consternation among some congressmen. The delegation from Japan expressed the hope that the organization of the League of Nations would offer opportunities to assert the equality of the races. Japan also desired to work out an alliance with China so that they could work in harmony on this ques-

47 Senate Document, No. 16, 55 Cong., 3 sess., p. 3.
48 Ibid., p. 13.
49 House Report, No. 350, 68 Cong., 1 sess., p. 8.

tion at the conference.[50] The amendment to the League Covenant
proposed by Japan read as follows:

> The equality of nations being a basic principle of the League of Nations,
> the High Contracting Parties agree to accord as soon as possible, to all
> aliens nationals of States Members of the League equal and just treatment
> in every respect, making no distinction, either in law or in fact, on account
> of their race or nationality.[51]

Some members of the United States Senate regarded the amendment by the Japanese as a trick to force their way into white countries. Woodrow Wilson was given credit, along with the delegates
from South Africa, Australia, and New Zealand, for frustrating the
proposal.[52] The Japanese feeling over the failure of the proposal to
get the necessary support led the marquis of Kuma to write to the
American ambassador to Japan that "permanent peace cannot be
achieved without first solving the question of the equality of treatment of races." The marquis wanted to know how Americans proposed to treat alien races in the future in her territory and insisted
"that Japanese emigrants be freely allowed to enter every country."[53]
    The above position showed the relevance of the Japanese position
at Paris to the treatment of Japanese in the United States. The Japanese delegation at Paris expressed its displeasure in the failure to get
adoption of the amendment through its spokesman.

> . . . I feel it my duty to declare clearly on this occasion that the Japanese
> Government and people feel poignant regret at the failure of the com-
> mission to approve of their just demand for laying down a principle aiming
> at the adjustment of this longstanding grievance, a demand that is based
> upon a deep rooted national conviction. They will continue in their in-
> sistence for the adoption of this principle by the League in the future.[54]

The action of Japan at the Peace Conference did little to help Hawaii to achieve statehood during the next decade. The large propor-

[50] *Foreign Relations: The Paris Peace Conference,* 1919, I, 490.
[51] *Ibid.,* III, 291.
[52] *Congressional Record,* 66 Cong., 2 sess., LIX, pt. 3: 3182–83 (February
20, 1920). Speech of Senator Phelan.
[53] Ambassador Morris to the acting secretary of state, January 2, 1919, *ibid.,*
p. 493.
[54] *Foreign Relations: The Paris Peace Conference,* 1919, III, 291.

tion of Japanese in Hawaii and the general attitude of Congress toward an "undesirable" population doomed Hawaii to remain a dependency.

The attitude of Congress toward the Japanese is shown in the Immigration Act of 1924. This act for the first time formally excluded Japanese from the United States and its possessions. Exclusion was a distinct diplomatic slap in the face for the Japanese nation. Secretary of State Charles E. Hughes thought the act undiplomatic.

It would be idle to insist that the provision is not aimed at the Japanese, for the proposed measure (Sec. 25) continues in force the existing legislation regulating Chinese immigration and the barred-zone provision of our immigration laws which prohibits immigration from certain other portions of Asia. The practical effect of section 12(b) is to single out Japanese immigrants for exclusion. The Japanese are sensitive people and unquestionably would regard such legislative enactment as fixing a stigma upon them.[55]

From the congressional point of view, legislation could not affect the Japanese, for they were already stigmatized by their dissimilar characteristics. When the measure passed the House of Representatives, the Japanese government entered a formal protest. The correspondence between the Japanese ambassador and the secretary of state was used very effectively by Henry Cabot Lodge and others to get the Senate to overwhelmingly pass the measure.

The relevance of the above acts to Hawaiian statehood is seen in the United States' exclusion of the two most prominent races of Asia. At the same time the United States held in a subordinate relationship a territory whose population was composed of a large contingent of these and similar peoples.

In an effort to "save face" the Japanese government enacted a measure which allowed Japanese born in other countries to hold citizenship in Japan. The measure went into effect December 1, 1924. It also had the effect of allowing Japanese to declare their intentions as to citizenship. While many opponents of statehood for Hawaii seized upon the measure enacted by the Japanese government per-

[55] *House Report*, No. 350, 68 Cong., 1 sess., pt. 2, p. 27.

mitting dual citizenship as the reason for their opposition, the real purpose of the measure was to clarify the status of the Japanese in foreign lands. American Edgar A. Bancroft wrote the State Department:

> . . . I have the honor to report that according to press statements not one of the forty children born to Japanese parents in Hawaii since December first has been registered at the Japanese Consulate-General.
>
> In commenting on the new Expatriation Law the Japanese Counsul-General at Honolulu, Mr. Keichi Yamazaki, . . . said that the new law represents the desire of the Japanese government to remove all objections which were raised to the former system of dual citizenship and that to this end he is personally urging the parents of those Japanese who are to reside in Hawaii to refrain from registering their children at a Japanese Consulate and thus define their status clearly as American citizens over whom the Japanese government has relinquished all claim to citizenship.[56]

The "gentlemen's agreement," the rejection of the racial equality clause in the Covenant of the League of Nations, the Immigration Act of 1924, and the Japanese dual citizenship act of December 1, 1924, all had racial connotations that affected Hawaii's efforts to gain admission to the Union.

Three-fifths of the population of Hawaii was of Asiatic origin and a large portion of the rest was of inferior quality, according to R. W. Neal. It was a considerable job to prepare the great mass of alien humanity for statehood and at the same time to make sure that America's hold on her key to the Pacific was secure. The problem centered around indoctrinating American ideals and standards into the population. Neal saw this as a three-part problem involving land, labor, and inferior races. The second part of the problem was "how to get rid of the portion of the population, especially the Oriental element, which cannot be Americanized, and how to make loyal Americans of the portion which cannot be got rid of?"[57] This aspect of the problem became more and more complicated because instead of the Oriental element decreasing, they were increasing in numerical

[56] Ambassador Edgar A. Bancroft to the secretary of state, March 24, 1925, *Foreign Relations*, 1924, II, 413.

[57] Robert W. Neal, "Hawaii's Land and Labor Problem," *Current History*, XIII (December 1920), 389–97.

strength. The possibility of political power was also developing as a result of citizenship acquired at birth.

The increase in the Oriental element in the population of Hawaii was cited by Lothrop Stoddard as evidence of the danger of imminent inundation from the yellow races of Asia. Stoddard wrote: "This mid-Pacific archipelago was brought under white control by masterful American Nordics, who established Anglo-Saxon institutions." The natives, because of the pressures of white civilization, died out. Therefore, Asiatic labor was imported; first, Chinese were brought in until annexation brought Hawaii under the exclusion laws, then Filipinos, Koreans, and, above all, Japanese. The Hawaiians and Americans could not compete with the ruthless undercutting of the Japanese and were pushed out. "Fully half the population of the island is Japanese," wrote Stoddard in 1922. "The Americans are being bitterly encysted as a small and dwindling aristocracy. In 1917 the births of the two races were: Americans, 295; Japanese, 5,000! Comment is superfluous."[58]

In 1936 Sydney S. Bowman found that the opponents to statehood for Hawaii felt that the 148,972 Japanese and the 54,668 Filipinos would immediately rush to California's golden shores, if statehood were granted. The only way to prevent this was to keep Hawaii a territory. Bowman felt that "except for the element of color in the island population, there would be little if any hesitation in saying to these petitioners 'Come on in, the Union's fine.'" According to Bowman, there were 300,000 people, including Hawaiians and part Hawaiians, who could not be classified as Caucasian. Out of a total population of 384,437, 254,808 were classified as Asiatic or part Asiatic. The figures were racial figures, however, because the so-called Orientals were, for the most part, citizens of the United States. He concluded that "the yellow peril is still a potent, mental factor in California and to a certain extent in Washington. It perhaps has an influence on the Congressional thinking which occasionally sees Hawaii as a possession or in extreme instances, as a foreign land."[59]

J. S. Phillips, in 1936, realized that the fear of Asiatic inundation was sufficient to cause petitions for statehood to go unheeded. The

[58] Stoddard, *The Rising Tide of Color*, pp. 279–80.
[59] Sydney S. Bowman, "Hawaii Knocks at the Door," *Forum*, XCV (June 1936), 350–51.

Hawaiian was some kind of quasi-citizen who enjoyed certain limited rights of citizenship as long as he remained in Hawaii, but upon migration to the mainland, he would receive the same treatment as the Japanese and Chinese.[60]

David L. Crawford suggested that the situation was one in which the opponents to Hawaiian statehood argued from a position of racial emotions while the Hawaiians argued "from a legally incontrovertible premise." The government, expressing the views of those who seemingly saw yellow spots before their eyes at the mention of statehood for Hawaii, answered, if at all, in irrelevant generalities. These generalities were sufficient to keep Hawaii out of the Union, despite the fact that Americans were being taxed without representation.[61] American imperial relations to the Hawaiian Islands could have been ended with the stroke of a pen signing an enabling act, but, as was the case in sections of the United States, American racism resulted in compromised ideals.

The Hawaiians realized that their basic problem was one of color. In a statement prepared for submission to Congress, the representative from Hawaii, Samuel Wilder King, submitted a brief which stated in part: "As in our case, some of the grounds of opposition to statehood for several of the western territories were based on racial differences."[62] The Hawaiian representative was pointing up the fact that racial preconceptions had previously played a part in America's continental expansion, just as they were then playing the dominant role in her imperial policy.

There was always the danger, assumed in the minds of the mainlanders, that persons other than Anglo-Saxon or Teutons were somehow given to bloc voting. Bloc voting was one of the charges leveled at Hawaii as an impediment to statehood. The danger was that the Japanese in Hawaii, by this method, would elect a Japanese governor and send Japanese senators and representatives to Congress.

The president of the University of Hawaii, David L. Crawford, conceded that this might occur but affirmed that race should not be

---

[60] J. S. Phillips, "Uncle Sam and His Asiatic Wards," *Contemporary Review,* CXLIX (March 1936), 349–50.

[61] David L. Crawford, "Hawaii—Our Western Frontier," *Review of Reviews,* XCI (January 1935), 60.

[62] *Hearings,* Sub-committee, Committee on Territories, House, 74 Cong., 1 sess., Statehood for Hawaii, H. R. 3034, p. 8.

a condition for Americans to gain the constitutional right of self-government. The right of representation in the House and Senate and the right to elect their governor rather than have him appointed by the President were constitutional rights. The problem of the Japanese vote was greatly exaggerated by those who expressed opinions on the subject. "The so-called 'Japanese Vote' probably would never be in the majority. It would never constitute a 'bloc' unless foolish and short-sighted attitudes on the part of other racial groups forced it as self-defense for the Japanese-American element."[63]

According to Lillian Symes, the success of the interbreeding of the races was a deterrent to statehood. An attitude opposed to "mongrelization" was to be found among the military and a small but growing group of lower middle-class residents who resented the competition of educated, native Orientals in business and politics. She contended that the large contingent of Southerners in the navy regarded a situation in which white and dark-skinned races lived side by side on a basis of political equality and mutual respect with great apprehension. Such individuals immediately started to visualize "orgies of mixed parties, wholesale inter-marriage, and general mongrelization."

The traditional prejudice of these groups was reinforced by military personnel and narrow nationalists who assumed that Asiatics were incapable of loyalty to America. These Americans had the kind of nationalism which they charged was possessed by the Japanese, the "world's most intense nationalists, loyal to the Mikado to the third and fourth generation."[64] Characteristic of this view was the statement of a naval officer who said, "Every Japanese born under our flag or not is always a Japanese. No matter how much he professes to be American he is always thinking Japanese thoughts, hoping secretly for Japanese victory." Waldon Webb asked, "Shall we admit to the dignity and power of statehood a territory where Japanese, secretly hoping for our overthrow, outnumber mainland Americans 13 to 1?"[65]

Louis Cain, in a statement before a House subcommittee on state-

[63] Crawford, "Hawaii," *Review of Reviews*, XCI, 74.

[64] Lillian Symes, "What About Hawaii?" *Harper's*, CLXV (October 1932), 533–34.

[65] Webb Waldron, "A New Star in the Union?" *American Magazine*, CXXII (April 1937), 36.

hood for Hawaii, reflected upon the fear held by many on the main-land that war with Japan was imminent and that the large Japanese population on the islands made it unwise to consider statehood at that time. The fears were based on the supposition that Japanese senators would be elected, thereby giving them access to all state documents. They would then automatically give the Japanese govern-ment knowledge of the United States' defenses in case of war. Cain conceded that this line of thinking sounded plausible, but noted, "It isolates the fundamental principles upon which the nation has been built, presupposes disloyalty of citizens of alien parentage, presumes that a minority voting as a racial bloc could prevail, and that traitors would be elected." Americanism contained the proposition in the Declaration of Independence that all men were created free and equal, Cain observed, and moreover,

no qualification regarding ancestors was included in that document. I submit to you, gentlemen, that you cannot indict a people, and loyalty, like honesty, must be presumed. . . . To hold race as a barrier to statehood is unreasonable, un-American, and will tend to destroy the racial tolerance which has made Hawaii the beacon light for the world of many races living together in peace and harmony. . . . I submit to you that you cannot breed loyalty with suspicion. To raise embargoes on citizenship because of an-cestry would tend to force the people so accused into racial blocs for self-protection. . . .

Replying to those who opposed statehood, advocates of the mea-sure pointed out that "little or no question is raised as to the possi-bility of Americanizing the immigrants from Europe and even less so in the case of their descendants."[66] However, the attitude that the Asiatics would not readily assimilate, as expressed by Walker Mathe-son, still persisted.

Hawaii knows that it is the "Japanese problem" that is barring the islands from statehood, despite a decrease in the alien Japanese population and an increase in island born Japanese. The argument is that if granted state-hood, the Hawaiians might send Japanese to the Governor's Mansion, the House of Representatives in Washington, and possibly the Senate itself.

[66] *Hearings*, Sub-committee, House, 74 Cong., 1 sess., H. R. 3034, Statehood for Hawaii, pp. 23–25.

. . . Hawaii does not deny that there is a preponderance of Japanese in the islands. It is proud of its Japanese population, and points out that in 1924, when Japan instituted a dual citizenship law by which everyone of Japanese blood born abroad could be registered at the Consulates as a subject of the Mikado, the great majority of the Japanese . . . ignored the ruling.

According to Matheson, racial prejudice concerning the loyalty of the Japanese population prevented the House Subcommittee on Territories from returning a favorable report on statehood for Hawaii in 1935. The subcommittee evidently saw too many Japanese for its liking and, in addition, believed the criticism it heard about the loyalty of Japanese citizens. The critics alleged that the Japanese were "all spies." Again in 1937 a committee consisting of twelve representatives and twelve senators turned down Hawaii's plea for statehood because of the Japanese element in the population.[67]

George H. Blakeslee pointed out that the army and navy were opposed to early statehood for Hawaii for two reasons: (1) American citizens of Japanese ancestry might be elected to the executive offices of the new state; and (2) if so elected, they would not co-operate fully with the army and navy.[68]

By 1940 the Chinese in Hawaii were not a source of opposition to statehood. They had merged into the life of the islands without any question and without criticism. The attitude towards the Japanese which prevailed among many was not based on the conduct of the Japanese in the Hawaiian Islands at that time but upon hostility to the nation from which their ancestors came. Ray Lyman Wilbur felt that "the sooner we bring these islands into statehood, and bring these citizens of diverse origins into all the responsibilities of statehood, the better it will be for our future in the Pacific."[69]

Ten successive congressional committees had visited the islands at the expense of the Hawaiian legislature and the general public to study the territory's qualifications for statehood. The average citizen of Hawaii felt that after forty-two years of subordinate relationship,

67 Walker Matheson, "Hawaii Pleads for Statehood," North American Review, CCXLVII (March 1939), 136–37.
68 George H. Blakeslee, "Hawaii: Racial Problems and Naval Bases," Foreign Affairs, XVII (October 1938), 97–98.
69 Ray Lyman Wilbur, "Statehood for Hawaii," Atlantic Monthly, CLXVI (October 1940), 497.

the territory should be put on an equal footing with other states. They carried their share of federal taxes. They were Americans in every sense of the word. Their standard of living, their thought, and their very life were American. They were no different from Americans in New York, California, Wisconsin, or Louisiana. Since they were the equal of the states in so many points of fact, why should they be inferior in point of law? The only conclusion that could be drawn was that race kept Hawaii in an inferior relation to the Union.[70]

Some of the racists were sure that, in the event of a war with Japan, the loyalty of the Japanese element in Hawaii would be put to the supreme test and that the Japanese fiber would be found wanting.[71] When the test came, it was the American government and some of the mainland Americans, motivated perhaps by the exigencies of war, who left much to be desired in loyalty to fundamental principles of democracy.

WORLD WAR II AND
DETERRENTS TO HAWAIIAN STATEHOOD

The Japanese attack on Pearl Harbor, December 7, 1941, had the effect of awaking Americans on the mainland to the real situation in Hawaii. The attack eventually proved the loyalty of the Hawaiian Japanese to the United States. The United States' avowed fundamental principles of equality and justice before the laws were seriously strained. Two situations were catalyzed as a result of that attack: (1) Japanese born in America eventually were looked upon as Americans; and (2) Americans (as a result of the treatment of the Japanese-Americans) became conscious of the erosion of fundamental American principles.

The Japanese element in the islands of Hawaii was not a serious problem because their loyalty was proved after the first months of the war. The Japanese on the West Coast, however, constituted a threat in the minds of some West Coast citizens, resulting in the program of "relocation."

Eugene V. Rostow found that the treatment of the Japanese and

[70] Lawrence M. Judd, "Hawaii States Her Case," *Current History,* LI (July 1940), 40–42.
[71] *Hearings,* Sub-committee, House, H. R. 3034, 74 Cong., 1 sess., pp. 37–38.

Japanese-Americans on the West Coast in the perspective of our legal tradition and facts was incredible. The relocation program was instituted on racial grounds. The recommendation on which the program was based, by General DeWitt to the secretary of war, stated:

In the war in which we are now engaged, . . . racial affinities are not severed by migration. The Japanese race is an enemy race and while many second and third generation Japanese born on United States soil, possessed of United States citizenship, have become "Americanized," the racial strains are undiluted. . . . There were no grounds for assuming that Japanese-Americans will not turn against the United States. . . .[72]

Partly for this reason, President Roosevelt issued an executive order in February, 1942, and in March of that year Congress passed a law authorizing military commanders to designate "military areas." The designation of military areas served as the basis for the relocation program. Other reasons for the order could be traced to the influence of economic factors in the prejudice against the Japanese.[73]

Groups that had long agitated against Japanese, after Pearl Harbor lost no time in making it known to Washington that the "presence of 110,000 Japanese on the West Coast, including about 40,000 'enemy alien' . . . was a grave threat to the safety of the country. . . . The Japanese who might have been a military danger were already known to the FBI and were taken into custody within a few days." That all the rest, "including 70,000 American citizens, should be treated as military threats was an act of unprecedented official racism in the United States."[74]

The Supreme Court received cases growing out of the relocation program after the complexion of the war had changed to favor the United States. Japan was on the defensive in the Pacific at the time. Therefore, the Courts were not operating under an immediate threat of danger. Yet the Courts reacted in a manner which "failed to uphold the most ordinary rights of citizenship, making Japanese-Americans into second-class citizens, who stand before the Courts on a different legal footing from other Americans."

[72] Eugene V. Rostow, "Our Worst Wartime Mistake," *Harper's*, CXCI (September 1945), 195.
[73] *Ibid.*
[74] Simpson and Yinger, *Racial and Cultural Minorities*, p. 132.

Rostow was alarmed about the decisions and refers to the case of
Ex Parte Milligan as an example of democratic procedure, forgetting
for the moment that there were only white men involved directly in
that case, while in the Japanese situation it was the white against the
yellow race. Again the Constitution was temporarily compromised
on racial assumptions.[75]

The war, relocation, and war propaganda, all left a bitter feeling
in the minds of Americans about Japanese in particular and Orientals in general. Against this background the campaign to make
Hawaii the forty-ninth state of the Union was begun. Monroe Sweetland wrote in 1944:

> Fear that some one group will dominate the State of Hawaii is offset by
> the way every nationality group has split in its political allegiances. The
> Island of Kauai, with its large Japanese-American majority, has repeatedly
> re-elected two men of Chinese ancestry to its most important financial post.
> The current Territorial Legislature is made up of four members of Chinese
> ancestry, seven of Hawaiian ancestry, seven of Portuguese ancestry, and
> three others.

It was argued that the United States needed the voice of Hawaii
in Congress. Two senators from Hawaii after the war would bring
invaluable knowledge of the people of the Pacific area. Their knowledge would aid in effecting a lasting peace. The congressional delegation from Hawaii would be defeated for re-election if they showed
the slightest bit of bigotry or racial discrimination. Internationalism
was considered the bone and fiber of Hawaii. "Chauvinism and nationalism are alien and anachronistic to pan-racial Hawaiians."[76] The
admission to statehood could be the American acknowledgment that
President Roosevelt spoke for the nation when he declared "Americanism is not and never was a matter of race or ancestry." It had long
been thought that the surrounding nations could learn a striking
object lesson in racial accommodation from Hawaii.[77] Here was opportunity for the United States to profit by one of her own possessions.

[75] Rostow, "Worst Wartime Mistake," *Harper's*, CXCI (September 1945), 198.

[76] Monroe Sweetland, "Our 49th State—Hawaii," *Asia*, XLIV (September
1944), 411.

[77] Elizabeth Green, "Race and Politics in Hawaii," *Asia*, XXXV (June 1935),
374.

By 1946 most factions in Hawaii were advocating statehood. It was believed that because the CIO, the Planters Association, the secretary of the interior, the President, and a congressional committee backed Hawaiian statehood, it was a good bet that something would happen in that session of Congress. Yet racial prejudice kept this hope from being realized for thirteen years.

J. A. Krug, secretary of the interior, wrote to the chairman of the House Committee on Territories that "on the basis of hearings and exhibits . . . despite the many racial groups . . . evidence of bloc voting as exists indicates that the practice has not assumed, and is not likely to assume serious proportion. . . ." He observed, "Your subcommittee concluded that the mixed racial complexion of Hawaii should not be considered an obstacle to statehood; that the people of Hawaii have shown themselves capable of self-government."[78]

Samuel Wilder King asked the committee, "If the prerequisites for statehood have already been met in all other respects, and if the doubt as to the loyalty of a portion of our population has been allayed by the war, then what remaining condition must we fulfill before we take our rightful place as the forty-ninth state?"[79] It was his belief that the continued denial of statehood for Hawaii would be a matter of criticism by world public opinion. He pointed this out by saying, "In other words, if our policy, our national policy toward Hawaii . . . [was] not in accord with our high principles in the United Nations of the World, our prestige [would] decrease by just so much." King thought that the system of recording nationality with the Board of Health was a poor one, in that it led to confusion. Children of mixed ancestry were listed as of the race of the mother. The racial background was tagged to them indefinitely. "Native born children of native-born parents, in other words, the second generation native-born are still called Japanese, or Chinese, and so forth. . . . Included in those listed as Japanese are large numbers of mixed ancestry, and thousands of the children of the second generation native born. . . ."[80]

Members of the House Committee on Territories in 1946 asked Professor Andrew W. Lind how long it would be "before the alien

[78] *Hearings*, Committee on Territories, House, 79 Cong., 1 sess., H. R. 3643, Statehood for Hawaii, p. 3.

[79] *Ibid.*, pp. 35–36.

[80] *Ibid.*, p. 37.

Japanese will have been eliminated, for the most part." Professor Lind stated, "At the present time they constitute somewhat less than 15 per cent of the entire Japanese group, and I think for practical purposes, one may say that within fifteen years—certainly that's liberal—their influence will have disappeared."[81]

Many exhibits were presented to the committee during the hearings on statehood for Hawaii in 1946. Most of the letters in opposition to statehood for Hawaii used race as their most potent argument. Despite this opposition, the subcommittee made the following findings:

1. Hawaii with its population of over 500,000 has a larger population than any other state at the time of admission to the Union with the exception of Oklahoma.
2. The heterogeneous peoples of the territory live and work together amicably, democratically, and harmoniously.
3. The mixed racial complexion of Hawaii existed at the time of annexation, was not regarded as an obstacle to annexation, and should not now be considered an obstacle to statehood.
4. The percentage of persons of Japanese ancestry reached its peak in 1940 and has steadily declined since then because of prohibition of immigration, lower birth rate, and the increasing immigration of other peoples.
5. The people of Hawaii have demonstrated beyond question their loyalty and patriotism to the government of the United States.
6. On the record of their behavior and their participation in the war, American citizens of Japanese ancestry can be little criticized.
7. Such evidence of bloc voting as exists among Americans of Japanese ancestry is not likely to assume serious proportions in our opinion because they, like all white peoples, are divided amongst themselves by differences, political and economic.
8. Hawaii has been a Territory for forty-six years, during which the people of Hawaii have shown themselves fully capable of self-government. . . .
14. The school system of Hawaii has been successful in instilling into people of many races and backgrounds the objectives and ideals of democracy, and has produced a literate population capable of discharging the duties of citizenship. . . .

[81] *Ibid.*, pp. 55–58. Andrew W. Lind, professor of sociology at the University of Hawaii.

16. A majority of the people of the territory are in favor of immediate statehood. No organized group has appeared in opposition. If a plebiscite were again held on the statehood question, in our opinion the people would vote for statehood in the same proportion as they did in 1940.[82]

The final recommendation of the subcommittee was "that the legislation to admit Hawaii to statehood be passed." Despite this recommendation, statehood was not granted.

Throughout the decades of the 1930s and 1940s statehood, with the concomitant right to proportional representation and two senators, was denied because many of the policy-makers thought that dissimilar peoples were incapable of understanding and appreciating the operation of Anglo Saxon republican institutions.

For most practical purposes, the Hawaiians were a part of the United States; yet, as in the case of the Negroes, they were not accepted on a basis of equality. Since it was repugnant to dispose of an Americanized Hawaii by expulsion, it became expedient to compromise basic constitutional principles until policy-makers were willing to accord to the Hawaiians a larger measure of self-government. It is important to note that progress was made during the 1940s and 1950s toward removing the impediments to full citizenship for dissimilar peoples in the United States. The movement toward full citizenship was given impetus during the Second World War. It continued into the 1950s culminating in the 1954 Supreme Court decision in *Brown* v. *Board of Education of Topeka, Kansas*, which ruled that segregation in the public schools was "inherently unequal" and denied Negro students equal protection as provided in the Fourteenth Amendment.

The 1954 decision was a repudiation of the doctrine of "separate but equal." This historic decision could be considered as important to the larger politics of the United States affecting imperial relations to Hawaii as the *Plessy* v. *Ferguson* decision was to the annexation of Hawaii. If the 1896 decision was a harbinger to annexation of Hawaii in 1898, the 1954 decision could be considered a harbinger to statehood for Hawaii in 1959. It was only a matter of time until Hawaii

[82] *Ibid.*, p. 43.

would become an integral part of the United States. The result would have a great effect on domestic politics as predicted by some earlier opponents to Hawaiian annexation. In close decisions in the House of Representatives and the Senate, Hawaii's representatives could be expected to favor democratic over nondemocratic procedures in both domestic and foreign politics.

IV

American Imperialism in the Philippine Islands

According to the report of the Schurman Commission, the native peoples of the Philippine Islands belonged to three distinct races—the Negrito, the Indonesian, and the Malayan. The Negritos were believed to be the disappearing remnants of a people which once populated the entire archipelago. They were, physically, weaklings of low stature, with black skin, closely curling hair, flat noses, thick lips, and large, clumsy feet. In the matter of intelligence they stood at or near the bottom of the human series and were believed to be incapable of any considerable degree of civilization or advancement. As a rule, they were found only on the forest clad sides of the higher mountains of Luzon, Panay, Negros, and Mindanao although they were said to inhabit the wooded lowlands near the coast of the northeastern part of Luzon. They led a nomadic life wandering almost naked through the forest, and lived on fruits, tubers, and such game as they could bring down with their bows and poisoned arrows. It was believed that not more than 25,000 of them existed in the entire archipelago, and the race was reported to be doomed to early extinction.

The Philippine tribes belonging to the Indonesian race were confined to the great island of Mindanao, the surface of which constitutes about one-third of the total land area of the archipelago. These tribes were considered physically superior to all other groups in the islands. They were tall and well developed, with high foreheads, aquiline noses, wavy hair, and often with beards. The color of their skin was quite light. Many of the Indonesians were considered clever and intelligent. None of the Indonesian tribes had been Christianized.[1]

---

[1] Schurman Report, *Senate Document,* No. 138, 56 Cong., 1 sess., pp. 11–16.

The great majority of the inhabitants of the Philippines were of the Malayan extraction although the race was not found in a pure state in any of the islands but was everywhere modified through interbreeding with Chinese, Indonesians, Negritos, Arabs, and to a limited extent, Spaniards and other Europeans. The individuals belonging to these Malayan tribes were of medium size, with straight black hair and skin darker than that of the Indonesians.

The inhabitants of the Philippines, ethnologically arranged under these three distinct races, were known by eighty-four tribal names or habitats, of which eight were regarded as civilized. Following is a list of tribes in order of population:

Race	Number
Visayans	2,601,600
Tagálogs	1,663,900
Bícols	518,100
Ilocanos	441,700
Pangasináns	365,500
Pampangos	337,900
Moros (civilized but non-Christian)	268,000
Cagayanes	166,300[2]

These were the peoples inhabiting islands some seven thousand miles from the United States—islands and peoples different in culture and political development from the peoples of the United States. In spite of American feelings about so-called inferior peoples, they were to come under the control of the American government.

RATIFICATION OF THE TREATY OF PARIS

In Senate debate on the ratification of the peace treaty between the United States and Spain, racism played an important part. Both the supporters and the opponents of the treaty used race to support their positions. The supporters were certain that there were but two alternatives, to ratify or to reject the treaty and that ratification did not commit the United States to a definite policy. They believed that Americans should be trusted as a people to deal honestly and justly

[2] Gazeteer of the Philippines, *Senate Document*, No. 280, 57 Cong., 1 sess., p. 66.

with the islands and their inhabitants. It was their hope and belief that the Senate would "have the wisdom not to attempt to incorporate those islands with our body politic or make their inhabitants part of our citizenship."[3]

This was the position of the faction led by Henry Cabot Lodge, who as chairman of the Committee on the Philippines must share some of the responsibility for the policy of conquest that ensued after the ratification of the treaty on February 6, 1899. The treaty was a departure from the customary practices of the United States in dealing with newly acquired territory. In previous acquisitions the inhabitants of the new territory had been collectively naturalized. This practice, perhaps resulting from the sparseness of population or the racial characteristics of the populations involved, had prevailed in the cases of the annexation of Louisiana, Florida, Texas, and Alaska.[4] The Treaty of Paris provided that "the civil rights and political status of the native inhabitants of the territories hereby ceded to the United States shall be determined by the Congress."[5]

In the debate on the treaty questions arose as to the right of the United States to gain by treaty territory which Spain did not actually possess. The Filipino leaders held, as did Senator Benjamin Tillman, that Spain did not have possession of the Philippine Islands.

The position held by this group was summed up in a memorial which set forth the grounds upon which the Philippine republic based its claim for recognition. The important points were summarized in the memorial and supported by various American government documents.[6]

The American Government for months has had in its possession . . . evidence of the actual independence of the Filipinos.

Spain could not deliver possession of the Philippines to the United States, being herself ousted by their people, and in fact at the present moment the United States holds only an entrenched camp, controlling one

[3] *Congressional Record,* 55 Cong., 3 sess., XXXII, pt. 1: 969 (January 24, 1899).

[4] Paul Charelton, "Naturalization and Citizenship in the Insular Possessions," *The Annals,* XXX (July 1907), 104–14.

[5] Treaty of Peace between the United States of America and the Kingdom of Spain, *Senate Document,* No. 62, 55 Cong., 3 sess., p. 10.

[6] Hearings, Affairs in the Philippines, *Senate Document,* No. 331, 57 Cong., 1 sess.

hundred and forty-three square miles, with 300,000 people, while the Philippine Republic represents the destinies of nearly 10,000,000 souls, scattered over an area approaching 200,000 square miles.

Spain having no possessions (except minor garrison posts), and no right of possession in the Philippines could confer no right to control them.

. . . .

Secretaries of State of your country (including Mr. Jefferson and Mr. Pinckney) have denied the right of an ally of America to acquire by conquest from Great Britain any American territory while America was struggling for independence. The United States Supreme Court has sustained this view. We deny similarly the right of the United States to acquire Philippine territory by cession from Spain while the Filipinos were yet at war with that power. . . .[7]

All efforts of the Filipinos to be heard either at Paris or Washington while the treaty was being negotiated were ignored.[8]

Could the destinies of 10,000,000 colored people be entrusted to a government which disregarded their aspirations and rights at the outset? Many of the senators opposed to ratification thought not and introduced resolutions to the effect that under the Constitution no power was given to the federal government to acquire territory to be held and governed as colonies. Not one of these resolutions passed both houses of Congress, but the debates shed light on the racial attitudes of the senators, who would have to work out a scheme of government for the Philippines if the treaty was ratified.

John W. Daniels of Virginia feared that ratification of the treaty would lead to the incorporation of the Filipinos into the body politic of the United States. This, he warned, would be a danger to the Republic. The inclusion of Filipinos under the treaty would make the Republic half-free and half-dependent, creating conditions similar to those that prevailed before the Civil War when the Republic was half-slave and half-free. Also the Philippines would never be fitted to become American states. "Their race forbid it; their climate forbid it; their condition in all respects forbid it. Therefore, if the gentlemen who deny them constitutional rights can have their way, it is for the creation of a perpetual dependency, of an absolute despotism

---

[7] Maxime M. Kalaw, *The Case for the Filipinos*, pp. 76–77.
[8] *Ibid.*, p. 61.

annexed to a Republic. . . . ."⁹ Senator Daniels was concerned that we were "breaking down our history, repudiating and belittling our principles, and seeking to subvert the whole theory and settled tenure of American progress and of American rule, just to get and embody in our commonwealth some scattered, barbarous, or savage islands and peoples of a mixed and non-descript race."¹⁰

Senator Desota Money of Mississippi, conscious of the disregard for the rights of the Filipinos in the ratification of the treaty, declared:

> . . . In the very exuberance of our strength we are about to exercise it without judgment or mercy; that we esteem but lightly the rights, the liberties, the sacrifices of a people who for one hundred years have groaned under the tyranny of aliens. . . . Are all these 10,000,000 people . . . unworthy of any consideration in this vast international transaction? . . .
>
> . . . .
>
> Is a Cuban to be cherished and to be the subject of anxious solicitude, for whom we pour out our blood and our treasure, and the Malay, at the other end of the world, under the same circumstances, with increased aggravation to incite rebellion, not only not to receive our sympathy but to be subject to our power? Have we gone into the business of buying men?

There was not a man in the Senate, he believed, who would take the Filipinos as citizens of the United States. If they were allowed to become citizens they would have representatives in the Senate and the House of Representatives. There was no one present in the chamber who wanted the Filipinos to have a voice in determining who the next President of the United States would be or in deciding the foreign or domestic policy of the United States.¹¹

Senator Donelson Caffery of Louisiana argued that the government of the United States was "of the people, by the people and for the people." As such it was inhibited from acquiring territory for the purpose of incorporating it into the Union without the consent of the inhabitants. The fourth part of his argument was distinctly racial in content, stating that "even if capable of self-government and they

⁹ *Congressional Record,* 55 Cong., 3 sess., XXXII, pt. 2: 1427 (February 3, 1899).
¹⁰ *Ibid.,* p. 1429.
¹¹ *Ibid.,* pp. 1418–20.

give their consent, . . . it would be impolitic, unwise, and dangerous
to incorporate . . . a distant country beyond the sea," whose inhabitants were of a "dissimilar race, with different religion, customs,
manners, traditions and habits. . . ."[12]

John L. McLaurin of South Carolina suggested that he was well
qualified to speak upon the question of incorporation of a mongrel
and semibarbarous population into the body politic. He thought that
a population "that, so far as I can ascertain, is inferior to, but akin to,
the negro race, . . . is pregnant with lessons of wisdom for our guidance in the Philippines." It seemed strange to McLaurin that senators
who favored universal suffrage and full enfranchisement of the Negro
should be advocating imperialism. Seeing the inconsistency in the
advocacy on the one hand of a policy of acquiring territory by treaty
or conquest, holding it as a colony, treating its inhabitants as vassals
instead of citizens, governing them by military rule or by legislation
that was unconstitutional, and, on the other hand, the advocation of
universal suffrage for the Negro, McLaurin suggested, "If they are
sincere in their views as to the Philippines, they should propose an
amendment to the Constitution which will put the inferior races in
this country and the inhabitants of the Philippines upon an equality
as to their civil and political rights, and thus forever settle the vexed
race and suffrage questions in this country as well as the outlying
territories."[13]

The opposition from Southern Democrats and some Northern Republicans left the fate of the treaty in doubt. Some senators felt that
the title to the archipelago was not clear. Senator Tillman, one of the
leading opponents of the administration's imperial policy, was called
the representative for Aguinaldo because he questioned the legality
of the treaty. He agreed with the Filipinos that possession was
ownership.[14]

When all efforts at disparaging the treaty on legal grounds seemed
to be of no avail, Tillman and other Southerners turned to racial
arguments. Tillman raised questions, he said, not as the senator from
"Aguinaldo but as senator from Africa, if you please, South Carolina with 750,000 colored population and only 500,000 whites, I real-

---

[12] *Ibid.*, pt. 1: 432–33 (January 6, 1899).
[13] *Ibid.*, p. 639 (January 13, 1899).
[14] *Ibid.*, pt. 2: 1529–34 (February 7, 1899).

ize what you are doing, while you do not; and I would save this country from the injection into it of another race question. . . ."[15] Tillman
directed the Senate's attention to the fact that those senators who
were then contending for a different policy in Hawaii and the Philippines were the same men who not only gave the slaves self-
government "but forced on white men of the South at the point of the
bayonet, the rule and domination of these ex-slaves. . . . Why the difference? Why the change? Do you acknowledge that you were wrong
in 1868?" The advocates of the Philippine policy were undertaking to
annex islands containing 10,000,000 of the colored race, of whom
more than one-half were barbarians of the lowest type.

"It is to the injection into the body politic of the United States of
that vitiated blood, that debased and ignorant people, that we object," Tillman argued, "and it is germane to the proposition, to the
question—the very vitals of it—to whether that shall be done or
whether we shall insist that this Government shall not annex those
people, but that we give them whatever necessary protection they
may need to keep other nations from gobbling them up, and thereby
relieve ourselves of any obligation. . . ."[16]

Senator William Teller of Colorado agreed that some kind of condition should be applied. He was opposed, "to begin with, of making
those people citizens of the United States," but he favored extending
to those people the protection of "those great principles which we
recognize in this country as essentials to the existence of free government. I am for treating them, not as citizens but, if you choose—
which is rather objectionable in a republic—as subjects; and that we
shall just as soon as possible give them all the blessings of a free government of their own."[17] He was sure no one wanted to make Cuba,
Puerto Rico, or the Philippines states and did not believe the American people were willing to admit these possessions into the Union.[18]
The senator seemingly contradicted himself in that he believed that
there was a great obligation resting on the United States to help these
people, despite his knowledge that there had never "been in a tropical country a government such as we believe ought to exist." And

[15] *Ibid.*, p. 1389.
[16] *Ibid.*, pt. 1: 837 (January 20, 1899).
[17] *Ibid.*, p. 969 (January 24, 1899).
[18] *Ibid.*, p. 327 (December 20, 1898).

there never would be a government in those areas that would come
up to "our idea of government. The people who live in the tropics
are not qualified," and, he feared, "never will be qualified to maintain such a government as is maintained by Anglo-Saxon people. . . .
A torrid climate [will] not develop high moral and mental qualities.
The Asiatic will never maintain such a government as the Anglo-
Saxon." He was not capable of it and, in addition, was already wed-
ded to tradition, seeing good in that which had gone before and not
making an effort to improve as did the Anglo-Saxon.[19]

If the Philippines were ever admitted to statehood, Senator Mc-
Laurin noted that the Congress would contain "about one-seventh
Japanese, Malays, Chinese, or whatever mixture they have out there.
We would have representatives with a voice in directing the affairs
of this country from another continent, speaking another language,
different in race, religion, and civilization—a people with whom citizens of the United States had nothing in common." He added that
an insuperable objection to the Philippines would be the difficulty of
governing a territory 8,000 miles away and a barbaric people, mongrel in race, religion, and character. A protectorate over the Philippines would cause more trouble than all of the domestic problems
then confronting the United States, since the three fundamental
principles upon which the United States was governed were "(1)
Citizenship, universal and coextensive with the country, (2) Local
self-government, (3) Freedom to travel, to labor, and to engage in
business in any part of the country." McLaurin thought that there
would be great difficulty in reconciling these principles with colonies
and wondered:

. . . Are these mixed races from the Orient, against some of whom we have
passed exclusion laws, to have all the rights of citizenship conferred upon
them? Shall they have a voice in the government of this country corre-
sponding to the voice we have in the government of theirs? Or is the right
of suffrage to be given to placate the spirit of the Constitution, while by
some legerdemain they are denied its practical fruits?

Of one thing I am sure—the American people will never consent for
these inferior races to flood our land and add another complication to the
labor problem. To permit cheap, Asiatic labor to come into competition with

[19] *Ibid.*, p. 329.

our intelligent, well-paid labor will be to degrade and lower our civilization. Already in Illinois negroes from Alabama have been shot and driven from the State, and such action defended by the governor.[20]

Opposition to ratification of the treaty based on racial prejudice was not confined to the senators from the South, as shown by Senator George Turner of Washington, who contended that the supporters of the treaty could not escape a violation of the basic principles in the Constitution by "a universal miscegenation of blood, of religion, and of government with the yellow Buddhists, Mohammedans, and Confucians over whom it is proposed to extend our protecting wing, and with whom it is proposed to attempt the process of deglutition and digestion disguised under the Christian and euphonious name of 'benevolent assimilation'." The alternative, he said, was not contrary to fundamental American principles of liberty. But it would do violence to the blood, the history, and the traditions of the race and would leave "such frightful results in mongrelizing our citizenship, that the advocates of the new movement in favor of a greater America prefer the alternative risk of debauching our institutions rather than do that, by an assimilating, miscegenation, which will certainly impoverish and debilitate our citizenship. . . ."[21]

Senator McLaurin, seeing the paradox in a situation which found supporters and opponents of ratification arguing from the same basic racial tenets, again took the floor. He argued that Senator Platt of Connecticut had

most amply vindicated the South, perhaps unintentionally, but we thank him the more heartily for his complete announcement of the divine right of the Caucasian to govern the inferior races.

When the question is brought home, the white man is the same everywhere. The Senator, perhaps unconsciously, shows that he realized that no other race in nearly equal numbers can live side by side with the Caucasian and enjoy such civil and political rights as under any circumstances render the domination of the inferior races a possibility. Hence his appeal to what he calls "inherent sovereignty," and in this he has to do what we did after reconstruction—pitch his tent outside the spirit of the fourteenth and fifteenth amendments of the Constitution. . . .[22]

[20] *Ibid.*, pp. 639–41 (January 13, 1899).
[21] *Ibid.*, p. 785.
[22] *Ibid.*, p. 639.

If Senator McLaurin's views were the same as those held by the American policy-makers, the Filipinos would not only have a difficult time gaining their independence, but their assumed rights would be nonexistent.

The outbreak of war between the Filipinos and American forces in the Philippines two days prior to the ratification of the treaty is credited by some senators as the reason for the shift of their position from opposition to the treaty to support for it. Some inferred that the hostilities were instigated in order to gain support for the treaty. Senator Rawlings charged, on the basis of Senate investigation, that the message about the start of the war against the Filipinos was sent to Washington at 10 P.M., two hours before actual hostilities began. He argued that the extra two hours were needed so that the dispatches could reach Washington in time to influence the vote.[23] Senator Tillman questioned to whose advantage the beginning of hostilities would be. He was of the opinion that the Americans stood to gain by it and that the senators who changed their votes were falling into the administration's scheme.

The United States, in the treaty, was purchasing from Spain islands which no longer belonged to her. It would take a war—one with racial implications—to establish the authority supposedly transferred by the ratification of the treaty.[24]

A number of individuals close to the McKinley administration had conducted a vigorous campaign of expansion. Their plan was to commit the country to a definite imperial policy. President McKinley seems to have adopted their plan and established a policy that resulted in an utter disregard for the people of the possessions sought.

As late as October, 1898, the *Nation* reported that the administration had not formally and officially declared its position, "but the series of speeches which President McKinley and members of his Cabinet have delivered on their Western trip virtually commit the Executive to the policy of demanding the whole archipelago."[25] He succeeded in getting this with the ratification of the treaty, but it

[23] *Ibid.*, 57 Cong., 1 sess., V, 4573 (April 23, 1902). See Testimony of General Arthur MacArthur, *Senate Document*, No. 331, 57 Cong., 1 sess., II, 890–91.

[24] *Congressional Record*, 55 Cong., 3 sess., XXXII, pt. 2: 1530 (February 7, 1899).

[25] *Nation*, LXVII (October 27, 1898), 306.

took a larger war, more men, and larger appropriations to "benevolently assimilate" the Filipinos.

Later in 1898 Lodge expressed fear that there would be trouble
over the treaty; how serious he did not know, but confessed that he
could not "think calmly of the rejection of that treaty by a little
more than one-third of the Senate. It would be a repudiation of the
President and humiliation of the whole country in the eyes of
the world, and would show we are unfit as a nation to enter into
great questions of foreign policy. I cannot believe that the opposition, which is, of course, composed of Southern Democrats, can
succeed. . . ."[26]

Though Lodge doubted that the treaty would receive the requisite
number of votes, McKinley proceeded as though the treaty had already been ratified. He appointed the First Philippine Commission,
headed by Jacob Gould Schurman. Schurman was opposed to the administration's Philippine policy, but in conversation with the President was persuaded that the alternatives to American acquisition of
the territory were worse. He became convinced that the President's
motive in compelling Spain to cede to the United States her sovereignty over the islands "was the humanitarian object of liberating
the Filipinos from misgovernment and oppression; and that in the
second place up to January, 1899, no definite Philippine policy had
been adopted or even thought out by the President, whose mind
had not indeed traveled beyond the first step of relieving Spain of
her sovereignty over the archipelago."[27]

Upon arrival in the Philippines, the Schurman Commission refused
to discuss with the leaders of the Filipino insurgents the question of
the sovereignty of the United States over the archipelago. "That matter," it was said, "had been already settled by the treaty of Paris, and
being so settled was a fact which was now beyond the realm of profit-
able discussion." The commissioners, after a careful consideration
and study, told the Filipinos, "It was the opinion of the commission
that the Philippine people were not capable of independent self-
government, and that independence, for which some of them said

[26] Lodge to Roosevelt, December 7, 1898, *Roosevelt-Lodge Letters*, I, 368.
[27] Jacob Gould Schurman, *The Philippine Affair: A Retrospect and Outlook*,
pp. 3–4.

they were fighting, was . . . an idea at present impossible, not only because of their unfitness for it, but because of their inability to preserve it among the nations even if it were granted."[28]

The commission brought back the kind of report that the administration desired. The Filipinos themselves, according to hundreds of witnesses, did not want independence. In view of their own ignorance and lack of political experience, the multiplicity of languages (none of which the American administrators spoke), the divergence of culture and mode of life, and the difficulties of communication, these witnesses were of the opinion that "an independent sovereign Philippine state was at the present time neither possible nor desirable. . . . The Philippine Islands, even the most patriotic declare . . . need the tutelage and protection of the United States."[29]

If King George III had sent a commission to the thirteen colonies under similar circumstances in 1783 to ascertain the capacity of the colonists to govern themselves and protect their independence, he would have received a similar report, unless he took the words of those fighting for independence. The Schurman Commission proceeded along the lines of ingrained preconceptions concerning the incapacity of inferior people to govern themselves. The commission even took the time to report on the ill effect of the Chinese on the Philippine people. There was evidence taken to the effect that the Chinese should be excluded

because they inter-marry with the Filipino women, and that they produced a race which does not furnish good citizens, that many of the great troubles of the islands are caused by Chinese and their descendants. Most of the witnesses concur in stating that it would not be advisable to let Chinese come into the country without restrictions. . . .[30]

Even with the report of the commission, there were doubts in some quarters as to the ability of the United States to give justice to the people of the Philippines, who were in the popular mind little more than savages. The United States ambassador to Madrid during the Spanish-American War, General Stewart Woodford, doubted that

[28] Schurman Report on the Philippines, *Senate Document*, No. 138, 56 Cong., 1 sess., pt. 1: 7–8 (January 31, 1900).
[29] *Ibid.*, pp. 82–83.
[30] *Ibid.*, pp. 154–55.

America would deal justly with the inferiors in the possessions acquired from Spain. General Woodford was placed by the *Nation* in that group of Americans who chose to believe that "destiny" had placed the Philippines on our hands. The general was honest enough, reported the *Nation*, to acknowledge that the Americans were not a people "trained to the very generous and considerate and thoughtful treatment of inferior races," and since America had not made a success of the Negro problem of the South, the country should have been reluctant to "hurry to assume the responsibility of governing inferior races whether they are in the Caribbean Sea or in the far off Pacific Islands." General Woodford did not have a solution to the problem of a more considerate attitude of Americans for inferior races in the Southern and Western states of the Union but did believe "that the clock of the world will not move backward, and that wherever our flag has gone there the liberty, the civilization, and humanity which that flag represents and embraces must remain and, God helping us, remain forever."[31]

Despite the doubts and misgivings of many Americans, the treaty was ratified with the aid of three Southern votes previously opposed to the treaty, but shifted at the suggestion of William Jennings Bryan. Henry Cabot Lodge wrote.

. . . When the Senate went into executive session on Monday, February 0, with the time for the vote fixed for three o'clock, the treaty had only 58 sure votes, 60 being needed for ratification; the opposition had 29 sure votes, and the remaining 3 were doubtful. At half past two, one of the doubtful voters was declared to be for the treaty, making 59, just before three o'clock another vote was promised, and the third doubtful vote was given to the treaty after the roll had been called. The final vote stood 57 to 27—including pairs, 61 to 29, just two-thirds and one vote to spare. . . .[32]

The implications that might be drawn from the ratification of that treaty and the difficulties which might ensue were pointed up by Senator Tillman. First, he called to the attention of the Senate a fact which had escaped the attention of senators, "that with five exceptions every man in the Chamber who has to do with the colored race in the United States voted against ratification of the treaty." He

[31] *Nation*, LXVII (October 27, 1898), 304.
[32] Henry Cabot Lodge, *The War with Spain*, pp. 231–32.

observed, "It was not because we are Democrats, but because we understand and realize what it is to have two races side by side that cannot mix or mingle without deterioration and injury to both and the ultimate destruction of the civilization of the higher. We of the South have borne this white man's burden of a colored race in our midst since their emancipation and before."[33]

The three Southern senators who changed their votes were McLaurin of South Carolina; McEnery of Louisiana; and Jones of Virginia. Of the other two senators—Morgan of Alabama and Grey of Virginia—Morgan was an out-and-out imperialist, and Grey had served on the peace commission.

ADMINISTRATION POLICY

An effort to avoid some of the difficulties assumed to be involved in the ratification of the treaty was made in the McEnery Resolution, which passed the Senate but was defeated in the House of Representatives. The first provision in this resolution stated that the inhabitants of the Philippines were not to be incorporated into citizenship of the United States. The second provision removed the possibility of territorial status for the Philippines and evolution into statehood. The islands were not to be permanently annexed as an integral portion of United States territory, and it was the intention of the United States, after establishing a government suitable to the wants and conditions of the inhabitants and preparing the inhabitants for local self-government, to make such disposition of the islands as would best promote the interest of the citizens of the United States and the inhabitants of the islands.[34]

However, the treaty had been ratified and the resolution could only reflect the sense of the Senate. The immediate task at hand was to extend the purchased sovereignty from Manila to the entire archipelago. In his message to Congress in 1900, President McKinley noted that the Articles of Capitulation of the City of Manila on the 13th of August, 1898, concluded, "This city, its inhabitants, its churches and religious worship, its education establishments, and

[33] *Congressional Record*, 55 Cong., 3 sess., XXXII, pt. 2: 1532 (February 7, 1899).
[34] *Ibid.*, p. 1529. S. D. McEnery was a senator from Louisiana.

its private property of all descriptions, are placed under the special safeguard of the faith and honor of the American Army."[35]

By some method of reasoning President McKinley extended the capitulation of Manila, which the Spanish forces controlled, to the whole of the Philippine Archipelago, which the Filipino insurgents controlled and claimed.[36] While the President was speaking to Congress, the United States Armed Forces were trying to "benevolently assimilate" the Filipinos—with bullet and bayonet at a ratio of ten Filipinos killed to one American.[37] To carry out the mission of liberating the Filipinos from themselves, a total of 74,021 officers and men were sent to the Philippines.[38] The figures given did not include the officers and men attached to the naval operation.

It was President McKinley's belief "that this purpose has been faithfully kept. A high and sacred obligation rests upon the Government of the United States to give protection for property and life, civil and religious freedom, and wise, firm and unselfish guidance in the paths of peace and prosperity to all the peoples of the Philippine Islands." Accordingly, he instructed the Second Philippine Commission, headed by William Howard Taft, to labor for the full performance of this obligation, which, he said, "concerns the honor and conscience of their country, in the firm hope that through their labors all inhabitants of the Philippine Islands may come to look back with gratitude to the day when God gave victory to American arms at Manila and set their land under the sovereignty and protection of the United States."[39]

---

[35] *House Document*, No. 1, 56 Cong., 2 sess., (December 3, 1900), pp. 12–15.

[36] Treaty of Peace between the United States and Spain, *Senate Document*, No. 62, 55 Cong., 3 sess. Also testimony of General Hughes, *Hearings*, Affairs in the Philippines, *Senate Document*, No. 331, 57 Cong., 1 sess. Also *Congressional Record*, 57 Cong., 1 sess., V, 4535 (April 22, 1902).

[37] *Hearings*, Affairs in the Philippines, *Senate Document*, No. 331, 57 Cong., 1 sess.; Moorfield Storey, *The Conquest of the Philippines*, p. 89. General MacArthur said the difference was due to the superior shooting of the Americans. Senator Rawlings called it slaughter resulting from orders not to take prisoners.

[38] *House Document*, No. 2, Annual Report of the War Department, 56 Cong., 2 sess., p. 4.

[39] *House Document*, No. 1, 56 Cong., 2 sess. (December 3, 1900), p. 13. The commission consisted of the Hon. William H. Taft of Ohio, Prof. Dean C. Worcester of Michigan, Hon. Luke Wright of Tennessee, the Hon. Henry C. Ide of Vermont, and Prof. Bernard Moses of California. The commission was to function as a board with Taft as president.

Soon after this the President outlined the kind of government desired for the Philippines, and the attack on his policy began. Senator Teller was concerned about the duty owed not the Filipinos or to the Puerto Ricans, but to the American people. Was the United States to have a colonial system? Or were the peoples of the Philippines and Puerto Rico to be made a part of the United States? One of these two policies had to be followed, and the senator, who regarded the latter as far more dangerous than the former, said, "I would a great deal rather make the Philippine Islands a colony, a province, a dependency, or whatever you may choose to call it, than to make their inhabitants citizens of the United States, . . . that they shall stand before the law on an equality with all other citizens of the United States. . . ."[40]

Alluding to the conquest of the Philippines in a Senate speech, Tillman asked if "the thirteenth, fourteenth, and fifteenth amendments" were "to be nullified in their essence because they had failed of their purpose in the South?" Were they for home consumption only? "Was the memorable conflict between slavery and freedom useless?" Had the nation not gained any lessons by it? Was the commercial greed which dominated in the councils and coerced "the President to do his bloody and horrible work to make the Constitution a new league with death and a covenant with hell, in the interest of oppression akin to slavery?" In order to do these things, we would have to "camp outside the Constitution." It would be necessary to "give the old interpretation of the Southern slaveholders to the Declaration of Independence and nullify all precedents and decisions of our Supreme Court."[41]

Tillman wondered if the nation had spent "the blood of seven hundred thousand" of "its best and bravest upon the altar of liberty" only to find within the short span of one man's life that "the sacrifice" had been "in vain, the Civil War a mistake, and that the colored race has no rights we are bound to respect at home or abroad?" Previously the South had enjoyed a monopoly "in the odium of shooting and hanging men of the colored race." Were the Northern people envious of the South, and were they now seeking to emulate the

[40] *Congressional Record*, 56 Cong., 1 sess., XXXIII, pt. 3: 2874 (March 14, 1900).

[41] *Ibid.*, pt. 2: 1261 (January 29, 1900).

South's bad example? The South, he contended, had been a victim of circumstances, and much of the blood of Negroes shed by white men of the South was a direct result of the attempt to place the Negro in control of the government of the Southern states. Though the conflict between liberty and slavery had destroyed slavery in the United States, it had left the South with "an irrepressible conflict between intelligence and ignorance, between vice and virtue, between barbarism and civilization." While the South had inherited its race problem, the advocates of the Philippine policy were wantonly going out in search of theirs and the nation's. Tillman believed that the sins of Southern fathers who had tolerated slavery were being visited upon Southern children to the third and fourth generations.

The ill consequences of having been bred in an atmosphere of slavery clings to us like the shirt of Nessus in our attempt to throw off the yoke and go forward with progress. But have we not enough of debased and ignoble people in our midst that we should seek by conquest, without any right other than a shadowy one, to incorporate 10,000,000 more colored people?

If the North was jealous of the "bad eminence" of the South in the murder of colored people, the North should note that almost the only protest against the policy of imperialism came from Southern senators. Tillman repeated, "We know whereof we speak. We are in contact with the race question at close quarters and have been and will continue to be. You know not what you do. We are tied to the 'body of death' represented by the presence in our midst of a debased and ignorant race. . . ." Could there be any reason, either in policy or in morals, he asked, why the "already hard task and hope less future of the blacks of the South, the burdens under which they bend should be increased by having the 'sullen silent peoples' [sic] of the East brought into direct competition with them . . .?"[42]

Senator Teller did not put much faith in the Congress or the American people giving justice and freedom to the newly acquired peoples. He was afraid McKinley's program of colonialism would get "the approval of the great American Senate and the American House of Representatives," and he stated:

42 Ibid.

I very much fear that the people of this country have so far forgotten
these great principles of liberty that it may receive the approval also of the
country. But nevertheless, it is our duty to raise our voices against it and
at least give warning to the American people that an outrage of this kind
perpetrated upon 10,000,000 men, who may not be citizens of this country, but who are under its jurisdiction, at least, must in the end reflect upon
every one of the 76,000,000 men who dwell under our flag. . . .[43]

Congressmen and senators were not alone in using racism to support or attack the Philippine policy of the McKinley administration.
Mrs. Jefferson Davis, writing in the *Arena* magazine for January,
1900, could not understand why the President persisted in conquering and retaining the Philippines. Why add several million Negroes
to the population when there were already eight million in the
country? The United States had not solved the problem of how best
to govern and promote the welfare of the Negroes already resident.
Mrs. Davis suggested that the Filipinos be given the right to govern
themselves, at least until the United States had solved the race problem at home.[44]

On the other hand, vice-presidential candidate Theodore Roosevelt, campaigning in 1900, compared the conquest of the Filipinos
to the winning of the West, saying, "The reasoning which justifies
our having made war against Sitting Bull also justifies our having
checked outbreaks of Aguinaldo and his followers."[45] Carried to a
logical conclusion, this meant that the Filipinos were no better than
the American Indians and deserved the same fate.

The policy of the McKinley administration was condemned by the
Democratic party in 1900. The Philippine plank read:

The Filipinos cannot be citizens without endangering our civilization;
they cannot be subjects without imperiling our form of government; and
as we are not willing to surrender our civilization, nor convert the Republic into an Empire we favor an immediate declaration of the nation's
purpose. . . .[46]

[43] *Congressional Record*, 56 Cong., 2 sess., XXXIV, pt. 5: 3109 (February
27, 1901).
[44] Mrs. Jefferson Davis, "The White Man's Problem," *Arena*, XXIII (January
1900), 1–4.
[45] Roosevelt, *Works*, XIV, 557.
[46] *Congressional Record*, 64 Cong., 1 sess., LIII, pt. 2: 1499 (January 25,
1916).

This purpose, according to the Democrats in 1900, should be a speedy release of the Filipinos.

The editors of *Outlook*, in criticizing a Senate speech made by Senator Hoar on April 17, 1900, dismissed his statement that the Filipinos were capable of self-government. In speaking of the so-called Philippine republic, they observed, "According to the undisputed testimony of Americans of spotless reputation, sent to ascertain and report the facts, this government, where it has possessed the power, has permitted, if it has not perpetrated, frequent assassinations and political robbery on a scale which made it little short of brigandage."[47]

Very few Americans of this period could look objectively at the Filipinos. The majority considered them to be in a class with the American Indians and Negroes. Americans, lacking the ability to be empathic where so-called inferiors were concerned, were unwilling to accord these peoples political rights, from which all other rights emanate.

In keeping with this view, Moorfield Storey felt that Americans at home could not be trusted with the task of deciding the destinies of several million Filipinos. "Nearly all the elements necessary for a real knowledge of the conditions existing in the Islands or for the creation of genuine sympathy with the aspirations of the Filipinos are sorely lacking in the hearts and minds of the American people."[48] Storey thought that the American people, knowing little and caring less about the Filipinos, "chose to believe what other Americans said about them because the latter were of their own race."[49]

Former President Benjamin Harrison was one of the few who could be empathic. He observed that if the present conditions were correct, then the old answer to the Southern slaveholder was wrong. It was not "a question of kind or unkind treatment, but of human rights, not of the good or bad use of power, but of power." He said the founding fathers had given the same answer to the claim of absolute power made on behalf of the British Parliament. Harrison insisted that a government of unlimited legislative or executive power was un-American. Speaking of the founding fathers, he said,

[47] *Outlook*, LXIV (April 28, 1900), 947.
[48] Storey, *Conquest of the Philippines*, p. 197.
[49] *Ibid.*, p. 264.

"They would write the law of liberty truly, and suffer for a time the just reproach of a departure from its precepts that could not be presently amended. It is a brave thing to proclaim a law that condemns your own practices. . . . The fathers left to a baser generation the attempt to limit God's law of liberty to white men." In regard to the instructions to the Taft Philippine Commission, he noted:

> The benevolent disposition of the President is well illustrated in these instructions. He conferred freely—"until Congress shall take action"—upon the Filipinos, who accepted the sovereignty of the United States and submitted themselves to the government established by the Commission, privileges that our fathers only secured after eight years of desperate war. There is this, however, to be noted, that our fathers were not content to hold these priceless gifts under revocable license. They accounted that to hold these things under tenure of another man's benevolence was not to hold them at all. Their battle was for rights, not privileges—for a Constitution, not a letter of instructions.[50]

The inability of many Americans charged with governing the Philippines to understand the inhabitants of those islands may be seen by the following dialogue taken from the hearings conducted by the Senate Committee on Affairs in the Philippines.

SENATOR CULBERSON: Let me reverse the case. Suppose the relative strength of the United States and the Philippine Islands was such that the Filipinos had the power to direct, and suppose they should undertake to force upon the United States, and the people thereof, their language, their civilization, and their laws, upon the ground, as they believed that they were best suited to our capabilities. What would you say about that?
GOVERNOR TAFT: . . . I am very free to say that I should resist it.
SENATOR CULBERSON: That is what I wanted to get at. I thought you would, and I presume that is why the Filipinos are resisting.[51]

Yet Taft would deny the Filipinos the full rights of citizenship, claiming that "the condition of the people of the Philippine Islands . . . is such that the extension of the constitutional restrictions which

---

[50] Benjamin Harrison, "The Status of Annexed Territory and Its Free Civilized Inhabitants," *North American Review*, CLXXII (January 1901), 12.
[51] *Hearings*, Affairs in the Philippines, *Senate Document*, No. 331, 57 Cong., 1 sess., pt. 1: 348.

apply in a State would very much interfere with the establishment of a stable and successful government."[52]

Had the American people been able to get the facts about the Philippines, perhaps they would have brought early pressure to bear upon the officials to withdraw and leave the Filipinos to themselves, with United States protection. Instead, the racial prejudices of the majority of the American people dictated handling the Philippines as President Schurman of the First Philippine Commission recommended. Insofar as the United States governed the islands, that commission strongly stated it should govern them at arm's length:

> Anything like the mingling of Philippine affairs with American affairs would . . . prove a serious mistake. . . . As it is the policy of our republic to maintain a national development unmixed with Asiatic immigrants, so it is to the interest of the Filipinos to have opportunity for full and independent development of their own individual capacities, their own racial characteristics and their own civilization.

Schurman hoped that "the Federal Constitution could be amended so as to provide for the perpetual exclusion of Asiatic countries from partnership in our great American Republic." Whether or not the Constitution would be amended, Schurman was certain it was the policy of the American people not to admit an Asiatic country to the status and privileges of statehood or to the conditions of a territory.[53] He was also sure that no political party would propose so unsure a program as statehood for the Philippines; no statesman would ever venture to support a policy so repugnant to American sentiment. The hostility against any such proposal was ingrained in the American fabric and ineradicable, causing Schurman to conclude: "The grounds of this antipathetic attitude are fundamental and all-embracing; they are physical, psychological, . . . ethnological, historical, social, and political. Every aspect of human existence enters its protest against a union so unnatural and so unwise."[54]

If this was any indication of the way the average American felt about the Philippines, one is inclined to wonder why the war of conquest and the long retention. The answer lies somewhere in the

[52] *Ibid.*, p. 322.
[53] Schurman, *Philippine Affair*, pp. 41–42.
[54] *Ibid.*, p. 88.

secrecy surrounding the operations in the Philippines and in the callousness of Americans for those they considered their inferiors. Information concerning this imperial adventure was allowed to come out piecemeal and was then edited. It took a congressional resolution and investigation to finally make public much of the information. Add the contempt for a race considered inferior, and an army thirsty for glory and at the same time frustrated by a distasteful job—certainly under these circumstances the Filipinos could not have gotten a fair and impartial hearing.

Harold Martin thought that the Manila censorship was never maintained in accordance with the only justification of a censorship, namely, "to keep the enemy in ignorance." Rather, it existed "to prevent the people of the United States from being informed of what was happening in the islands; its keynotes being partisan politics and military pride."[55] Behind the keynote of military pride, the racism of Americans in the service conditioned the activities of the army.

Many of the military leaders were aware of the problem. General Thomas M. Anderson attributed the attitude of racial superiority, carried to the Philippines by American forces, as one of the causes of the continuing conflict. General Anderson thought that had the Americans known something more of dealing with Asiatics, hostilities could perhaps have been avoided. The whole concept that the administration seemed to practice—not respecting, or ignoring altogether, the rights of the peoples of the possessions acquired from Spain—influenced the conduct of the individual soldiers in the Philippines. General Anderson wrote, "Our soldiers, to get what they considered trophies, did a good deal of what the Filipinos considered looting. A number made debts which they did not find it convenient to pay. They called the natives 'niggers,' and often treated them with good-natured condescension which exasperated the natives all the more because they feared to resent it. . . . Thus, it happened that the common people, from at first hailing us as deliverers, got to regarding us as enemies. . . ."[56]

[55] Harold Martin, "Manila Censorship," *Forum*, XXXI (June 1901), 463.
[56] Thomas M. Anderson, "Our Role in the Philippines," *North American Review*, CLXX (February 1900), 282. See also *Hearings, Affairs in the Philippines, Senate Document*, No. 331, 57 Cong., 1 sess., pt. 1: 77.

Support for the attitudes described by General Anderson as characteristic of the military can be seen in the conduct of the war as reflected in the Senate hearings.

SENATOR PATTERSON: When a war is conducted by a superior race against those whom they consider inferior in the scale of civilizations, is it not the experience of the world that the superior race will almost involuntarily practice inhuman conduct?

GOVERNOR TAFT: There is much greater danger in such a case than in dealing with whites. There is no doubt about it.[57]

James A. Le Roy wrote that Americans in the Philippines drew the color line based on the "nigger" theory in vogue in the United States. It was the usual thing among Americans who had visited the Philippines "and imbibed a contempt or dislike for the people to betray in their conversation the fact that their theories of the situation are based upon popular notions at home as to the negroes' shortcomings and incapacity."[58]

These theories were reinforced by the technique of hearing only what one wished to hear and seeing only that which one wished to see. Arthur Llewllyn Griffiths reported, "Men came to the Philippines at their own expense and at the expense of the government for the sole purpose of studying the Philippine situation from the Filipinos' standpoint. After being wined and dined at the various officers' clubs in the principal parts of the archipelago, hearing speeches by Filipinos prepared for the occasion, as a minister prepares his sermon to conform to a certain text, they return 'knowing the Philippine situation' but in truth loaded with hearsay."[59]

David H. Doherty in a paper on conditions in the Philippines found that the "benevolently despotic" civil government in the islands was saved from tyranny only by virtue of its personnel. The government was attacked by American adventurers and a "yellow press" interested in exploiting the islands. There was an attitude of resent-

[57] Also see the answers to the charges of cruelties to the Filipinos, *Senate Document*, No. 205, 57 Cong., 1 sess., pt. 1.

[58] James A. Le Roy, "Race Prejudice in the Philippines," *Atlantic Monthly*, XC (July 1902), 101.

[59] Arthur Llewllyn Griffiths, "The Philippine Insurrection, Why?" *Arena*, XXII (November 1904), 497.

fulness on the part of the military toward the civil authorities, resulting from the feeling that they could do a better job of governing the islands than the civil authorities were then doing. There were also the ex-soldiers who boldly asked for another chance "to wipe out the 'niggers'." Doherty asserted:

> The most lamentable condition in the Philippines is the discontent which shows itself in ladronism and foolish insurrection, and still worse in passive resistance or sullen obedience. . . . The causes are the following:
> First, the lack of a definite political status; . . . of ultimate independence or assimilation under the Constitution. The dread of colonial subjection weighs upon the people, who know very well the decisions of our Supreme Court and the acts of Congress. . . .
> Third, the social taboos which some Americans . . . enforce against the brown man, and the oriental habit of abusive treatment of servants, in which many have already become adept. . . .[60]

Perhaps it should have been apparent to the Americans who advocated a policy of conquest of the Philippines that on the anvil of war and racism they were hammering a divided people into a united people. However, the leaders found reason after reason for the failure to bring peace to their ill-gotten possessions. Felix Alder observed that first the people of the country were told it was the ambition of the leader of the insurrection, Aguinaldo, that prolonged the war. Aguinaldo was captured, but the war still continued. Then the country was told it was the ambition of a Tagálog oligarchy to acquire control of the islands that kept the war alive. It was found that the Visayans were as stubborn in their resistance as the Tagálogs. Alder could only conclude, "No, it is not Aguinaldo, it is not a Tagálog oligarchy, it is the awakened national consciousness of a people that opposes us, a spiritual force which survives defeat, which the dispersion of organized armies cannot disintegrate, which, like a fire, goes on smouldering beneath the ashes, breaking out anew ever and ever again until either it achieves its aim or those who harbor that aim are exterminated. . . ."[61]

[60] *Senate Document*, No. 170, 58 Cong., 2 sess., p. 19.
[61] Felix Alder, "The Philippine War: Two Ethical Questions," *Forum*, XXXIII (June 1902), 397.

RACE—THE COMMON DENOMINATOR

Racism, embodied in the concept of the "White Man's burden," was partly responsible for conditioning American imperialism in the Philippines. In the legislation whch determined the Filipino position as a political entity, the recommendations of the Schurman Commission were followed. The act to provide temporarily for the administration of civil government in the Philippine Islands left the Filipinos suspended between citizenship in the United States and citizenship in the Philippine Islands, whch had no sovereignty. Section 4 made the Filipino a citizen of the Philippine Islands but left him without the ability to become a citizen of the United States.[62]

Two policies emerged, embracing the philosophies of the Republican party on one hand and the Democratic party on the other. Needless to say, adherents of both philosophies were to be found in both parties. The Republican party was for retention of the islands until such time as the inhabitants were capable of self-government; the Democratic party favored Philippine independence as soon as possible, with some measure of protection by the United States. On one thing both parties were agreed—that the Filipinos were incapable of governing themselves in the manner of the Anglo Saxons.

The McKinley policy was instituted in 1899 with the appointment of the Second Philippine Commission headed by William Howard Taft. Taft was in positions of great influence over a long period of time to implement that policy, first as president of the Second Philippine Commission, then governor general of the Philippines, secretary of war, President, and finally as a member of the Supreme Court. The policy pursued by Taft was one designed to tie the Philippines to the United States economically, making it impossible for the Filipinos to sever the relationship. Yet Moorefield Storey wrote that his policy "creates a new race problem because his position rests entirely upon the assumption that the Filipinos, being unfit to govern themselves, should be governed by a race of superior people."[63]

The question of policy was raised by senators investigating affairs in the Philippines in 1902. They asked Taft, then the governor gen-

[62] Act of July 1, 1902.
[63] Storey, *Conquest of the Philippines*, p. 206.

eral, about the future of the islands and their inhabitants. Senator Edward W. Carmack of Tennessee wanted to know if it was an "open question whether the people of the Philippine Islands—islands populated with eight or ten million Asiatics—should be admitted to full rights of American citizenship, or whether or not an archipelago so populated should be admitted to statehood in the Union?" Governor Taft answered that he did not think so, although "the question would not have to be answered for two or three generations." Senator Carmack implied that the question of statehood for the Philippines should not be considered for a hundred years. In order to avoid the dangers of possible statehood, the question demanded immediate attention.

Taft's attitude concerning the Filipinos' ability to appreciate and use Anglo-Saxon methods was illustrated by his opposition to the extension to the Philippine Islands of the rights and privileges which the Constitution granted to incorporated territories.[64] In a speech in 1903, Governor Taft indicated that he sympathized with the aspirations of the Filipino people for independence. However, he did not think that their struggles were to be equated with similar struggles for independence by Anglo-Saxons. The United States had decided that the people of the Philippines "were not able themselves to bring about any beneficial results which would secure an efficient government." That the Filipinos had, through their educated leaders, breathed "the inspiration of liberty and free government" was noted by the governor. In their struggle for independence many of the inhabitants had "fought, bled, and given up their lives." The struggle was a mistaken one, but the sacrifice and bravery were worthy of admiration and suggested "a people capable of greater things."[65] Although Taft seemed to hold out to the Filipinos some hope of ultimate independence, his actual policy worked toward retention of the islands through the attraction of capital investment, tariff regulations, and trade.

President Theodore Roosevelt and Governor Taft were in agreement on the nation's Philippine policy. Roosevelt stated in a message

---

[64] *Hearings,* Affairs in the Philippine Islands, *Senate Document,* No. 331, 57 Cong., 1 sess., pt. 1: 322–23.
[65] *Senate Document,* No. 191, 58 Cong., 2 sess., p. 3.

to Congress in 1903 that "the Philippines should be knit closer to us by tariff arrangements."[66] Seemingly, Roosevelt desired to continue in the belief that the Filipinos were not a united people, as shown by his message to Congress in 1904.

"The Philippine people," he said, "or, to speak more accurately, the many tribes, and even races, sundered from one another more or less sharply, who go to make the people of the Philippine Islands, contain many elements which we have a right to hope stand for progress. At present they are utterly incapable of existing in independence at all or of building up a civilization of their own. I firmly believe that we can help them to rise higher and higher in the scale of civilization and of capacity for self-government."[67]

The Democrats throughout the McKinley administration opposed the Philippine policy instituted in 1899. This opposition continued into the election year 1904, when the Democratic Philippine plank stated

that no government has a right to make one set of laws, for those "at home" and another and different set of laws, absolute in their character, for those "in colonies." All men under the American flag are entitled to the protection of the institutions, whose emblem the flag is. If they are inherently unfit for those institutions, then they are inherently unfit to be members of the American body politic. Whenever there may exist a people incapable of being governed under American laws, in consonance with the American Constitution, the territory of that people ought not to be part of the American domain.

But Theodore Roosevelt was elected in his own right, and Philippine policy continued unchanged.

The election year 1908 found the Democrats condemning the Republican policy of retention and advocating a policy of independence for the Philippines. Their platform read:

We favor an immediate declaration of the nation's purpose to recognize the independence of the Philippine Islands as soon as a stable government can be established, such independence to be guaranteed by us, as we guar-

[66] *House Document*, No. 1, Message of the President, 58 Cong., 2 sess., p. xxv.
[67] *Foreign Relations*, 1904, *House Document*, No. 1, 58 Cong., 3 sess., p. xlvi.

antee the independence of Cuba, until neutralization of the islands can be secured by treaty with other powers.[68]

On the strength of a popular vote of 7.7 million for the Republican standard bearer, as opposed to 6.4 million votes for the Democratic presidential candidate, the Republicans were continued in office. William Howard Taft could now direct the Philippine policy from the White House.

Before leaving office, Roosevelt said that within a generation the Filipinos might be able to determine for themselves whether or not they wanted independence. He observed, "It would be worse than folly to try to set down such a date in advance, for it must depend upon the way in which the Philippine people themselves develop the power of self-mastery."[69] Although the closeness of the popular vote in 1908 may indicate that some Americans were not satisfied with the Philippine policy of the Republicans, Taft's election was probably the result of other factors.

Horatio W. Seymour, along with a growing number of Americans, debunked the suggestion that the Filipinos were incapable of self-government. He was sure that there were people in Luzon who were qualified to vote. He thought that there were more of that class than there had been in the Northwest Territory and Louisiana when the Constitution was extended over them. "On the other hand, there is not one American there or elsewhere who is qualified to govern without law and without responsibility."[70]

Filipino adherents to the policy of retention pressed for inclusion as a territory. However, they soon realized the racial basis of their plight, that the American or European observers would not, or could not, concede that the Filipinos were capable of sustaining an independent government. It was known, said Juan Sumulong,

that not a few Americans insist that control of the government and its administration shall remain in the hands of American functionaries; while others, not content with appropriating the lion's share, throw upon the

[68] *Congressional Record,* 64 Cong., 1 sess., LIII, pt. 2: 1499 (January 25, 1916).

[69] *Foreign Relations,* 1908, pp. xlvi-xlvii.

[70] Horatio W. Seymour, "Democratic Expansion," *North American Review,* CLXXIX (July 1904), 103.

whole Filipino race the shadow of distrust, and with injurious intent openly declare, or covertly insinuate, that it is incapable of understanding and
organizing a republican system of government. When we learn of these
things, we infer that there is in some Americans prejudice that does not
permit them to render full justice to other peoples. . . .[71]

In the minds of some Americans the racial preconceptions tended
to outweigh the economic and military considerations on Philippine
policy. Indicative of this view were the writings of Major John H.
Parker, who believed that the United States already had abundant
territory yet to be developed. There were few citizens to spare for
"the deadly perils either of Asiatic jungles or of Filipino trickery." He
suggested that the Philippine Islands might be used to channel the
unwanted immigrants from Japan and China "to those Eastern shores,
insuring the development of these islands under some interested
power, and perhaps at the same time turning the gaze of neighbors,
already semi-hostile, to an Asiatic rather than Occidental expansion."[72]

John Sharp Williams of Mississippi, the Democratic leader of the
House of Representatives, contended:

We have annexed a new race problem. . . . Where there is no mutual will-
ingness for legal blood mixing there is no fraternity, and where there is no
fraternity there can be no true equality, and where there is none of these
Government must, in form, or in spirit or in both, be a Government by
actual or by reserve force. . . . Men differ about the right of the white man
to maintain by forcible methods, if necessary, his own peculiar civilization
and race supremacy in his own country. Surely, wise and good men cannot differ about the Unrighteousness of it in the brown man's country,
which we can leave not only without sacrifice, but with profit to ourselves.
. . . Let us acknowledge the Right of the Filipino not to be Race-Ruled by
us in his own country.[73]

The consternation that gripped many Americans at the very mention of statehood for the Philippine Islands is illustrated in questions

[71] Juan Sumulong, "The Philippine Problem from a Filipino Standpoint,"
North American Review, CLXXIX (December 1904), 861.
[72] John H. Parker, "What Shall We Do with the Philippines?" *Forum*, XXXII
(February 1902), 670.
[73] John Sharp Williams, "Why Should a Man Vote the Democratic Ticket
This Year?" *The Independent*, LVII (October 13, 1904), 965.

raised by Senator Carmack, commenting on a speech by General Luke
E. Wright, a member of the Second Philippine Commission. The
Manila Times reported General Wright as saying:

Whatever difference may have existed among the American people in
principle as to holding these islands, there never has been a doubt that
Filipinos would not in time enjoy the same liberties and become part of
our nation. . . .

The [Federal] party is welcomed into the field because the policy it an-
nounces is in accordance with American principles. . . . You will [in pur-
suing that policy] be engaged in preparing yourselves to be worthy of
citizenship in the great American Republic.

Senator Carmack said that this was an expressed endorsement

by an American member of the Philippine Commission, of the platform
and declaration of purposes of the Federal Party which includes citizenship in the United States. . . .

. . . When men in the confidence of the administration can make these
open and public declarations, practically promising the people of the
Philippine Islands that they shall be given American citizenship, . . . it
becomes a matter of duty for the party in power, . . . to make a declaration
of its purposes; not to make a declaration to the Filipinos but to make a
declaration to the American people as to whether or not it intends that
8,000,000 or 10,000,000 Malays 10,000 miles from our seat of Government shall be incorporated into the body of our citizenship, and as to
whether a Malay archipelago 10,000 miles away shall be admitted to
statehood in the American Union.

Alarmed at the possibility of citizenship for the Filipinos, Carmack
introduced an amendment, which did not pass, to the bill to provide
a civil government for the Philippine Islands. The proposed amendment stated:

That the United States regard with extreme disfavor any movement having for its object the early or ultimate admission of the Philippine Islands
as a State or States of the Union; and any action on the part of persons
holding office under the authority of the United States that gives sanction
or encouragement to such movement is hereby condemned.

That to confer the rights and privileges of citizens upon the inhabitants of the Philippine Islands would tend to destroy the integrity of the citizenship and to degrade the character of the Government of the United States. That to maintain the relation of sovereign and subject between the Government of the United States and a people under its dominion would be repugnant to the principles of the Constitution.

The Federal party of the Philippines was considered by Senator Carmack to be an adjunct of the Philippine Commission. Three of the members of the Federal party advocated annexation, American citizenship, territorial status, and ultimate admission to the Union, expecting full constitutional rights to be granted to all of the Filipino people.[74]

Despite affirmations that all was well in the Philippines and that the Filipinos were happy with American rule, information to the contrary was occasionally called to the attention of the country in congressional debate. Such was the case when Representative James L. Slayden of Texas pointed out that in the years between the tenure of William H. Taft as civil governor and the tenure of Governor General Smith, race relations in the Philippine between the Americans and the Filipinos had deteriorated. Smith, in a speech before the Philippine assembly February 1, 1909, was reported as deploring the "growing gulf between the Americans and the Filipinos in the Philippines."[75]

Senator Newlands implied that the number of "inferior" inhabitants affected his attitude on the annexation of the Philippines. "It is one thing," he said, "to get a commercial port, or naval station [Hawaii] with 100,000 people attached to it, who are inferior, and quite another thing to get one with 7,000,000 inferior people attached to it."[76]

The Filipino press called attention to American efforts to gain economic rights in an Oriental land, while denying the same rights to Orientals in America. An editorial from the Manila newspaper, *El Renacimiento*, for November 13, 1908, entitled "To Caesar All or

[74] *Congressional Record,* 57 Cong., 1 sess., XXXV, pt. 6: 6176–77 (June 2, 1902).

[75] *Congressional Record,* 60 Cong., 2 sess., XLIII, pt. 3: 2750 (February 19, 1909).

[76] *Hearings,* Revenue for the Philippine Islands, *Senate Document,* No. 277, 59 Cong., 1 sess., p. 52.

Nothing," alluded to the problem of American injustices based on race—injustices which aroused the fear that Americans would not be able to deal justly with the Filipinos.

What we are afraid of is absorption, monopolies, special privileges given "for good," the death of our nationality, our annihilation as a nation, economic slavery, the most barbarous of all slaveries. When you with your energy, your skill and labor efficiency, your wealth, and your national power, close your door to the Oriental who comes to your country, not in search of equal chance, but of any chance at all, for making a living, lest your own welfare should be jeopardized ever so little, why should we Filipinos not be afraid when we are challenged to what you choose to call a battle of "equal chances?" . . . The true meaning of the principle of equal chance applied to subjugated countries is . . . "To Caesar everything or nothing."[77]

During the campaign of 1912 the Republicans and Democrats continued to differ on Philippine policy, with the Democrats declaring that they were in favor of "an immediate declaration of the nation's purpose to recognize the independence of the Philippine Islands as soon as a stable government could be established."[78] Because of the split in the Republican ranks, the Democratic candidate, Woodrow Wilson, whose views we have already discussed,[79] emerged as the victorious candidate. The new President, however, adhered to the traditional Democratic view on the Philippine question. In his message to Congress he said of the Philippines, "We must hold steadily in view their ultimate independence, and we must move toward the time of that independence, as steadily as the way can be cleared and the foundations thoughtfully and permanently laid."[80] The Democrats had already stepped up activity during the lame-duck session under Taft to carry out their platform pledge in regard to the independence of the Philippines.

The majority of the House Committee on the Philippines thought that retention was repugnant to republican ideals and disastrous to

[77] *Congressional Record*, 60 Cong., 2 sess., XLIII, pt. 3: 2751 (February 19, 1909).

[78] Democratic Platform of 1912, "Philippine Plank," *Congressional Record*, 64 Cong., 1 sess., LIII, pt. 2: 1499 (January 25, 1916).

[79] Wilson, *Constitutional Government*, pp. 52–53.

[80] *Foreign Relations*, 1913, pp. xii–xiv.

American interests. They regarded the question of independence primarily from the standpoint of the best interests of the American people. They found the idea of holding and "governing against their consent any people who aspire to independence and capable of governing themselves" incompatible with the principle on which the American government had been founded. Traditionally, the United States had expanded into contiguous territory "inhabited by a homogeneous people, and never into land in another hemisphere, . . . inhabited by an alien people differing from us in manners, customs, civilization and race." The Spanish-American War had been fought to "free Cuba and not to enslave the Philippines; to erect a republic in the Occident, not to establish a subject colony in the Orient." The majority found that the Filipinos were capable of self-government and should be given a specific date when independence would be granted.[81] On the other hand, the minority members of the committee expressed the Republican view.

. . . He must be a credulous person who believes that within 16 years a collection of tribes, inhabiting separate islands, speaking different tongues, adherents of different religions, ranging in enlightenment from the lowest savagery to the highest civilization, can be welded into a homogeneous people capable of establishing and maintaining themselves among the nations of the world.[82]

Before the government changed hands, the outgoing administration did everything in its power to prove that after thirteen years of tutelage the Filipino people had not improved in their capacity to govern themselves and should, therefore, be kept as subjects, not citizens, of the United States. The Jones Bill aimed at granting qualified independence to the inhabitants of the Philippines. Its author, William A. Jones of Virginia, observed that the outgoing administration's propaganda campaign was "bringing to bear every possible influence, commercial, political and ecclesiastical, in its effort to defeat the declared purpose of the Democratic Party to give the Filipinos their independence." The country was being told that the incoming Democratic administration was not sufficiently informed to attempt to change a policy which was inaugurated and pursued for

[81] *House Report*, No. 499, 64 Cong., 1 sess., pp. 4–8.
[82] *Ibid.*, pt. II, 5.

more than a decade by the Republican party. "All those who have any personal and intimate knowledge of the Philippine people and of real conditions existing in the islands are unanimously of the opinion that it would be 'suicidal' to recognize the independence of the Philippines."

The Jones Bill was to be the instrument by which the Democrats were to keep their platform promise. Various versions were debated between 1912 and 1916. The debates give abundant evidence that the two parties were not far apart on their basic racial viewpoints, differing only in the Republican's desire to retain control over the Filipinos as opposed to the Democrat's wish to relinquish control.

Before leaving office, President Taft, addressing the Ohio Society of New York, attacked the proposed Jones Bill on the ground that such a measure was "suicidal and highly defective." After proposing that the United States keep the islands as colonies, the President said, "I always will be opposed to any measure looking to their freedom."

Representative Jones implied that the Republicans had consciously gathered opinions supporting their position for retaining control of the Philippine Islands. "I readily admit that there is apparently great unanimity of opinion in respect to this subject on the part of the people from whom the administration secures its information," he said, "but I absolutely deny that its sources of information are either the most dependable or the only sources."

The Democrats leveled criticisms at the administration of civil government in the Philippines by Anglo-Saxon superiors. The most striking was the attack on Governor General Forbes. In an interview, former Judge Charles B. Elliott of Minnesota said of the Forbes administration, "I have said and still say that it is an infernal outrage to run the government of the Philippines with so little regard for law."[83]

The commissioner from the Philippines, Manuel L. Quezon, noting the racial nature of the debates, succinctly pointed out the difficulty which Americans had of gaining an adequate knowledge of Filipinos or of the aspirations of the Filipino people. Alluding to the technique of the opponents of the Jones Bill, who had acted as authorities on the Philippine problem, Quezon stated, "To know a people you must not

[83] *Congressional Record*, 62 Cong., 3 sess., XLIX, pt. 3: 2149–53 (January 28, 1913).

only live with them for a number of years but share their feelings, possess a sympathy for their aspirations, and most important of all, be broad-minded enough to abandon race prejudice and fixed views on the superiority of one civilization over another. You must be so elastic as to take the place of those whom you are studying, and from their point of view consider their life and deeds."[84] The commissioner's appeal had little effect on either the advocates or the adversaries of Philippine independence. Both continued to proceed from the same racial axioms. And both continued to see the Filipinos merely as a potpourri of "inferior" races incapable of self-government in the Anglo-Saxon tradition. They differed only on the proper disposition of the islands and their inhabitants.

Quezon blamed Taft for the Republican policy on the Philippines. According to the commissioner, Taft was responsible for the attitude of Theodore Roosevelt, who had never been to the Philippine Islands. Quezon also attributed to Taft propaganda the American concepts of the civilized or uncivilized nature of the inhabitants of the Philippines. Under Taft the first Philippine census was taken. "The director of the census himself—Major General Sanger, United States Army, retired—was appointed at the request of Governor Taft, and was placed at the head of this important work without any previous connection or knowledge of the Filipino people. . . . General Sanger believed with Mr. Taft and with a majority of his army comrades that the Filipinos were better fitted to be governed than to govern themselves."

Quezon graphically pointed out that government by an oligarchy of Americans appointed by the President was considered good American government for other people who had no voice in their own government. According to the advocates of Philippine retention, there was a danger to good American principles of government if only 15 percent of the Filipinos had a voice in their own governmental affairs. Quezon inquired if "it is not Americanism to permit that so small percentage of the population shall have in their hands the sole guidance of the ship of state? If it is not Americanism to permit 15 per cent of the Filipinos to govern their countrymen, what is it to permit five Americans to govern the whole population?"[85]

[84] Ibid., pt. 5: 191 (February 13, 1913).
[85] Ibid., p. 197.

The blunt racial arguments were resumed in the debates of 1916 on the question of Philippine independence. The Republican platform of 1916 continued the advocacy of the "White Man's burden" in their Philippine plank.

We renew our allegiance to the Philippine policy inaugurated by McKinley, approved by Congress, and consistently carried out by Roosevelt and Taft. Even in this short time it has enormously improved the material and social conditions of the islands, given the Philippine people a constantly increasing participation in their government, and, if persisted it will bring still greater benefits in the future.

We accept the responsibility of the islands as a duty to civilization and the Filipino people. To leave with our task half done would break our pledge, injure our prestige among nations, and imperil what has already been accomplished.

We condemn the Democratic administration for its attempt to abandon the Philippines, which was prevented only by the vigorous opposition of Republican Members of Congress, aided by a few patriotic Democrats.[86]

Thus, the Republicans in Congress claimed credit, with the aid of "a few patriotic Democrats," for saving the Filipinos from the tragedy of independence. Senator William E. Borah of Idaho, when asked in debate if it was the intention of the United States to give the Filipinos their independence, replied, "I do not know what the nation intends to do. . . . I do not know whether our successors will do it or not, but I know that the disposition of the Anglo-Saxon race is not to let anything loose it has gotten hold of. . . ." Borah suggested that it would be an act of insincerity to the people of the Philippines to talk to them about independence many years in advance of their capacity to enjoy it. He took for granted, however, the ability of the representatives of the American people to judge the capacity of other peoples to govern themselves. Borah stated that the present Congress had no intention of giving the people of the Philippines their independence and that it was impossible for that Congress to impose upon their successors the obligation to grant it to them.[87]

[86] Republican Platform of 1916, "Philippine Plank," *Congressional Record,* 64 Cong., 1 sess., LIII, pt. 15: 2018–19 (September 2, 1916).
[87] *Ibid.*, pt. 2: 1440 (January 24, 1916).

Senator Borah was of the opinion that the Filipinos could not be readied for self-government within a century.

> ... We may spend our time and our means and our energy for the next 15 or 20 years, and so far as permanent results are concerned, they will be no different than if we should leave the Philippines within the next three or four years.

. . . .

> ... We ought to eliminate, once and for all, all discussion of independence and let the Filipino people understand that the first lesson which they must learn is the lesson of self-government before they shall be permitted to assume the right of independence, and they must be permitted to know from us in plain but kindly language that they will not acquire that capacity for self-government within the next 50 or 100 years; that it is a long, tedious lesson requiring patience and persistence beyond anything they seem to have contemplated.[88]

Senator Borah was not averse to saying in the presence of the Senate or "in the face of history" that the Filipino people would not "be fitted for self-government, upon any standard which has ever prevailed in a free government inside 200 years."[89]

Senator James K. Vardaman of Mississippi, though on the opposite side of the political fence from Senator Borah, held the same views about the characteristics of the Filipinos. Nevertheless, he advocated a policy of independence. To Vardaman the talk about qualifying "the Filipino or any other mongrel race for the duties of citizenship, for self-government as the American white man understands that term" was a thing that could not be done in a hundred thousand years, because it was not in their strain of blood to accomplish it. The Filipino had never shown any capacity for self-government as it was practiced in the United States. Nevertheless, it was their country and they had a God-given right "to control that country for their own good and for their own betterment; or probably to their own detriment, from our standpoint."[90]

[88] *Ibid.*
[89] *Ibid.*, p. 1446 (January 24, 1916).
[90] *Ibid.*, pt. 1: 773 (January 10, 1916).

Vardaman assumed that the Filipino would fall short of the Anglo-Saxon standard of capacity for self-government and said it was unfair to attempt to measure the Filipino by Anglo-Saxon standards. He based this belief on the consideration that "no race has ever reached the standard of Anglo-Saxon excellency in the art of self-government." He was positive that the Filipino

would not be capable of self-government if every one of them were a college graduate. . . . The fact is I do not believe that the best educated Filipino in the world is as capable as the average illiterate sane, sound-minded Anglo-Saxon living in the rural districts of this Republic. . . . It is not a question of school book learning, but a question of race. . . . I do not think the annals of history contain an instance where a mongrel race has ever been able to maintain for any great length of time a stable form of government, and it is not fair to expect too much of the Filipino. Give the Filipino a chance and he will take care of himself. . . .[91]

Although he agreed with the advocates of retention about the incapacity of the Filipino for self-government, Vardaman maintained that "you cannot have one form of government for the Filipino under the American flag and another form of government for Americans under the same flag without doing violence to the very fundamentals of our government." Since the Filipinos were congenitally and racially incapable of understanding the form of government practiced in the United States, it was impossible to make citizens of them. The victory of the Democratic party and its Philippine plank was a testimonial to the fact that the Filipinos should be granted independence. Vardaman reminded the senators that the United States had experimented with the race problem, and all agreed that the nation could not stand "any more black virus of incompetency. We all know that race political equality means ultimate social equality—social equality will be followed in turn by race amalgamation—race amalgamation will produce race deterioration—race mongrelization, and that will be followed inevitably by disintegration and death of our civilization. . . . I am speaking of races as diametrically different as the Negro, the Mongolian, and the white race. . . ."[92] At the same time Vardaman argued

[91] *Ibid.,* pt. 2: 1500 (January 25, 1916).
[92] *Ibid.,* p. 1501.

that the Filipinos would never learn self-government by being governed by Americans.[93]

DEMOCRATIC PROCEDURE

The Democrats' new policy in the Philippines was instituted with the inaugural address of Governor General Francis Burton Harrison. The first step taken was to make the appointive commission predominantly Filipino, which gave control of both branches of the Philippine Assembly to the Filipinos. Harrison's policy was a step in the direction toward true realization of a policy based on consideration of racial differences.

Senator John F. Shafroth of Colorado pointed out the racial problems associated with colonial government. The first difficulty stemmed from the usual arrogance and supercilious conduct of the officers and citizens of the conquerors stationed in or residing in a subjugated country. This attitude was offensive to the native inhabitants. In the second place, the families of the service personnel of the controlling nation assumed an air of aloofness which set them apart from even the most highly educated members of the conquered race. These two situations were much in evidence in the Philippines under American control. Senator Shafroth saw independence for the Philippines as the only logical solution to the problem because the United States would never treat the Filipinos as citizens entitled to statehood. As a state in the Union they would be entitled to forty representatives in Congress, and none of those who favored retention were in favor of that.[94]

In continued occupation of the Philippine Islands, there was the danger that a situation would develop leading to their admission as states. Senator Charles Thomas of Colorado warned, "If our constant occupation of these islands should lead to such a result, the votes cast by an alien people 10,000 miles away might determine an election of a President of the United States at a most critical period in our political affairs."[95]

The contradictory position of the retentionists was vividly illus-

[93] *Ibid.,* p. 1075.
[94] *Ibid.,* pt. 1: 653–54 (January 7, 1916).
[95] *Ibid.,* pt. 2: 1449 (January 24, 1916).

trated by a question raised by Senator Williams of Mississippi, who asked, "Do you imagine that anybody is absurd enough to suppose the Filipino can mount to our standard of self-government within a hundred years?" The congressional answer to this question was, obviously, no. He then asked, "Are you absurd enough to say that he shall have no self-government because he cannot do it?" The retentionists' answer to the second question was yes. Williams found the answers foolish because in one breath they asserted American superiority to the whole world and in the next breath demanded that the Filipinos measure up to that standard.

To solve the problem, Williams favored acquisition of the Philippines by the Japanese because they were of a similar race. The Japanese would interbreed with the Filipinos. There was at least potential equality between Japanese and Filipinos, where there was none between Filipinos and Anglo-Saxons. Williams did not believe that a successful government could be carried on where potential equality did not exist between two diverse races. Voluntary mating was one of the essentials of a genuine fraternity which contributed to equality. Since the Japanese were seeking an outlet for their population, the Philippines could "relieve the pressure upon Hawaii and upon the Pacific Slope." The development would "recognize the right of the brown and the yellow men to rule the brown and yellow men's country," while the United States "asserted the right of the white men to rule the white man's country."

The problem of the Philippines could be solved in one of three ways, according to Williams. One was to let the Filipinos go and in that way preserve the country from reaction against democratic institutions; a second way was to embody them as part and parcel of the American body politic; the third way was to keep and govern them as "King George dremt [*sic*] that he could govern" the thirteen colonies. If the third choice was made, then army and navy officers would have to be trained to regard free institutions with contempt. Once inferior races were embodied in the politics of the Republic, "you poisoned the body politic with an inalienable and a nonassimilable blood." A democratic structure had to be founded on the four pillars of liberty, fraternity, equality, and justice. "No race," Williams said, "believing itself to be superior and being superior can

really meet in genuine equality and fraternity a race [with] which it
refuses to mix blood in lawful wedlock. You may take the statement
for all it is worth in the Philippines and for all it is worth in Mississippi. It is worth its weight everywhere."[96]

The advocates of retention were attempting to compel the Filipinos
to remain in subjection until "such time as they" reached "an arbitrary
standard of mental and political qualification" which, according to
Senator Harry Lane of Oregon, would be pleasing to the policy-
makers, and "for which no other standard is set, but which must needs
make them conform to a sliding scale of indefinite length, manipulated by an interested referee." If the nation continued that policy,
the Filipinos' only hope of attaining their independence, Lane continued, would "rest on successful revolution." Further, such a position would be an insult, "a self-righteous assumption of superiority
which, whether based on facts or not, cannot with good taste be
urged by a people who acquired their own independence only after a
bloody revolt against a country which urged the same reasons for not
freeing us from their subjection."[97]

Of course, the traditional motives for imperialism played an important part in the attitude of the Congress toward Philippine independence—such motives as strategic considerations, raw materials,
markets for finished products, and capital investments. Against these
factors, race played a qualifying role, conditioning the attitude of the
congressmen.

In their eight years in office, 1913 to 1921, the Democrats made
progress toward the granting of independence to the Philippine people, even though some Democrats considered it the duty and mission
of the United States to civilize the Filipinos. Despite the earnest
pleadings of the Filipinos and of others on their behalf—that they
were already civilized and could conduct their own affairs—their
pleas went unheeded.

It had been the practice under the various Republican administra-
tions to suppress the views of the Filipino freedom fighters. All former
fighters for Philippine independence were under oath not to talk
politics. When the Democrats gained control of the administration,

96 *Ibid.*, pt. 1: 723–24 (January 8, 1916).
97 *Ibid.*, pt. 2: 1803 (January 31, 1916).

they asked these men how they felt about independence. This gave an opportunity for the Filipinos to carry their plea to the American people.

After years of silence on the subject, Aguinaldo was asked his opinion on the matter of Philippine independence. His response would have been the same twenty years before in the heat of the war. He conceded that the people of the Philippines were happy, contented, and more prosperous as a result of American rule. But he flatly stated, "Now we want the independence which was promised us." The territorial form of government which some Americans in the islands were advocating did not satisfy the Filipinos, even though they appreciated the honor of becoming American citizens. He reminded the advocates "that Congress had decided that it would be impossible for the Philippines to become American territory."[98]

The eight years of Democratic administration allowed light to be focused on a relationship which was repugnant in many aspects to the sensibilities of the American people. However, with the return of the Republican party to power in 1921, a reversal of the Philippine policy ensued. Again, the Republicans sent a special mission to investigate conditions in the Philippines, and as before, care was taken to select investigators who agreed with the Republican philosophy of retention.

The mission consisted of W. Cameron Forbes, former governor general of the Philippines, and Leonard Wood, former military governor of Cuba—hardly disinterested investigators. Both men had supported Republican principles on imperialism. Their report found the "people happy, peaceful, and in the main prosperous." The Christian Filipinos were generally in favor of independence "under the protection of the United States. The non-Christians and Americans [were] for continuance of American control." The Filipinos, they found, could not appreciate the fact that a protectorate was not true independence. There were "underlying causes which result in the destruction of government," and the efficiency of the government was "relatively inefficient, due to lack of inspection and to the too rapid transfer of control to officials who have not had the necessary time for proper training." The report found that the people were

[98] "Aguinaldo on Philippine Independence," *Current History*, XIII (October 1920), 112–13.

"not organized economically nor from the standpoint of national defense to maintain an independent government." It was the feeling of the investigation that the Filipino "experience of the past eight years, during which they have had practical autonomy, has not been such as to justify the people of the United States relinquishing supervision of the government of the Philippine Islands, withdrawing their army and navy, and leaving the islands a prey to any powerful nation coveting their rich soil and potential advantages."[99]

Wood and Forbes were convinced that it would be a betrayal of the Philippine people, "a misfortune to the American people, a distinct step backward in the path of progress, and a discreditable neglect of our national duty were we to withdraw from the islands and terminate our relationship without giving the Filipinos the best chance possible to have an orderly and permanently stable government." The subsequent recommendations were designed to reverse the work of the previous eight years under the philosophy of the Democrats. For example, one of them stated, "We recommend that under no circumstances should the American government permit to be established in the Philippine Islands a situation which would leave the United States in a position of responsibility without authority."[100]

Leonard Wood, the chairman of the mission making the report, was subsequently appointed governor general of the Philippine Islands. The action was a callous disregard for the rights of so-called inferior peoples, for in Anglo-Saxon terms the appointment was tantamount to a court case in which the prosecutor, the judge, and jury were embodied in the same person.

The Filipinos took exception to the reversal of policy regarding independence and petitioned President Coolidge through an independence mission sent to the White House. In reply, the President used the altruistic arguments of the "White Man's burden," pointing out that "there were some Americans who believed that immediate independence for the Philippines would be best for both countries." The strongest argument that had been used in the United States in support of immediate independence of the Philippines was "not the argument that it would benefit the Filipinos but that it would

[99] W. Cameron Forbes, *The Philippine Islands,* II, 520–47.
[100] *Ibid.*

be of advantage the United States." The old argument was that slavery was good for the slave and injurious to the master, but the altruistic master was willing to endure injury for the inappreciative slave. Shorn of extraneous words, Coolidge's reply proved that the standards of measurement, determinants of capacity for self-government, had been changed in the middle of the game and that the Filipinos would have to meet new standards before independence would be granted.

A part of the problem of Philippine independence stemmed from the American attitude, developed over many years of dealing with people held in an unequal status before the law, of not hearing what the so-called inferiors have to say, or hearing, but not believing, that the assertions made by these people are worthy of respect or serious consideration. It is the attitude of unenlightened father to child. Everything was done, through official censorship and managed news, to show Americans that the Filipinos were incapable of self-government without giving the Filipinos an equal chance to plead their own case, even before a jury that consisted of members of the ruling group. Again, the philosophy was children should be seen and not heard—especially illegitimate children such as the Filipinos.

President Coolidge dealt undemocratically with the voice of a people by not allowing the Philippine people to vote on the question of independence in 1927. In a long letter rejecting the Plebiscite Act of the Philippine Assembly, he refused to allow the Filipinos to register their opinion under American supervision. The opinion they sought to register had been misrepresented by Americans as in favor of a continuation of the existing relationship between the Philippines and the United States. The letter in some passages took Senator Vardaman's approach to the problem.

The ability of a people to govern themselves is not easily attained. . . . It cannot be learned from books. . . . The degree in which they are possessed determines the capability of a people to govern themselves. In frankness and with utmost friendliness, I must state my sincere conviction that the people of the Philippine Islands have not as yet attained the capability of full self-government.[101]

101 *Ibid.*, p. 564.

In 1924 the Republican platform stated that the time for Philippine independence had not arrived, and the Republican platform of 1928 did not contain a Philippine plank. The Democratic platforms of 1924 and 1928 reiterated their desire for immediate independence for the Philippine people.[102]

Senator William King of Utah saw danger in retention which would not lead to ultimate independence when he observed that if independence was postponed for a decade, it was possible that it would never be granted. There would then be a growing agitation in various parts of the United States that would add to the bitterness and confusion between the two countries. The immigration laws would be extended to exclude the Filipinos at the insistence of many persons, especially labor leaders.[103]

In 1933 a bill known as the Hare-Hawes-Cutting Act, granting the Philippine Islands independence, was passed over the veto of President Hoover. The bill failed to be ratified by the Philippine Legislature because of lack of support from Manuel Quezon.[104] The commissioners from the Philippines, Pedro Guevara and Camilo Osias, agreed that Manuel Quezon was responsible for the rejection of the Hare-Hawes-Cutting Act, Osias asserting that the Filipino people had not been given an opportunity to act on the measure. He contended that "the Philippine Legislature under the domination of Mr. Quezon, resolved to decline to accept the law in its present form and appointed a committee to proceed to the United States to seek amendments of the law or new legislation."

Osias pointed out that Quezon belonged to a group in the islands known as "antis" because of their rejectionist policies toward the independence law. However, he observed that there was another group, to which he belonged, known as the "pros." This group recommended that the law be accepted making it clear that "acceptance of the law will not prevent the Filipino people from subsequently petitioning Congress for a modification of its provisions, if such modi-

102 *Ibid.*, p. 570.
103 *Congressional Record*, 73 Cong., 2 sess., LXXVIII, pt. 3: 3408 (February 28, 1934).
104 *Ibid.*, pt. 1: 129–30 (January 4, 1934). See Bemis, *A Diplomatic History of the United States.*

fication were desired by them."[105] The opposition of Quezon and his
followers centered around the following four points: (1) The trade
relations which the act established pending final withdrawal of
American sovereignty were considered by the Filipinos to be unfair
to them; (2) The reservation of American military and naval bases
in the islands was considered a curtailment of Philippine independence; (3) The powers which the act vested in the President of the
United States and in the high commissioner during the period of
transition were considered excessive and destructive of Philippine
autonomy; and (4) The ten-year period between the establishment
of the Commonwealth of the Philippines and the granting of independence was considered by some Filipinos to be too long.[106]

Quezon secured the support of the Roosevelt administration in the
passage of another bill similar to the previous measure which became
known as the Tydings-McDuffie Act. President Roosevelt made the
bill more acceptable to the "antis" in the Philippines by removing
one of the major objections and allowing for another to be negotiated. President Roosevet said:

> As to the military bases, I recommend this provision be eliminated from
> the law and that the bases be relinquished simultaneously with the ac-
> complishment of final Philippine independence.
> As to the naval bases, I recommend that the law be so amended as to
> provide for ultimate settlement of this matter on terms satisfactory to our
> own Government and that of the Philippine Islands.[107]

However, the only major change in the Hare-Hawes-Cutting Act
which became the Tydings-McDuffie Act, according to Representative John McDuffie of Alabama, co-sponsor of the bill, was to agree
when independence was accomplished "to remove our Army reserva-
tions. We [would] continue to retain our naval bases and coaling stations, but agree to enter into negotiation with the new independent
government to determine the feasibility of further maintenance of
our navy in the islands."[108]

105 *Ibid.* p. 639.
106 *Congressional Record,* 73 Cong., 1 sess., LXXVII, pt. 2: 1418 (April 10,
1933).
107 *House Document,* No. 272, 73 Cong., 2 sess., p. 2.
108 *Congressional Record,* 73 Cong., 2 sess., LXXVIII, pt. 5: 4834 (March
19, 1934).

The measure passed both houses of Congress and received presidential approval March 24, 1934. The Philippine Legislature ratified the act on May 1, 1934. The developments of 1933 and 1934, seemingly, reflected through the senators and representatives of the United States the views of the Democratic party on the solution of the Philippine question. The bill had the support of producers of sugar, tobacco, and fats. In general, it also had the support of labor unions. These indicated a reluctance on the part of Americans to compete with products produced by Asiatic labor.

The Tydings-McDuffie Act as passed provided for complete independence ten years after the ratification and acceptance of a Philippine constitution. The act also pointed up the fact that the Filipinos were considered to be undesirable as potential citizens of the United States:

(1) For the purposes of the Immigration Act of 1917, the Immigration Act of 1924 (except Section 13(c)), this section, and all other laws of the United States relating to the immigration, exclusion, or expulsion of aliens, citizens of the Philippine Islands shall be considered as a separate country and shall have for each fiscal year a quota of fifty. . . .

(2) Citizens of the Philippine Islands who are not citizens of the United States shall not be admitted to continental United States from the Territory of Hawaii (whether entering such territory before or after the effective date of this section) unless they belong to a class declared to be non-immigrants by Section 3 of the Immigrant Act of 1924 or to a class declared to be non-quota immigrants under the provisions of Section 4. . . .

After actual independence the act provided in Section 14:

Upon the final and complete withdrawal of American sovereignty over the Philippine Islands the immigration laws of the United States (including all the provisions thereof relating to persons ineligible to citizenship) shall apply to persons who were born in the Philippine Islands to the same extent as in the case of other foreign countries.[109]

In these provisions the immigration acts of 1917 and 1924 were made to apply to the Filipinos in the same manner as they applied to

[109] The Tydings-McDuffie Act. United States, *Statutes at Large*, 73 Cong., XLVIII, pt. 1: 464.

other persons of Asiatic origin with the minor concession that fifty Filipinos a year would be admitted until final independence. Then the exclusion would become total. The Filipinos were then to join the Japanese and Chinese as undesirable persons who were practically excluded from the United States.

As provided in the Tydings-McDuffie Act, the constitutional convention met in Manila in July, 1934. The convention completed its work in February, 1935. The draft of the constitution was approved by President Roosevelt on March 23, 1935, and subsequently ratified May 14, 1935, by popular vote of the citizens of the Philippine Islands.

After the cessation of hostilities in the Philippines and the proclamation of the liberation of the Philippines in 1945 by General Douglas MacArthur, general elections was held in April, 1946. Manuel Roxas y Acuna was elected president of the Philippine Commonwealth. When on July 4, 1946, the Philippine Republic was proclaimed, he became the first president of that republic, and the United States completed its retreat from an imperial relationship to the Philippine Islands.

V

Cuba: An Enigma of American Imperialism, 1893-1946

The United States has always shown a keen interest in Cuban affairs. The question of its annexation was discussed in the administration of John Quincy Adams. This came, in part, from the desire to keep the island from passing to the control of another European power and in part from the desire to expand slave territory.

Interest again manifested itself in the Southern states during the Mexican War, and in 1854 the "Ostend Manifesto" declared that "the possession of Cuba by a foreign power would be a menace to the peace of the United States, and that Spain should be offered tho alternative of taking $200,000,000 for her sovereignty over the island or having it taken by force."[1] President Grant expressed his belief that only independence and emancipation would settle the Cuban question. During the Ten Years' War in Cuba, from 1868 to 1878, Grant thought that intervention might be necessary to end the war and repeatedly offered the good offices of the United States in obtaining peace.

When rebellion in Cuba broke out again in 1895, the rebels found many sympathizers in the United States. Despite this, Congress limited itself to a concurrent resolution of strict neutrality coupled with a declaration that the United States was willing to offer its good offices to help end the war.[2]

While manifestly friendly to Cuba, the United States found herself in a peculiar position because of her ideas about the superiority and inferiority of races. The racial preconceptions had a definite

[1] *Report on the Census of Cuba, 1899,* p. 39.
[2] *Ibid.*

effect on America's attitude and relation to Cuba. The nation was sympathetic to the aspirations of the Cubans for republican principles but unwilling to concede political independence.

Henry Cabot Lodge explained the condition of mind that permeated the relations of the United States with all of the Latin areas that came under her imperial sway. It was a condition which found the United States not the champion but rather the suppressor of freedom. As Lodge explained, "The Latin mind is severely logical in politics, which accounts in a measure for its many failures in establishing and managing free governments. Being of this cast of mind, the Spanish-American states, when they rose to free themselves from Spain, also freed their own slaves, and in this instance they were not only logical, but right."[3] The political logic of the Latin mind stood in sharp contrast to the political logic practiced in the United States. This is evident when one realizes that the United States, in securing her own independence, contradicted the basic principles of freedom by recognizing in her Constitution the opposite of freedom—slavery —which compromised the political rights of black men. As Lodge pointed out:

The people of the United States, on the other hand, were at once illogical and wrong, and they held just then that white men should be free and black men slaves. So they regarded with great disfavor this highly logical outcome of South-American independence, and from this cause Southern hostility brought the Panama Congress, fraught with many high hopes of American solidarity, to naught. The sinister influence of slavery led the United States to hold Cuba under the yoke of Spain, because free Negroes were not to be permitted to exist upon an island so near their Atlantic seaboard.

It was a cruel policy which fastened upon Cuba slavery to Spain as well as slavery of black men to white, when both might have been swept away without cost to America. . . .[4]

Keeping in mind this conception of the American attitude concerning Cuba, one can understand the qualified sympathy which led to the Spanish-American War—a war which was fought for Cuban freedom, yet which failed to make Cuba a fully independent country.

[3] Henry Cabot Lodge, "The Spanish-American War," *Harper's*, XLVIII (December 1898–May 1899), 451.
[4] *Ibid.*

As the rebellion continued into 1896, both the Republican and Democratic national conventions expressed sympathy for the Cuban people and demanded that the federal government take some action. In May, 1897, Congress appropriated $50,000 for the purchase of supplies for *reconcentrados.* At the same time, the United States requested Spain to recall General Weyler because of his allegedly cruel treatment of the Cubans.

Into this situation was injected the destruction of the American battleship *Maine* on February 15, 1898, with the loss of 266 officers and men.[5] The imperialist campaign in the United States was at its height, and all the ingredients were present to precipitate the war.

RACE AND GEOGRAPHY

Cuba, the largest and most populous of the West Indian Islands, is located directly south of Florida. To the east of Cuba lies Hispaniola, the second largest island in the West Indies, and to the south lies the island of Jamaica. On its west coast, Cuba is separated from the Yucatan Peninsula of Mexico by the 130-mile-wide Yucatan Channel. From a military point of view, Cuba occupies a strategic position, controlling the Windward Passage between Cuba and Hispaniola and the Yucatan Channel, which connects the Gulf of Mexico with the Carribean Sea.

Located entirely within the north tropic zone, the island's characteristic climate influenced its economic, social, and political life. Cuba's main industry centered around plantation agriculture, with its great demand for abundant cheap labor. This demand brought about the introduction of African slavery, an institution that persisted until 1887.[6]

Because the Spanish masters were not as adverse to miscegenation as the Anglo-Saxons, the population of Cuba developed into a mixed race. Lieutenant R. L. Bullard, U.S.A., said that the Spaniards with countless women at their will contributed to the development of a race of mulattoes, who, contrary to American custom, were free because of the master's blood in their veins. Hence, slave women sought honor or favor by giving birth to the master's children.

[5] *Census of Cuba, 1899,* pp. 38–40.
[6] *Ibid.,* p. 97.

"This blood was sought," according to Bullard, "and the pure blood of their own race disdained by the female blacks and mulattoes. It spread until it filled the land, approximated white and can no more be traced. It has made impossible all clear distinctions between races. We may know the extremes but the means blend. But free or slave, black or mulatto, the mother's side . . . has been essentially negro and has made, the type. . . ."[7]

The Census of 1899, taken under the direction of the United States Military Occupation, used United States statistical methods but disregarded the racial method by which the United States designated citizens. The United States classifies those persons with a fraction of Negro blood as nonwhites. The color of the skin has nothing to do with the classification; therefore, there are white Negroes. In Cuba, the color of the skin was used as the basis for racial determination. The results of the census showed that the native whites of Cuba constituted 57.8 percent of the population. The foreign-born whites made up 9 percent; the colored, including Negro and mixed elements, amounted to only 32 percent. According to this census, the native whites formed a majority in every province. In the city of Havana, native and foreign white elements made up a little more than half of the population. The proportion of native white was greatest in the province of Puerto Principe, the sparsely settled pastoral province where it reached 75.2 percent. The second largest percentage of whites in the population of a province could be found in Pinar del Río, basically a farming province, where it reached 65 percent. In Santo Clara the whites constituted 60 percent of the population; in Havana, 57.3 percent; and in Matanzas, 50.7 percent. The census report of 1899 showed that the Negro element in the population had decreased from a high of 58.5 percent in 1841 to a low of 32.1 percent in 1899. The census analysts explained the relative decrease of Negroes on the basis of the "survival of the fittest" concept then current in the United States. "Doubtless," the report held, this was "but another illustration of the inability of an inferior race to hold its own

[7] Robert L. Bullard, "The Cuban Negro," *North American Review*, CLXXXIV (March 15, 1907), 624. Bullard was colonel of 3d Alabama volunteers (colored) in the war with Spain. His command gained a high reputation in the War Department for discipline and excellence of conduct. From 1907 to 1908 he served as special aid and investigator for the American provisional government of Cuba and as supervisor of public instructions and fine arts of that republic.

in competition with a superior one, a truth which is being demon-strated on a much larger scale in the United States."[8]

Needless to say, the foregoing characteristics of the population of Cuba affected the social and political climate in Cuba, both before and after the United States extended its control over the island. Although the Negroes constituted about 30 percent of the popula-tion, they made up 50 percent of the insurgents in 1898 and 80 per-cent in 1906.[9]

Cuba, despite a population considered inferior by training, race, and environment, was coveted by some elements in the United States. These elements justified their covetousness on military, commercial, or humanitarian grounds. They intended to disregard race in con-sidering the annexation of the island.

CUBAN INTERVENTION

If the McKinley administration considered Hawaiian annexation as a step in a policy, then intervention in the affairs of Cuba was an extension of the same policy.

Two years after the republican revolution in Hawaii in 1893 the last of a series of revolutions against Spanish authority erupted in Cuba. Both the Cuban and the Hawaiian revolutions were reactions against monarchical rule; both were of interest, militarily and com-mercially, to the United States; and both involved countries in-habited largely by "inferior" races in the eyes of the inhabitants of the United States. But a great difference also existed in that Hawaii's revolution pitted American residents against a native regime.

Cuba's revolution in 1895 elicited from Spain a determined effort to suppress the insurgents. The policy was pursued with such vigor that it awakened the sensibilities of the Congress, which reacted by passing a series of resolutions reported by the Senate Committee on Foreign Relations.

Joint Resolution No. 2 requested the President of the United States "to issue a proclamation recognizing the political independence of the Republic of Cuba"; Senate Resolution No. 40 instructed the Com-mittee on Foreign Relations "to inquire what obligations the United

[8] *Census of Cuba, 1899*, p. 97.
[9] Bullard, "The Cuban Negro," *North American Review*, CLXXXIV, 624.

States have assumed toward the people of Cuba by asserting and maintaining the right to prevent the acquisition of that island by any European power and compelling its people to remain subject to the dominion of Spain"; Joint Resolution No. 132 recognized "the political independence of the Republic of Cuba"; Joint Resolution No. 133 recognized "the independence of the Republic of Cuba" and "declared war against the Kingdom of Spain"; Joint Resolution No. 134 recognized "the independence of the Republic of Cuba and provided for intervention by the United States"; Joint Resolution No. 135 empowered the President "to terminate, by intervention, the hostilities between Spain and the people of Cuba" and favored "the independence of said people"; Joint Resolution No. 145 authorized the President "to take such steps as are necessary to put an end to hostilities in Cuba and to establish a republican form of government on that island." In addition to the above resolutions, the Committee on Foreign Relations was given the President's messages on March 28 and April 11, 1898, to consider. The purpose of the consideration was to determine the obligation of the United States to the people of Cuba.

The majority of the committee submitted a report which resolved:

That the people of the island of Cuba are, and of right ought to be, free and independent.

That it is the duty of the United States to demand, and the Government of the United States does hereby demand, that the Government of Spain at once relinquish its authority and government in the island of Cuba and withdraw its land and naval forces from Cuban waters.

That the President of the United States be and he hereby is directed and empowered to use, the entire land and naval forces of the United States, and to call into actual service of the United States the militia of the several states, to such extent as may be necessary to carry these resolutions into effect.[10]

Although the several resolutions tended towards a recognition of an independent Cuban republic, the majority of the committee chose to follow the President's suggestion not to recognize a government in the island.[11] A minority of the committee concurred with the majority but stated, "We favor the immediate recognition of the Repub-

[10] *Senate Report*, No. 885, 55 Cong., 2 sess., "Affairs in Cuba," p. xxii.
[11] *House Document*, No. 405, 55 Cong., 2 sess., p. 8.

lic of Cuba, as organized in that island, as a free, independent, and sovereign power among the nations of the world."[12]

The ensuing debate on the form of the final resolution saw Senator Benjamin Tillman of South Carolina support a position that would recognize the absolute independence of Cuba. This would keep Cuba from paying the war debt incurred by Spain in suppression of the insurrection. The question, as Tillman saw it, was "whether we shall recognize the existing government, whatever may be its obligations, or whether we shall recognize no government, but declare in general terms that the people of Cuba are free, and then go there and have an election under our control and direction so as to set up a government of our making."[13]

Senator William Lindsey of Kentucky felt the same way as Senator Tillman and observed that there was no objection to making the Cuban people allies of the United States unless "we intend, through the process of intervention, to put them under military constraint while we usurp the function of setting up a government for the island of Cuba."[14]

Senator Stewart M. Williams of Nevada, reacting to the suggestion that the Cubans had no government worthy of recognition, stated that the contention was "refuted by every document before us, and more strongly by the President's message than any other document."[15] The senator could not understand the denial on the part of Congress of the existence of a Cuban government "although the President tells us that Cuba is forever lost to Spain and that it is impossible for Spain to regain it." Even after the Committee on Foreign Affairs and the President had affirmed that Spain no longer controlled Cuba, they were "unwilling to follow the logic of that declaration and to recognize the independence of Cuba, recognize a fact which both the message of the President and the report of the Committee make known."[16]

Senator Teller of Colorado compared the struggle of the Cubans for freedom to the struggle for freedom by the United States. The

[12] *Senate Report,* No. 885, *op. cit.,* p. xxiii.
[13] *Congressional Record,* 55 Cong., 2 sess., XXXI, pt. 4: 3890 (April 15, 1898).
[14] *Ibid.,* p. 3785 (April 13, 1898).
[15] *Ibid.,* p. 3901.
[16] *Ibid.,* p. 3902.

Cubans had assembled more men in the defense of Cuban freedom than the United States had mustered in the contest with Great Britain over United States independence. Spain had, according to Senator Teller, dispatched four or five times as many troops to Cuba as "Great Britain sent to compel us to yield obedience to her mandate." And yet, "that government is said not to be a government capable of being recognized by the people of the United States. . . ."[17]

Even though administration spokesmen denied that there were ulterior motives in not recognizing a Cuban republic, the government's actions belied its pronounced intentions. The administration seemed to believe the Spanish propaganda which had "assured the world that the Cubans cannot govern themselves." Spain had predicted that the independence of Cuba would result in "another Negro republic" and "a relapse into barbarism, constant revolutions and a loss of civilization."[18]

Representative William W. Grout of Vermont, a supporter of the administration's position of nonrecognition of a Cuban government, declared, "Should intervention lead . . . to the landing of troops in Cuba, recognition would put the commander of such troops under General Gómez as commander-in-chief of the sovereign state which we shall have already recognized."[19] To understand the racial implications of this statement, one has to take into consideration the fact that General Gómez was a mulatto and the caste system that existed in the United States Armed Forces. General Thomas J. Morgan explained the situation in the United States, where he advocated the elevation of qualified Negroes to the rank of officers. "The only caste or class, with caste distinctions, that exists in the Republic is found in the Army," said Morgan. "Army officers are, *par excellence*, the aristocrats; nowhere is class feeling so much cultivated as among them; nowhere is it so difficult to break down class lines."[20] To ask American Army officers to serve under Gómez would not have gained many votes for Cuban independence.

Some senators supported the idea of a Cuban republic on the

[17] *Ibid.*, p. 3898.

[18] "Is the Cuban Capable of Self-Government?" *Forum,* XXIV (September 1897), 120–23.

[19] *Congressional Record,* 55 Cong., 2 sess., XXXI, pt. 8: 301 (April 11, 1898).

[20] Thomas J. Morgan, "Epaulets or Chevrons?" *The Independent,* L (June 30, 1898), 846.

grounds of presenting an opportunity to the Negro race. Senator George F. Hoar said that he supported the cause of Cuba because "it is well understood that the aspiration of Gómez is for a black republic in the West Indies. If he should get control of Cuba, and if Haiti and Santo Domingo join him, and perhaps Puerto Rico, he aspires to give an example to mankind where the men of the colored race may rule themselves as equals socially and politically."[21] Ironically, Cuba was to be the entering wedge that would see by 1916 all of the islands named by Senator Hoar under the control of the United States.

Senator Tillman complained of the haste with which the country was going into war without deliberating on the effects of an ill-defined policy toward the Cubans. The failure to recognize the Cuban republic would create a situation, similar to the Reconstruction of the South after the Civil War, in which the United States would reconstruct Cuba.[22]

The Senate finally adopted the so-called Teller Amendment which failed to recognize a government in Cuba, controlled by the Cubans, but committed the United States to a policy of ultimate "liberation."[23] The amendment demanded the wihdrawal of Spanish authority and power from the island of Cuba and vicinity, and gave the President the power to use the militia to carry the resolution into effect and to declare the following policy:

The United States hereby disclaims any disposition or intention to exercise sovereignty, jurisdiction or control over said island, except for the pacification thereof, and asserts its determination, when that is accomplished, to leave the government and control of the island to its people.[24]

On April 25, 1898, Congress declared war on Spain as of April 21, 1898.

THE OCCUPATION OF CUBA

The war was of short duration, lasting from April 21 to July 22, the date on which overtures for peace were first made. Russell H. Fitz-

[21] *Congressional Record*, 55 Cong., 2 sess., XXXI, pt. 4: 3833 (April 14, 1898).
[22] *Ibid.*, p. 3890.
[23] See *Senate Report*, No. 885, *op. cit.*, p. xxii for report which desired immediate recognition of Cuban independence.
[24] Approved April 20, 1898.

gibbon observes that "so far had the aims of the United States as contemplated in the Congressional resolutions been completed by July 13, that on that date the President's communication to the Secretary of War defined the rights and duties of the United States as a military occupant of Cuba."[25]

The President's interpretation of the Teller Amendment gave the United States a greater amount of latitude in dealing with the Cubans. In doing this, he was in line with many of the imperialists who looked upon the Teller Amendment as a nuisance, to be disregarded because the United States had the duty of teaching self-government to a people who were incapable of governing themselves.

The victory of its armed forces enabled the United States to dictate the terms of the peace treaty. In keeping with the demands of the resolution of April 20, 1898, Spain was required to relinquish all claim of sovereignty and title to Cuba. The treaty further provided:

> Since the island is upon its evacuation by Spain, to be occupied by the United States, the United States will, so long as such occupation shall last, assume and discharge the obligations that may under international law result from the fact of its occupation for the protection of life and property.[26]

Despite the Teller Amendment, the first article of the peace treaty gave the United States the power of occupation and control of Cuba and the destinies of its people until such time as she decided to withdraw. Although the administration spoke of rights and duties in Cuba, Charles E. Magoon stated that the Treaty of Paris imposed duties, but "did not confer rights upon our Government."[27] If this was the correct interpretation, then the United Sates was either in violation of Cuban rights, or the Cuban had no rights that the United States was bound to respect. The latter view seemed to prevail.

Major General John R. Brooke became the first military governor of Cuba under the United States control. General Brooke seems to have taken the Teller Amendment seriously, putting Cubans in places of authority. The Cubans did not complain of a lack of posi-

[25] Russell H. Fitzgibbon, *Cuba and the United States*, p. 27.
[26] Henry Steele Commager, ed., *Documents of American History*, pp. 187–89.
[27] *Senate Report*, No. 234, 56 Cong., 1 sess., pp. 9–11.

tions in the government, but of the change of customs under General Brooke from the Spanish system of doing things to the American. Secretary of Finance Pablo Desvernine, a Cuban, complained of the American officials' disregard for the customs of the Cubans. He pleaded for Cuban participation in the dispersing of public monies, commensurate with the proper legislative organs and controls. In a rather indirect way, Desvernine accused the United States of withdrawing the most important branches of finance from Cuban administration because of a "lack of confidence on the part of the United States government in the ability and honesty of Cubans to manage their own finances."[28]

The Cuban people felt that American officials discriminated against Cubans. Desvernine asserted that it would not be an "easy task to disabuse the people of this inaccurate notion as long as the Department of Finance should be maintained in the condition of restriction and limitation" in which it was placed as a result of a changeover to an unfamiliar American system.

Brigadier General James H. Wilson reported that Cuba was one of the tropical isles where the white race could become acclimatized. On the basis of eight months' observation, General Wilson was of the opinion that the white race had "in no degree lost its social efficiency." Wilson suggested annexation to the United States after a period of economic adjustment, which would give time "for the Cubans to show that they are not tropical and revolutionary, not a mongrel and vicious race, not disqualified by religion or impaired social efficiency for carrying on a stable government, or becoming American citizens."[29]

It seemed as though General Brooke was not treating the Cubans as though they had to learn self-government by looking on, but was actually letting them learn by doing. For this he was severely criticized in an article by Major J. E. Runcie. The primary reason for the removal of Spain from the island of Cuba, in the major's mind, was for the United States' advantage and only incidentally for Cuba's benefit. Runcie contrasted the Cubans with the Americans in con-

[28] *House Document*, No. 2, VII, 56 Cong., 1 sess. Report of Major-General John R. Brooke; Report of Pablo Desvernine, secretary of finance of Cuba, October 1, 1899, p. 238.
[29] *Ibid.*, pp. 338–39.

tending that "where Americans have been allowed to work, with American methods, the result has been distinguished success. On the other hand, whenever Cubans have been allowed to proceed, by any method of their own choice, they have invariably clung to the methods of Spain . . . and the result [has been] disastrous failure for which Americans are responsible."[30]

While articles such as Major Runcie's did little to help Americans understand the problems associated with governing Cuba, other army officers charged the Americans with causing the Cubans to distrust and dislike them. One such article observed, "It is difficult for the average American to understand fully the nature of the irritation caused by our military occupation." In the first place, it had to be remembered that the Americans were an alien race, and American methods were different from those of Cuba. The Americans were characterized by brusqueness, as were the Cubans by politeness. This caused Americans to offend Cubans unconsciously.[31]

General Thomas Morgan, writing in June, 1898, saw the dangers that would befall American troops in the islands of the Caribbean and suggested that their attitude would not permit them to become good occupation troops. His solution to this problem was at least fifty years ahead of its time.

The war with Spain is primarily and professedly a humanitarian crusade, undertaken for the redressing of the wrongs of the Cubans, multitudes of whom are negroes. The Republic can hardly afford to incur the sharp criticism of inconsistency by inflicting a wrong upon its own soldiers, and perpetuating in its own army an invidious discrimination against brave men, while going out ostensibly in the rights of others. I think the keenest thrust which has been made against the Republic since it entered upon this new career of humanitarianism has been that of the Spanish caricaturists who represent us as rushing off to liberate negroes in Cuba while lynching negroes at home. . . .

General Morgan also suggested that the colonization or control of the West Indian and Philippine Islands would require a large army of occupation. "Such an army could with advantage be made up

---

[30] J. E. Runcie, "American Misgovernment of Cuba," *North American Review*, CLXX (February 1900), 284–94.

[31] John T. Morgan, "The Logic of Our Position in Cuba," *North American Review*, CLXIX (July 1899), 111.

largely if not exclusively of negro soldiers. They would be better suited for tropical and semitropical climates, would be more contented than white men in that far away service, and would not be objectionable to the native inhabitants of the islands in either ocean. . . ."[32]

The official and unofficial attitude on race in Cuba was to play down the Negro element. The Negro was a decreasing element in the population according to Richard Hinton. The figures Hinton used were taken from the Census of 1899 and showed the whites to outnumber the Negroes in almost every province.[33]

George Kennan endeavored to dispel the stereotype view of the Cuban, perhaps to make Cuba acceptable to America as an area fit for annexation. He took exception to the view "that the Cubans are naturally lazy and improvident; that they will not work if they can help it, and as long as the government furnishes them with . . . rations they will make no effort to support themselves or their families." Kennan found the statements to be untrue and unfair. He conceded that the Cuban "may not be as efficient a laborer as the Anglo-Saxon," but an observer could not walk through the markets or drive through the countryside without being convinced that the Cuban did work, and worked hard.[34]

The administration of Cuban affairs was turned over to Major General Leonard Wood on December 13, 1899. General Wood's "instructions left him practically a free agent." It was his duty to prepare the Cubans for a republican form of government so that the United States forces could get out of Cuba as soon as safety could be assured.[35] In attempting to carry out this order, Wood, acording to one observer, was changed from an annexationist to an advocate of independence for the Cubans.[36]

If misgovernment was charged to the Brooke administration by Major Runcie, the Wood administration came under attack from Senator August O. Bacon of Georgia, who criticized the excessive

[32] Morgan, "Epaulets or Chevrons?" *The Independent,* L, 846.
[33] Richard J. Hinton, "Cuban Reconstruction," *North American Review,* CLXIII (January 1899), 93.
[34] George Kennan, "The Regeneration of Cuba," *Outlook,* LX (June 1899), 202.
[35] Hermann Hagedorn, *Leonard Wood, A Biography,* I, 204.
[36] *Ibid.,* p. 266.

expenditures of the military government and the discrepancies in the Cuban Post Office Department. The blame was charged to the American administrators and to the new imperialism.

Bacon prophetically questioned whether it was America's "duty to go to Santo Domingo and to Haiti—which are infinitely below Cuba in point of development and intelligence and in character of population—and to civilize these people? Do we propose to remain in Cuba until we have raised the inhabitants to a pitch of civilization such as we will approve?" The questions raised by Senator Bacon as to the two Negro republics pointed to a continuation of the policy begun with the Cuban intervention.[37]

CUBAN INDEPENDENCE

A number of circumstances—the forthcoming presidential election, the Teller Amendment and world public opinion, and anti-imperialist agitation—combined in 1900 to cause the McKinley administration to consider a qualified independence for Cuba. Because of these circumstances General Wood was instructed to begin preparations for the transfer of government from the Americans to the Cubans. General Wood reports that during his visit to the United States in July, 1900, the conditions in Cuba were presented fully to the President and the secretary of war. It was decided by them "that, everything considered, the time had arrived for the preliminary measures for a general election to be held throughout the island for the election of delegates to a convention to be assembled for drawing up and adopting a constitution for the island of Cuba, agreeing on the relations which were to exist between Cuba and the United States, and providing for an election law." Accordingly, Order 301, authorizing the election, was published on July 25, 1900, and Order 316, establishing the regulations to govern the election, was published on August 11, 1900.

In discharging its duty to the Cubans, the United States treated their leaders as puppets to be moved by the manipulation of strings from Washington without regard for the rights of the Cuban people. Under these conditions it is not surprising that General Wood re-

[37] *Congressional Record*, 56 Cong., 1 sess., XXXIII, pt. 6: 5596 (May 16, 1900).

ported that the election was held on September 15, without any disorders and "without interest." The result was the election of a radical
element to the Cuban constitutional convention.

The constitutional convention assembled on November 5 and
listened to an address by General Wood in which he stated the duties
of the convention.

All friends of Cuba will follow your deliberations with deepest interest,
earnestly desiring that you shall reach just conclusions and that, by the
dignity, individual self-restraint and wise conservatism which shall charac-
terize your proceedings, the capacity of the Cuban people for representative government may be signally illustrated. . . .

The fundamental distinction between true representative government
and dictatorship is that in the former every representative of the people, in whatever office, confines himself strictly within the limits of defined powers. Without such restraints there can be no free constitutional
government.

Wood made sure that the delegates understood that they had no
"authority to take part in the present government of the island" and
that their powers were limited by the terms of the order under which
they were elected and convened.[38]

In the United States it was public knowledge that the forthcoming
Cuban republic would be of a conditional nature. The policy of the
McKinley administration, as explained by Walter Wellman, allowed
Cuba to become "an independent republic." However, it was to be
limited in its power, in reality a self-governing colony under the
"aegis of the United States." According to Wellman, all the Cuban
needed was imagination, for with that attribute he could rationalize
for himself an independent republic. By looking inward at his island
he could say that he had a nation. But if he looked outward, he would
have to admit that his nation was a dependency. The policy "as to the
reconstruction of Cuba" had been considered over a long period of
time, and the administration had worked it out in harmonious detail.
It was designed to persuade the Cubans to believe that they were the
masters of the situation as long as they "proceeded to do all that it is
wished they should do." The success of this persuasion would reflect

[38] Annual Report of the War Department, *House Document,* No. 2, 56 Cong.,
2 sess., XII, pt. 1, Civil Report of Major General Leonard Wood, U.S.V., 626.

"credit to the skill and patience of the directing government and its agents in the island." Wellman envisioned a relationship of Cuba to the United States "almost precisely what the dominion of Canada is to Great Britain." It was his opinion that the Teller Amendment was a mistake and should not have been passed since it was done in haste. Wellman succinctly summed up the situation when he wrote:

> What shall be done with the Constitution when the convention agrees upon one? Everything depends upon whether the organic act does or does not contain provisions called for by the Administration's policy. First of all, the Constitution will come to the President. If it does not meet with his approval, nothing can be done, and the convention will have to try again; or, a new convention called. By force of circumstances, the President is the ruler of Cuba, and he will not withdraw till he is fully convinced that a strong and enduring government is ready to take the reins of power.[39]

Official Washington knew that they were creating a puppet government in Cuba. The Cuban delegates tried to act like self-governing men and refused to give serious consideration to the aspect of the instructions relating to what the future relations of Cuba to the United States should be. Charles Warren Currier thought that the United States was presumptuous in sending instructions to the Cuban constitutional convention. Currier, in support of the Cubans, observed, "The Constitution of every free and independent government is, and must be, unhampered by foreign relations. What can the constitutional relations of Cuba to the United States be but one [*sic*] of dependency? Were they merely those of nation to nation, upon a basis of equality, there would be no need of embodying them in the Constitution." He implied that the United States had limited the number of delegates to thirty-one because "the limited number renders independent action more difficult, and facilitates outside pressure." A group that small would be easier to control than a larger body. "As for myself, I am a firm believer in the sincerity and in the good intentions of Mr. McKinley, but," he warned, "I fear outside

[39] Walter Wellman, "The Cuban Republic Limited," *Review of Reviews*, XXII (December 1900), 708–12. Wellman was a journalist, explorer, aeronaut, founder and publisher of the Cincinnati *Post*. From 1884 to 1911 he was the Washington correspondent of the Chicago *Herald* and its successor, the *Record-Herald*.

pressure and the network of influences which the annexationists may weave around him. I hope, however, for the honor of our country, that we shall be true to ourselves and our promises, and that we shall be just to a weaker people. . . ."[40]

The Cubans chose the Constitution of the United States as their model. A more absolutely independent document could not be found anywhere. The administration wanted to make sure that the Cubans were dependent and not independent. Therefore, on February 15, 1901, General Wood received an official communication from Washington which instructed him to insist that the five basic provisions which later became the Platt Amendment be incorporated in the Cuban constitution.[41]

Utter contempt and lack of respect for the rights of the Cubans is aptly illustrated by the method through which the chief American administrator in Cuba conveyed the administration's message to the relations committee of the convention. On February 15, 1901, the day that Wood received the communication from Washington, he had planned an alligator-hunting trip, something apparently more important to him than Cuban rights. Therefore, he sent for or ordered the committee to accompany him. On very short notice the Cubans were forced to accompany their "master" for "thirty miles of railway, upon part of his trip, to receive that which he had to give them. This may have been democracy; but the Cubans, not without warrant under the circumstances, took it as a discourtesy. They rode the thirty miles, ate a poorer dinner than they would have had at home, and returned at midnight, hurt and offended, to talk about the manner in which suggestions, which they neither wanted nor needed, had been 'pitched at' them."[42] It is inconceivable that General Wood would have acted similarly with Anglo-Saxons.

The importance of the desired relationship to the United States was pointed out by Secretary of War Root, who said, "No one familiar with the traditional and established policy of this country in respect to Cuba can find cause for doubt as to our remaining duty."

[40] Charles Warren Currier, "Why Cuba Should Be Independent," *Forum*, XXX (September 1900), 145–46.

[41] Annual Report of the War Department, *House Document*, No. 2, 57 Cong., 1 sess., pp. 44–45.

[42] Albert G. Robinson, "The Work of the Cuban Convention," *Forum*, XXXI (June 1901), 410–11.

This policy establishing the relationship of the United States to Cuba had been stated in uncompromising and clear terms, that the "United States would not under any circumstances permit any foreign power other than Spain to acquire . . . Cuba."[43] Therefore, the provisions in the note of February 15, 1901, were a necessary addition to the Cuban constitution. The instructions contained the following:

The people of Cuba should desire to have incorporated in her fundamental law provisions in substance as follows:

1. That no government organized under the Constitution shall be deemed to have authority to enter into any treaty or engagement with any foreign power which may tend to impair or interfere with the independence of Cuba, or to confer upon such foreign power any special right or privilege without the consent of the United States.
2. That no government organized under the Constitution shall have authority to assure or contract any public debt in excess of the capacity of the ordinary revenues of the island after defraying the current expenses of government to pay the interest.
3. That upon the transfer of the control of Cuba to the government under the new Constitution, Cuba consents that the United States reserve and retain the right of intervention for the preservation of Cuban independence and the maintenance of a stable government, adequately protecting life, property, and individual liberty, and discharging the obligations with respect to Cuba imposed by the Treaty of Paris on the United States and now assumed and undertaken by the government of Cuba.
4. That all the acts of the military government, and all rights acquired thereunder shall be valid and shall be maintained and protected.
5. That to facilitate the United States in the performance of such duties as may devolve upon her under the provision and for her own defense, the United States may acquire and hold the title to land for naval stations, and maintain the same at certain specified points.

The note concluded that the provisions "may not, it is true, prove to be in accord with the conclusions which Congress may ultimately reach." But until Congress considered the subject, it was necessary for the executive branch to act "within its own sphere of action" and

[43] *House Document,* No. 2, 57 Cong., 1 sess., Annual Report of the War Department, Report of Secretary of War Root, p. 44.

be controlled by its own judgment. General Wood, with the committee, was further instructed, "Your actions should now be guided by the views above expressed."[44]

Under these circumstances the Cuban relations committee met, drew up what they considered an independent country's course should be, and submitted it to the convention. They saw their first duty as "interpreting the will and heeding the interest of our country." They stated that inasmuch as the suggestions of the Executive Department of the United States appealed to what should be the desire of the people of Cuba, the committee interpreted that to mean "that the desires of the Cubans are the ones which are to prevail." They observed that the suggestions did not "absolutely have a definitive or legal character." The note had recognized the fact that Congress had the sole responsibility for fixing the relations between the United States and Cuba.

In rejecting the principles which were to be later incorporated in the Platt Amendment to the Army Appropriation Bill of March 2, 1901, the Cubans failed to take into consideration the fact that if they possessed any rights whatsoever, few Americans in positions of authority were concerned enough to try to change the course of events.

The relations committee quoted the secretary of war as saying, "that the United States must have the assurance that the island of Cuba is to forever be an independent country." Taking that assertion literally, the committee insisted:

Some of these stipulations are not acceptable, exactly because they impair the independence and sovereignty of Cuba. Our duty consists of making Cuba independent of every other nation, the great and noble American nation included, and, if we bind ourselves to ask the government of the United States for their consent to our international dealings, if we admit that they shall reserve and retain the right to intervene in our country to maintain or precipitate conditions and fulfill duties pertaining solely to Cuban governments, and, lastly, if we grant them the right to acquire and preserve titles to lands for naval stations and maintain these in determined places along our coast, it is clear that we could seem inde-

[44] Annual Report of the War Department, *House Document,* No. 2, 57 Cong., 1 sess., pp. 46–47.

pendent of the rest of the world although we were not in reality, but never would we be independent with reference to the United States.

The relations committee suggested to the constitutional convention that the answer to the American demands might be "the aspirations you have, and for which we have been and are willing to zealously care, that the independence of the island of Cuba is attained." The United States, the committee suggested, should not be apprehensive about the future stability of Cuba. Then the independence-minded commitee suggested a five-point program of its own for consideration by the constitutional convention:

First: The Government of the Republic of Cuba will make no treaty or convention with any foreign power or powers which compromises or limits the independence of Cuba or in any other manner permits or authorizes any foreign power or powers to obtain, by means of colonization or for military or naval purposes, or in any other manner, settlement of authority, or rights, over any portion of Cuba.

Second: The Government of the Republic of Cuba will not permit that its territory serve as a basis of war operations against the United States nor against any other foreign nation.

Third: The Government of the Republic of Cuba will accept the Treaty of Paris of December 10, 1898, in its integrality, the same in what affirms Cuba's rights as with regard to obligations it limitedly assigns her, and especially those obligations imposed by international law for the protection of lives and properties substituting the United States in the obligation they acquired to that effect in conformity with . . . said Treaty of Paris.

Fourth: The Government of the Republic of Cuba will recognize as legally valid the acts done for the good government of Cuba by the American military government in the representation of the Government of the United States during the period of its occupation, likewise the rights proceeding therefrom, in conformity with the Joint Resolution and Section 2 of the United States Army Bill for the fiscal year 1899 to 1900, known as the Foraker Amendment, or with the laws existing in that country.

Fifth: The Government of the United States and the Republic of Cuba should regulate their commercial relations by means of a convention based on reciprocity and which, with tendencies toward free trade in their natural and manufactured products, will mutually assure them ample and special advantages in the respective markets.[45]

[45] Papers Relating to Foreign Affairs, *House Document,* No. 1, 57 Cong., 2 sess., p. 363.

The statement of principle submitted to the Cuban constitutional convention assumed that the United States would treat with the Cubans as equals. That this assumption was erroneous soon became evident. On the very day that the committee submitted its five principles, February 26, 1901, the United States Senate, with little debate, fixed the relationship between Cuba and the United States. This was done without the senators' having seen the official draft of the Cuban constitution. Senator John T. Morgan of Alabama charged that the administration had received a draft of the original Cuban constitution and was purposely withholding it from the Senate. Evidently, to the majority of this august body, the deliberations of the delegates to the Cuban constitutional convention were not important.

Ironically, it was the senators from states which disregarded the rights of colored people who opposed the Platt Amendment. Among them was Senator Morgan, a supporter of imperialism, who said in debate, "We come at [the Cubans] with an ultimatum, not laid down after a discussion and presentation of their side of the case at all, but an ultimatum fixed in an act of Congress, which neither the President nor anybody else can escape from ordering, and they shall stand up now and subscribe to what we prescribe . . . or else." Although Senator Morgan needed only to look to his home state's legislation for precedents which disregarded the rights of colored people, he attacked the amendment on the ground that it was "a legislative ultimatum to Cuba." The United States ordered the Cubans, "Take this or die, for [you] cannot resist. Take this and abandon your hopes of an independent, sovereign, autonomous government. Take this and lay your national and your race pride beneath the feet of the Anglo-Saxon and let him walk over you." Morgan was prophetic in his criticism of Article II of the Platt Amendment which implied that the United States acted "toward the government and people of Cuba as if we supposed they were children." He felt that the Cubans should be treated on the assumption "that they have intelligence enough to take care of themselves when we propose to give them autonomy, and yet that second branch of this amendment assumes everything else."[46]

The method of forcing the amendment through, as a rider to the

[46] *Congressional Record*, 56 Cong., 2 sess., XXXIV, pt. 4: 3038–40 (February 26, 1901).

appropriations bill in the closing days of Congress, came under attack on the ground that the proper place for defining relations between nations was in treaties, which required a two-thirds vote of the Senate. The amendment was nevertheless adopted, and for Cuba it was tantamount to securing a contract under duress, an illegal practice in Anglo-Saxon countries. The administration used the Treaty of Paris as justification for its decision not to work out its relations with Cuba through diplomatic channels[47] and explained that intervention under the Platt Amendment was "not synonymous with intermeddling or interference with the affairs of a Cuban Government."[48] The Cubans were concerned about the actions of an administration which had not kept faith with promises made before the world. In an effort to confer with President McKinley and Secretary of War Root, they sent a committee from the constitutional convention to Washington to try to modify the provisions of the Platt Amendment. The committee was politely told that the amendment would remain as legislated. To soothe the wounded feelings of the Cuban emissaries trade concessions were held out to the committee. Representative Chester I. Long of Kansas observed that Secretary of War Root had told General Wood, "The Platt Amendment, being a law of the United States, the President is bound to execute it, and to execute it as it is. He cannot change or modify, add or subtract from it."[49]

The Cuban constitutional convention resisted the incorporation of the provisions of the Platt Amendment into the Constitution of Cuba. The administration began to apply pressure, causing the *Nation* to observe, "The President thinks to frighten the Cubans into bending to his will by telling them that if they do not, there will be danger of their having the rights of American States given them." To the editors of the *Nation*, the threat was amusing; for if annexed, Cuba's inhabitants would have self-government and have a voice in the operation of United States affairs. "They would enjoy constitutional immunities and privileges and there would be a rule, not of superior beings,

[47] Fitzgibbon, *Cuba and the United States*, p. 82.
[48] Annual Report of the War Department, *House Document*, No. 2, 57 Cong., 1 sess., p. 47.
[49] *Congressional Record*, 57 Cong., 1 sess., XXXV, pt. 4: 4010 (April 11, 1902).

but of the Cuban people just as they are."[50] According to Senator Platt, however, the Cubans were not to be considered for statehood. In discussing the question of possible annexation of Cuba, he said, "The project of annexation may, and ought to be, dismissed. It should not for a moment be considered, except in case of the direst necessity. The people of Cuba, by reason of race and characteristic, cannot be easily assimilated by us. In these respects they have little in common with us. Their presence in the American union, as a state, would be most disturbing. . . ."[51]

The senator from Connecticut was now mouthing the views of the Southern congressmen on the question of race; he was now committed to the Southern viewpoint regarding the right of the government to participate in their government. If he believed in the amendment that carried his name,[52] then he would deny the Cubans the right of independent government. If he would not consider the Cubans material for statehood in the Union, he would deny that they had any right to help govern Anglo-Saxons. Clearly, the relationship between the Cubans and the United States was similar to that of the Southern Negroes and the Southern states.

Marriam Wilcox described the impossible situation facing the Cubans in their efforts to gain their independence as "a few months of wavering indecision and feeble protest—then the plunge into error. The priceless thing that the Constitutional Convention sold in 1901—the independence of Cuba—was sold for the pitiful price of tariff concessions."[53]

John W. Foster, former secretary of state, did not believe that the American people were so enamored of a policy of annexation that they desired to complicate problems yet unsolved. The Cuban population contained a large proportion of Negro or mixed blood. In addition to that, Cuba's slaves were the last to be emancipated in American countries. He asked, "With the negro problem in our

[50] *Nation*, CLXXII (May 2, 1901), 347.

[51] Orville H. Platt, "Solution of the Cuban Problem," *World's Work*, II (May 1901), 729.

[52] See Fitzgibbon, *Cuba and the United States*, p. 81, on the authorship of the Platt Amendment. Fitzgibbon credits authorship to Secretary of War Root.

[53] Marriam Wilcox, "The Situation in Cuba," *North American Review*, CLXXV (December 1902), 822.

Southern States pressing upon us for solution . . . do we desire to aggravate the situation by adding a million more of the despised race to our voting population?"[54]

The people of the United States were not in favor of any plan of annexation of Cuba that might result in ultimate statehood. *World's Work* considered that the American people would never favor Cuban annexation "unless the great commercial interests wage a successful campaign to change public sentiment." Annexation without hope of ultimate statehood was totally unacceptable to the Cubans because "this would indefinitely defer hope of self-government."[55]

After the administration had achieved its goal of incorporating the principles of the Platt Amendment into the Constitution of Cuba, the traditional respect for promises made and pledges given to peoples of color began to appear. The Cubans were not people to whom pledges or promises were seriously made. Support for this contention can be seen in the many attacks on the Teller Amendment. With this attitude existing in the United States at the time, the only thing that saved the Cubans from being swallowed up by the Republic was the large percentage of color in the population.

There were some factions in the United States who were willing to overlook the color question to gain additional territory; hence, the continued agitation for annexation. Edmond Wood considered the Teller Amendment responsible for what would "prove to be an opéra bouffe government" in Cuba unless the inhabitants of that island had "learned from the mistakes of other Spanish-Americans" and were able to develop the necessary character and capacity "never yet displayed by any nation of Spanish descent" which was prerequisite to self-government.

But the architects of States need more than bravery in order to build for generations yet to come. Neither Spanish colonists nor their descendants, whether of pure or mixed blood, have ever developed the constructive faculty and executive capacity that are necessary in order to establish a stable government. The evolution of Constitutional liberty, the sanctity of the ballot, the purity of courts of justice, and the ability to administer na-

[54] John W. Foster, "The Annexation of Cuba," *The Independent*, LXI (October 25, 1906), 967.
[55] "Talk of Cuban Annexation," *World's Work*, II (October 1901), 1249.

tional finances are matters of slow growth and development. They cannot be secured by imitation, and they have never been successfully exercised by people of Spanish origin or training. . . .[56]

Under laws established by the military occupation, the Cubans were not given much chance to govern. After the municipal elections of June 1, which were supposed to be completely in the hands of the Cuban people, eight of the mayors elected were put out of office by United States "military rulers." The basis of this action was the alleged fraud that took place during the election.

The *Nation*, in reporting the situation, conceded, "This may have been the case, though the election law was framed by our officers expressedly to guard against fraud. . . .

"The incident shows how hollow is the pretense that Cuba is under anything but a regime of force."

The fact of this regime was recognized by the president of the Cuban constitutional convention when he notified General Wood that the Platt Amendment had been adopted "In conformity with the order from the Military Governor of the island." The *Nation* concluded that "this is the fulfillment of our promise never to control Cuba."[57]

The acceptance of the Platt Amendment by the convention was noted by President Roosevelt in his message to Congress. A casual reader of that message would be led to believe that the Cubans accepted the measure without pressure from the United States. President Roosevelt said, "Cuba has in her constitution affirmed what we desired, that she should stand, in international matters, in closer and more friendly relation with us than with any other power. . . ." Then, leaving the impression that the United States had unconditionally retired from Cuba, the President declared, "Our attitude in Cuba is a sufficient guaranty of our own good faith. We have not the slightest desire to secure any territory at the expense of our neighbors." The reader would assume from one of Roosevelt's statements that the Platt Amendment was nonexistent: "The peoples of the Americas

[56] Edmond Wood, "Can Cubans Govern Cuba?" *Forum*, XXXII (September 1901), 66–67.

[57] *Nation*, LXXII (June 27, 1901), 501. Also Annual Report of the War Department, *House Document*, No. 2, 57 Cong., 1 sess., p. 126.

can prosper best if left to work out their own salvation in their own way."[58]

The relations of the United States to Cuba from the American point of view were again illustrated in 1902. In his message to Congress, Roosevelt observed that on May 20, 1902, the United States had kept its promise to the island by vacating Cuban soil and turning Cuba over to her representatives. He stated that Cuba's interests were also the United States' interests. The closeness was so ingrained in the feeling of the United States that "in the Platt Amendment we definitely took the ground that Cuba must hereafter have closer political relations with us than with any other power." Roosevelt was in favor of closer economic ties between Cuba and the United States. He urged the adoption of reciprocity with Cuba, saying, "It is eminently for our own interest to control the Cuban market and by every means to foster our supremacy in the tropical lands and waters south of us, but also because we, of the great republic of the North, should make all our sister nations of the American continent feel that whenever they will permit it we desire to show ourselves disinterestedly and effectively their friend."[59]

To say that the United States was manipulating effectively in Cuba is an understatement. The government of the United States had created a situation under which no Cuban government could live, as demonstrated by the downfall of the first Cuban government.

RACE AND CUBAN RECIPROCITY

The government of Cuba was turned over to the elected representatives of the people on May 20, 1902. Thus, the United States fulfilled a part of the pledge made to the Cubans in 1898. The pledge made by the McKinley administration, in return for the incorporation of the provisions of the Platt Amendment in the Organic Law of Cuba, depended upon the action of the Congress. The pledge was aimed at granting favorable trade concessions, especially for their principal commodity—sugar. The ensuing debates are both interesting and instructive: first, because of the role of racism in United

[58] Papers Relating to Foreign Affairs, *House Document*, No. 1, 57 Cong., 1 sess., pp. xxxi–xxxvii.
[59] *Ibid., House Document*, No. 1, 57 Cong., 2 sess., pp. xix–xx.

States relations with Cuba; and second, because two basic principles of the Republican party, protective tariff and territorial expansion into noncontiguous areas, were brought into irreconcilable conflict. The Republican leaders in Congress felt morally responsible for Cuba's economic well-being since the Platt Amendment had left Cuba somewhat less than independent. The efforts of the administration leaders to meet this moral responsibility were in the direction of a 20 percent reduction on the tariff for Cuban sugar imported into the United States. This reduction would enable the sugar producers of Cuba to make a profit. The Democrats charged the Republicans with helping the sugar trust at the expense of the Cuban people and the infant beet sugar industry of the United States. Since the protective tariff was a basic Republican principle, a reduction of duties on Cuban sugar was considered by both parties as a break in the vaunted protective dike. This proposal found many Republicans in opposition because it belied one of their party's basic principles. Many Democrats opposed the measure because the proposal did not go far enough toward free trade. Thus, in the first session of the Fifty-seventh Congress there was extensive debate on Cuban reciprocity but little action on the measure.

Senator Orville Platt charged Republican senators from the beet sugar states of siding with Democrats to defeat the desire of the American people to create an economic market for Cuban sugar in return for Cuba's adoption of the Platt Amendment. A failure to live up to that promise would be interpreted as a break of faith.[60]

The administration blamed the Congress for the failure to fulfill a pledge to a weaker people. The subsequent failure of Cuban governments as a result of the Platt Amendment would be blamed on the incapacity of the Cubans to govern themselves. The Cubans who had opposed the Platt Amendment believed that the United States had never paid the price (trade concessions) of the incorporation of that amendment in their constitution. Therefore, the contract had never been consummated, and the Cubans were released from any "obligation to observe the conditions prescribed by the United States in those preposterous articles."[61]

[60] Orville H. Platt, "Cuba's Claim Upon the United States," *North American Review*, CLXXV (August 1902), 147–49.
[61] Wilcox, "The Situation in Cuba," *North American Review*, CLXXV, 822.

The zeal of the earlier Republican expansionist sentiment was dulled by the dominance of color in Cuba. Democratic Representative Francis G. Newlands of Nevada voiced the position of the beet sugar producers, arguing that any agreement granting reciprocity to Cuba would be unfair because it would give Cuba an opportunity to produce in a free trade market using labor acquired in a free labor market. He alleged that the Republicans sought to meet the opposition of the American sugar producers "by imposing our immigration and contract-labor laws upon Cuba." He was opposed to that proposed method of equalizing the labor market conditions. If Cuba was, as the Republicans asserted, an independent republic, the United States had already gone "sufficiently far in controlling and regulating her autonomy. The Platt Amendment was certainly an invasion of her sovereignty. To go farther would be indefensible." Though the United States was justified in passing the Chinese exclusion acts, it was unfair to regulate and control the growth of another country's population through measures passed by the Congress. Newlands charged that the Republicans pursued the policy "to wait until economic distress shall drive Cuba into an application for annexation and then to accept Cuba simply as a military dependency instead of a territory or infant state."

To frustrate the intent of the Republicans and to remove Cuban fear of American imperialism, he felt that American intentions should be made known to the Cubans. Representative Newlands suggested that "an invitation was required from us because we have lately entered upon a policy of imperial expansion, and Cuba will be reluctant to apply for annexation, fearing that her fate will be that of Porto Rico and the Philippine Islands." The United States, Newlands continued, was claiming a right "to annex territory which is to be appended to the United States and subject to its jurisdiction, but not a part of it." The peoples of such territories "shall be subjects, not citizens. . . ." Cuba could not be expected to chance an inferior relationship such as that between the United States and the Philippines, and since Cuba was seeking a commercial union, he saw "no reason why he should not make a counter proposition and invite her into a political union which will ultimately make Cuba one of the wealthiest, most prosperous, and most powerful states in the Union." Cuba was believed to be capable of supporting a population of twelve or fifteen million people because of the richness of her soil. This meant that the people of the United States could "live there without degeneration." In order to ward off the development of an undesirable population, the sooner annexation took place, the better it would be for both Cuba and the United States. Accordingly, Cuba was not as undesirable in 1902 as she would be after ten or fifteen years of independence. Newlands suggested that Cuba be combined with Puerto Rico and other West Indies Islands and be admitted as a single state in the Union "to prevent over representation in the Senate."

In a similar minority view, Representative Samuel M. Robertson of Louisiana noted that the bill reported by the House Ways and Means Committee provided "that the President be authorized to enter into a reciprocal trade agreement with Cuba when there shall be enacted by said Government immigration, exclusion, and contract-labor laws as 'fully restrictive' of immigration as the laws of the United States." In his opinion, the proposed law gave the President even more power to compromise the sovereign rights of Cuba.[62]

The administration's view was expressed by the chairman of the House Ways and Means Committee, Representative Sereno E. Payne of New York, who pointed out that the American people had become linked to the Cuban people, believed that the destiny of the two countries could not be separated and that the most intelligent people of Cuba were looking toward annexation with the United States. He expressed his hopes when he said, "They may come in a year, they may come in five years. When they come I pray God they will be in no worse condition than they are today. If we can keep out this horde of immigrants, if we can keep out undesirable labor as we are keeping it out of our country . . . it is a consummation devoutly to be wished. . . ." Since the United States was committed to giving good government to Cuba, which would eventually lead to annexation, it was to the advantage of Americans to get "Cuba without Asiatic hordes forcing themselves in with her. . . ."[63]

Support for the administration's position on reciprocal relations with Cuba came from Representative Samuel W. McCall of Massa-

[62] Reciprocity with Cuba, *House Report*, No. 1276, 57 Cong., 1 sess., pt. 3: 7–10; pt. 4: 1–4.

[63] *Congressional Record*, 57 Cong., 1 sess., XXXV, pt. 4: 3855–56 (April 8, 1902).

chusetts, who preferred to have Cuba flourish as an independent republic "rather than to have her take a part in the government of the
people of the United States. Under the protection of this nation in
foreign affairs, with the instability of the races which inhabit her
regulated and tempered by people of American birth . . . I think she
can flourish as an independent government in a way that will make
her the model of the other Latin American States."

Representative Wayne R. Parker of New Jersey, in answering the
question whether Cuba should be annexed to the United States, commented, "When Cuba has been, if she ever will be, Americanized and
wishes to come to us, yes; until then, no; I believe that the policy in
regard to Texas was right—the policy by which we first recognized
her independence—then filled her with Americans, and then took
her in." Parker opposed the idea of sending Southern Negroes to
Cuba. He asked, "Do you want to put on Cuba all the difficulties
which now result from the race question in the South?" The question,
he believed, was "whether there shall be pursued in Cuba a policy
which will attract and bring to her people who shall renew her life
and make her cease to be the thorn in our side. . . . whether there shall
be created in the island a condition which will people it with those
who will help us to carry out the agreements that we have made for
the independence of Cuba and her freedom from foreign control . . .
whether she shall be made the home of the coolie or the home of the
independent farmer and citizen."[64]

Representative Rudolph Kleberg of Texas observed that the proposed treaty demanded "as a condition precedent, of Cuba, the enactment of immigration, exclusion, and contract-labor laws of the
United States before our government [would be able] to enter into
negotiations of reciprocal trade relations. . . ."[65]

As the race question was injected into the debate, it became apparent that the administration's program was to restrict undesirable
Asiatic, or Southern Negro immigration. Cuba was, evidently, to be
reserved for white immigrants.

Some Democrats proposed immediate annexation of Cuba. United
States exclusion laws would then apply to Cuba, preventing Chinese
and other Asiatics from being imported into Cuba. The Republicans

[64] *Ibid.*, pp. 4123–25.
[65] *Ibid.*, p. 3967. Speech of Representative Rudolf Kleberg of Texas.

who championed tighter imperial control felt that the puppet Cuban government, in return for a treaty of reciprocity, would be forced to adopt Chinese exclusion laws fully as restrictive as those of the United States. The promise of trade had worked in getting Cuba to incorporate the provisions of the Platt Amendment into the Cuban constitution. Why not use the same proposal to get Chinese excluded from the island?

Since the United States was to turn over the government of Cuba to its duly elected president and representatives on May 20, 1902, Congress did not have the necessary time to enact the reciprocal trade legislation affecting Cuba in the Fifty-seventh Congress. Instead, the Executive Department, acting through the secretary of war and the military governor of Cuba, extended the Chinese exclusion laws of the United States to Cuba.

The fear of undesirable Asiatic labor was only one of the racial factors conditioning the United States' imperial relations with Cuba; another factor was concern over the large percentage of Negroes and persons of mixed blood already in the Cuban population. The number of persons of Negro blood in the Cuban population was variously estimated from less than half to three-quarters. Southern Democrats had succeeded to their own satisfaction in controlling their racial problem by excluding Negroes from political activity. The Negro in the South was relegated to an inferior status, not only politically, but socially and economically as well. The situation found the South living under an "Athenian democracy." Under these circumstances some Democrats had little fear of annexing Cuba. Because they were sure that nearby Cuba would become a Southern state with white people from the South migrating there, there was some Southern Democratic support for outright annexation.

The administration was dubious about the Southern methods and preferred to set up a quasi-independent puppet state in Cuba that could be controlled from Washington. To achieve this end, the administration compromised the political rights of citizens of color in the United States by failing to investigate the election laws of states accused of violating the Fourteenth and Fifteenth Amendments to the Constitution.

The relationship between the administration's imperial policy and its domestic racial policy was brought to the attention of the Congress by Representative William P. Hepburn of Iowa. Using an article from the *Washington Post* as his authority, he alleged that Republican leaders had approached Representative O. W. Underwood of Alabama in a caucus of Democrats and Republicans on Cuban reciprocity with a plan by which "it was to be agreed that the Republican leaders would abandon the Crumpacker Resolution to investigate the Southern election laws if the delegates from the States concerned (North Carolina, South Carolina, Mississippi, Louisiana, and Virginia) would aid the majority to close debate and would vote against appeals which would be taken from the decisions of the chair when the motions to open up the bill to general amendment are offered."[66]

As debate opened in the Senate on reciprocity with Cuba, a joint resolution, introduced by Senator Newlands, brought into clear focus the contrasting views of Republicans and Democrats concerning the implications of Cuban racial conditions for the United States' imperial relations to that island. The resolution would have made Puerto Rico a county of Cuba and the president and vice president of Cuba the governor and lieutenant governor of the State of Cuba. The senator denied that there were any ulterior motives in offering his resolution and stated that "the national interests of the two countries and . . . the interests of the States composing the Federal Union and Cuba are identical, and that they can best be secured by equal terms and be governed by equal and indiscriminating laws, insuring freedom of trade and equality of rights and privileges."

This position was attacked by the spokesman of the administration as a reversal of the traditional Democratic position on expansion. Senator Newlands replied that it had always been Democratic policy to expand the Republic as opposed to the expansion of the Empire.

Senator Platt opposed the resolution. "I do not believe there is," he said, "and I hope there never will be, any considerable sentiment in this country looking to the annexation of Cuba as a State in our Union, or to any new development of the policy of expansion of our territory. And it is a little strange that this new theory or sentiment of expansion shall come from those who in so recent years have been the loudest in the denunciation of that policy."

Senator Henry Cabot Lodge was more skilled in presenting the

[66] *Congressional Record,* 57 Cong., 1 sess., XXXV, pt. 5: 4382 (April 18, 1902).

Republican position. Without direct reference to race, he observed that Cuba "has observed toward us the most absolute good faith. She has embodied in her constitution the clauses of the Platt Amendment. In further assurance she has embodied those same clauses in a treaty, which is now before the Committee on Foreign Relations. She has done all that we have asked her to do. . . . We have all the control in a military and political point of view that we can possibly desire in regard to that great island."[67] By the Republican methods the United States had all of the advantages of the Democratic methods without the distasteful aspects of having the Cubans incorporated into the Union.

Supporting the position held by Senators Platt and Lodge was Senator Chauncy M. Depew of New York. Depew felt that the United States had been far too careless in admitting states to the Union, as our government was constituted "with each State, no matter what its population or what its interest, equal to every other State in the Senate." He held that Cuba should be kept out of the Union until she became Americanized, for in five years enough Americans, "especially from the Southern States, would go to Cuba to Americanize the island. Then Cuba could come into the Union as a State."

The clearest portrayal of America's desire for Cuba, but not for the Cuban people, was made by Senator Newlands, who observed, "I hear it often said that Cuba would be desirable if for a half hour she could be sunk into the sea and then emerge after all her inhabitants had perished. . . . The objection that is urged is to the people themselves. And yet today Cuba has been practically dipped into the sea."[68] As a result of her civil war, Cuba's population had been diminished by almost half; so that if Cuba were now incorporated into the Union, she would "be incorporated at a period of her lowest development as to population." Cuba, Newlands contended, had a population of "only 1,500,000 people, but was capable of supporting twelve or fifteen million people." In the event of Cuba's annexation as a state, United States immigration laws would apply and would prevent undesirable people from populating the island. "Then," Sena-

[67] *Ibid.*, 58 Cong., Special sess., XXXVII, pp. 419–23 (November 23, 1903). A reciprocity treaty was ratified in 1903.
[68] *Congressional Record*, 58 Cong., 2 sess., XXXVIII, pt. 1: 167–68 (December 12, 1903).

tor Newlands predicted, "the population of our country would pour into that island, and within three, four or five years that island would be thoroughly Americanized. . . ." Hence, he insisted that the "speedy and practicable way to Americanize Cuba is to take her into the Union as soon as possible."[69]

It is a melancholy fact that racial antipathy was more and more affecting the relations between Cuba and the United States. The wish expressed by some Americans that an entire people might be disposed of in order that their homeland might be taken over by Anglo-Saxons tortures the mind in search of one glimmer of the vaunted principles of American democracy and fair play. Yet both major parties were, by different methods, trying to gain control of a Cuba devoid of colored people.

RACE AND THE SECOND INTERVENTION

In giving a brief résumé of events leading up to the second intervention in Cuba by the United States, one should point out the failure of Congress to enact reciprocal trade legislation in the closing session of the Fifty-seventh Congress, a failure which left many Cubans dissatisfied with their own government. However, the administration of Estrada Palma was like a calm before a storm. On the surface Palma was able to steer the ship of state steady and true on a course of stable government, but beneath the surface conditions were such that shipwreck was imminent.

Upon his installation in office, President Palma pursued an independent course, avoiding affiliation with any political faction. He chose his cabinet from men of either party or men who were not associated with any political party. The constitution required that the Cuban congress pass certain laws. One such law would have made the officers of the municipalities elective; a second would have made the judiciary independent of and irremovable by the executive; and a third would have secured minority representation in both houses of congress. These laws were not enacted in compliance with Palma's request, and the Palma administration resorted to the Spanish practice of appointing and removing mayors from office. The judges also came under the will of the executive.

[69] *Ibid.*

President Palma was able to continue as an independent executive until the spring of 1905. He then became affiliated with the Moderates in the hope of securing the needed laws for the operation of republican government. He appointed a new cabinet composed of members of the Moderate party. The Liberal party opposed the president's action, charging that the new cabinet was committed to carrying the next election by force. When election time arrived in 1905, President Palma had lost the support of the Cuban people. In a last effort to maintain himself in power, he used force to carry the election in favor of the Moderates and himself. The Liberals took to arms, feeling that they could not win with ballots, but that they could with bullets.

The Moderates entertained the notion that the United States would intervene and sustain in power the elected government, no matter how elected. The Liberals hoped for American intervention which would force the Moderates out of office and bring about a new election.[70]

An American observer, Talcott Williams, was of the opinion that "the insurrection in Cuba is both over-estimated and underrated by Americans." Williams noted that revolutions were a traditional political phenomena among Latin Americans. They were far less serious in Cuba and Latin America than in more advanced countries. Williams contended that the "stability of Spanish-American rule is in almost exact proportion to the share of white population present." Cuba, according to Williams, was at that time "two-thirds white, though in 1846 the races were evenly divided"; therefore, its prospect of escaping disorders was quite strong. The black faction in Cuba was mostly descended from Negroes who had been brought from Africa during the nineteenth century and constituted a greater proportion of the population of Cuba than in most areas of the southern United States. Wherever such Negroes were found in the United States, such regions were noted for "notorious disorders and race issues."

Williams stated that Gualberto Gómez, a Negro leader during the

[70] Report of William H. Taft, Secretary of War, and Robert Bacon, Assistant Secretary of State, of what was done under the instructions of the President in restoring peace in Cuba. Report of the War Department, *House Document,* No. 2, 58 Cong., 2 sess., I, Appendix E, p. 451.

Revolution of 1895–98, was a malcontent during the whole of President Palma's administration. Much of the unrest in Cuba, he charged, resulted from the introduction of American capital and various other influences "which have brought the first signs of a division on the color line." The insurrection leaders were, according to Williams, largely Negroes, and the real issue in Cuba was not "between this or that party or between President Palma and his opponents, but whether the new Cuba of independence . . . has the leadership and fighting force to suppress wandering bands of Negro laborers led by politicians out of a job and seeking one, or whether, being unable to do this, Cuba shall drift into disorder which will render intervention necessary."[71] By inference, Williams suggested that the Negro and mixed elements in Cuba were beyond the ability of native or resident white Cubans to control without American help. Significantly, as the Americans came in, it seemed that colored persons were relegated to minor political consideration, and Asiatics were excluded entirely from the country.

A Cuban, writing six years earlier, saw the necessity of American control to prevent a situation in which black ruled white. The only way to prevent "the submergence of the white race in Cuba would be by annexation to the United States." He observed that this method of preservation of the white rule in the Dominican Republic had failed, resulting in Spain's effort to annex this republic. A "most furious war, without removing the menace from the future of Santo Domingo" followed the downfall of white rule in this case.[72]

Captain M. Carnillo Aldama wrote that, generally speaking, the rebel forces were composed of "the lower strata of Cubans—Spanish laborers, negroes, disgruntled and discontented office seekers, and others who prefer the excitement of an insurrection to honest work."[73]

President Roosevelt was quite reluctant to intervene in Cuba in 1906. There was fear that a second intervention might ultimately result in annexation. Many Republicans in Congress were satisfied to continue to control Cuba without the threat of annexation. Roosevelt

[71] Talcott Williams, "The Causes of Cuban Insurrection," *Outlook*, LXXXIV (September 15, 1906), 111–14.
[72] "A Plea for Annexation of Cuba," *Forum*, XXX (September 1900), 208.
[73] M. Carnillo Aldama, "The Cuban Government's Side," *The Independent*, LXI (September 20, 1906), 663.

reflected this view when he asked Taft to ascertain "to what extent Americans were furnishing funds for the revolutionists."[74]

Whether the racial problems that beset the administration at home and abroad affected Roosevelt's response to the Cuban situation is hard to ascertain. Resentment over the Panama episode had not completely died down in Latin America. At home the Japanese were a problem on the West Coast; the Negroes were causing riots over voter registration at Atlanta, Georgia; and the Negro soldiers were a distinct sore spot in Brownsville, Texas. To worsen the situation, Negroes were allowing themselves to be lynched in the most uncivilized manner. John Hope Franklin states that few regarded these manifestations of violence as an inherent part of an industrial imperialism in which the subjection of the black men to caste control and wage slavery was an integral part, an industrial imperialism to which America was committed.[75]

President Roosevelt had said that a man could never be the same after having taken part in a lynching. Merely to have seen the hideous sight implied "degradation." He felt that the wrong done by the mob to the community was greater than that done to the individual victims. In reporting on the President's views, the *Nation* asserted, "If a severe logician were to apply the doctrine rigorously to the action of this nation since 1898, he might find reason for saying that the wholesale contempt for the rights of 'niggers' in the Philippines, of which this Government has been guilty, has had a great deal to do with the outbreak of savagery against the colored man in this country."[76]

Roosevelt's reluctance to intervene in Cuba is pointed up in his instructions to Taft and Bacon as well as in a letter to the Cuban people. His views are given force in the attitude of Assistant Secretary of State Robert Bacon, who was definitely opposed to military intervention and carefully weighed every step, saying, "It is . . . a very serious thing to undertake forcible intervention, and before going into it we shall have to be absolutely certain of the equities of the case and of the needs of the situation; meanwhile, we assume that every effort is being made by the Government to come to a work-

[74] Taft-Bacon Report, p. 469.
[75] Franklin, *From Slavery to Freedom*, p. 431.
[76] *The Nation*, LXXVII (August 13, 1903), 126.

ing agreement which will secure peace with the insurrectios, provided they are unable to hold their own with them in the field. Until
such efforts have been made we are not prepared to consider the
question of intervention at all."[77]

Further reluctance to intervene is shown in the plan of the peace
commission for returning Cuba to a stable condition. The plan provided for "the resignation of the vice-president, all senators and
representatives," and other public officials elected in December,
1905, and for the laying down of arms by the insurgents upon the
signing of a compromise agreement. A commission composed of three
members selected by the Moderate party, three selected by the Liberal
party, and one appointed by the President of the United States was to
be established for the purpose of drafting laws. New elections were
to be held January 1, 1907, under laws drafted by the commission.
From the first the plan was to get out of Cuba fast.[78]

The peace commission was unable to effect the compromise despite
President Roosevelt's personal appeal to President Palma. President
Palma resigned, causing the whole government to fall and making
intervention a necessity. Secretary of War Taft proclaimed himself
provisional governor after consulting Roosevelt and stated, "If the
insurrectionary habit persists, if again the Cubans divide into armed
forces, the strong hand of our Government will have to be imposed
at whatever cost of life and property, and permanent peace should
then certainly ensue because it should be in our keeping."[79]

On October 6, 1906, President Roosevelt designated Charles E.
Magoon as the provisional governor of Cuba replacing Secretary of
War Taft. Magoon took office on October 13, 1906, proclaiming a con-
tinuation of the policies inaugurated by Taft.[80]

The existence of annexationist sentiment in Cuba during the second intervention was noted in the report of Governor Magoon, who
stated that during the early months of the provisional administration
there was some discussion of the advisability of annexing Cuba to
the United States. As a result of that agitation, fears developed among

[77] Taft-Bacon Report, p. 445.
[78] Annual Report of Charles E. Magoon, Provisional Governor of Cuba, *House
Document*, No. 155, 60 Cong., 1 sess., p. 11.
[79] Taft-Bacon Report, p. 485. See also Fitzgibbon, *Cuba and the United States*,
pp. 120–21, for official attitudes on impending intervention.
[80] Magoon Report, p. 12.

some Cubans that the United States had designs on the island. Magoon reported that the Cubans realized "the strategical importance, from a military standpoint, of Cuba to the United States. . . . Doubtless the desire to be brought under the jurisdiction and direction of the United States continues to prevail among the large alien contingent and a small number of Cubans who own property and fear a recurrence of disorder."[81]

The second intervention was to be a short one. Roosevelt wanted it to end before he left office. At first the Cuban elections were to be held in January, 1907, but "by general consent" they were moved to May, 1907.[82] The President's desire to get out of Cuba as soon as possible is pointed up in his note to Secretary Taft on January 13, 1908, in which he said, "I direct that the installation of the President and Congress of Cuba, who will be elected next December, and, turning over the island to them, take place not later than February 1, 1909." It seemed that by the end of the first decade of the twentieth century, both Roosevelt and Lodge had lost some of their earlier zeal for taking up the "White Man's burden." Others, however, were ready to take it up where they had left off.

The change in policy after the second intervention ending in 1909 is attributed by Fitzgibbon to "approbrium heaped upon the United States in all Latin-America as well as Cuba for the alleged character of the Provisional Government." The criticism was not minimized by the American withdrawal in 1909.[83] Roosevelt interpreted the Platt Amendment with restraint; thus, intervention was cautiously undertaken. The Taft policy in interpreting the Platt Amendment was termed a preventative policy. It was considered a policy of interfering with the internal affairs of the Cuban government.[84]

The election was held as prescribed and resulted in a sweeping victory for the Liberals, who carried the presidential and vice-presidential positions as well as electing every member of the senate. The date for the inauguration was January 28, 1909, "a day sacred to Cuba as being the anniversary of the birth of José Martí, the great

[81] *Ibid.*, p. 31.
[82] David A. Locmiller, *Magoon in Cuba: A History of the Second Intervention, 1906–1909*, pp. 174–75.
[83] Fitzgibbon, *Cuba and the United States*, p. 145.
[84] Sydney Brooks, "Some Impressions of Cuba," *North American Review*, CXCIX (May 1914), 744.

apostle and martyr of Cuban independence."[85] However, the underlying causes for insurrection were still present. In fact, the election of
the Liberals left the veterans and Negro elements in Cuba very
disgruntled.[86]

Early in 1912 the conditions were such that a new insurrection
seemed imminent to the American minister, Arthur M. Beaupré.
Minister Beaupré appears to have been an alarmist whose interest in
effecting an intervention of United States military forces increased as
the year 1912 progressed. On January 12, he cabled the secretary of
state concerning the developing conditions in Cuba, suggesting that
the United States should make known its intention to support the
Cuban president, in order to "probably have a discouraging effect on
those wishing to promote intervention." He concluded that the "situation now" was more alarming "than at any previous time." The secretary of state instructed the minister to hand the Cuban president
the following note:

> The situation in Cuba as now reported causes grave concern to the
> Government of the United States. That the laws intended to safeguard
> free republican government shall be enforced and not defied is obviously
> essential to the maintenance of law, order and stability indispensable to
> the status of the Republic of Cuba, in the continued well-being of which
> the United States has always evinced and cannot escape a vital interest.

The note further stated that the President of the United States looked
to the president and government of Cuba to prevent a disruption of
law and order or "a threatened situation which would compel the government of the United States, much against its desires, to consider
what measures it must take in pursuance of the obligation of its relations to Cuba."[87]

As the situation worsened, American property holders in Cuba
began to favor annexation. Others objected because of the large
Catholic population on the one hand and the large Negro and mixed-
blood population on the other. A writer pointed out that America was

[85] Report of the Provisional Governor of Cuba, *House Document*, No. 1457,
60 Cong., 2 sess., p. 38.
[86] *Foreign Relations*, 1912, p. 242.
[87] *Ibid.*, p. 240.

inhospitable to both Catholics and Negroes. He imagined that the colored population of Cuba "might fear annexation and the increase of the American influence, which tended to put such a population into an inferior class."[88] That this assessment of Cuban fears concerning the racist policies of the United States was correct could be seen in the fact that the veteran soldiers, who were for the most part colored, began to work for peace in order to forestall intervention.

The insurrection, basically a Negro uprising, was due to the failure of the Gómez government to recognize any party organized along the lines of color. The leader of the party, Estenzo, alleged that he and other leaders of the Negro group arrested in 1910 were told that this was done on instructions from Washington.[89] According to the *Independent*, by late spring in 1912 the Negro uprising had taken an alarming character; the two leaders, General Estenzo and General Ironnet, were sought but could not be found. The reason for the uprising was, according to the Negroes, that although they had furnished the bulk of the manpower in the fight for Cuba's independence, "a fair share of the offices had not been given to them." The *Independent* reported that the Cuban Negroes were receiving arms from Haiti and were being urged by the Haitians to set up a Negro republic in eastern Cuba.[90]

On May 24, Minister Beaupré was calling for a battleship to be sent to Guantanamo. Beaupré thought it would be difficult "to say . . . what moral effect the presence of ships" would "have upon the irresponsible negroes, who were unlikely to be greatly concerned over the possible consequences of thier actions." He was certain that the movement was directed by some unknown interest because it was "highly improbable that the negroes at the head of the Independent Colored Party would be capable of engineering a movement on this scale."

President José Miguel Gómez did not agree with the American minister that the presence of the ships did not mean intervention. The very presence of the battleships, he said, was in reality intervention. He warned the American minister that a landing of foreign

[88] *The Independent,* "Editorial," LXXII (January 25, 1912), 209.
[89] *Foreign Relations,* 1912, p. 343.
[90] *The Independent,* LXXII (May 23, 1912), 1139.

troops would accentuate the character of the intervention and "that a determination of this serious character alarms and injures the feelings of a people loving jealously their independence."[91]

That the insurrection was being instigated and financed by American interests was a probability in the minds of at least two senators, who introduced resolutions directing the Committee on Foreign Relations or one of its subcommittees, to "inquire, investigate, ascertain, and report whether any persons, associations, corporation, or other interest in the United States have heretofore been or are now engaged in fomenting, . . . encouraging, or financing rebellion, insurrection, or other flagrant disorders in Cuba and Mexico against the lawful organized governments."

This resolution was introduced by Senator Knute Nelson of Minnesota, along with a similar resolution introduced by Senator August O. Bacon of Georgia. All the annexationists had to do to precipitate a revolution was to furnish a little money for certain leaders among the mulattoes and the colored people and have them burn a few cane mills and plantations. Then they could raise the hue and cry that peace and order could not be maintained in Cuba and that, therefore, it was necessary to annex Cuba.[92]

Senators Nelson and Bacon had only to look to the American legation to find just that kind of attitude. On June 5, 1912, four companies of marines from Guantanamo were landed despite the protest of the Cuban president. The Cuban minister of foreign affairs, Manuel Sanguily, in a long note to the American minister, protested, "In discharge of my conscience and in behalf of the Cuban government, to be so honestly frank with you as to say that the intervention which has been initiated and is being prepared is in no sense justified."

The annexationists' plan of operation seems to have been to use the Negro efforts to achieve political rights as a device to save the white minority from rule by peoples of color. It was their mistaken hope that the American aversion to the submergence of white men under Negro and mulatto domination would outweigh their aversion to the incorporation of more Negroes into the United States.

The American minister continued his alarmist campaign, reporting to the secretary of state that the disorders in Havana and suburbs

[91] *Foreign Relations*, 1912, pp. 247–48.
[92] *Congressional Record*, 62 Cong., 2 sess., XLVIII, pt. 8: 7838 (June 8, 1912).

had for some days been assuming the nature of a race war. Threats on the part of the government to deal severely with troublemakers were not enough. According to the minister, the authorities were showing weakness, and Americans and other foreigners, as well as Cubans, were extremely apprehensive. Beaupré appealed for the sending of more war vessels. He reasoned, "The size of our colony and the large number of American women it contains places heavy responsibility upon our government as regards possible consequences of racial trouble." He urged that a war vessel be sent immediately for moral effect and to "calm general apprehension."

The minister was using every device known to racists to precipitate intervention, for if the Americans were concerned about anything, it was the safety of their women from the danger of contamination by Negro men. He succeeded in getting the war vessels, which were ordered to Havana on June 9, 1912. The Cuban minister and president appealed to the American officials, arguing that it was extremely important that the Cuban government be allowed to crush the insurrection if they were to forestall the possibility of future insurgents hoping for success through American intervention.

It seemed as though the reports of Minister Beaupré were grossly exaggerated. Yet, he accused the Cuban government of never having been frank with him. The end result was that "a number of Negroes were attacked by crowds of whites armed with revolvers." At least one was killed in the center of town and two or three more in various parts of the city and suburbs. The minister reported, "Large numbers of negroes were beaten and the receiving hospitals were kept busy until a late hour of the night." He reported on June 13 that wholesale arrest of Negroes in Havana and vicinity had been made on charges of conspiracy. The Cuban government contended that the remainder of the county of Havana was absolutely quiet. Yet, Minister Beaupré reported that Negroes were "conspiring almost openly in various parts without interference from the authorities." The final attempt to force a takeover was the circulation of a story to the effect that the President was planning to "send General Wood or General Crowder to Cuba to look into the justice of the negroes' demands, and if so advised, the American government will insist that the negroes be given the upper hand in the government." Beaupré realized that the story was ridiculous but saw fit to repeat it in an official dispatch, saying that it was creating a "surprising amount of consternation and resentment even among intelligent classes who would welcome intervention."

The so-called race war ended on June 28, 1912, with the report that the rebel leader, Estenzo, had been killed in a battle at Micoma and his body had been brought to Havana to be identified.[93] The efforts to achieve annexation by the threat of a black takeover in Cuba failed; however, some of the racial patterns in the United States were being introduced into Cuba. Under the guise of fear, whites shot and beat Negroes with impunity in order to keep them from disturbing the social order.

An American observer wrote that the "Negro Revolution" in Cuba had been caused by a failure of the Gómez government to keep promises made to the Negroes and mulattoes, who constituted 75 percent of the electorate. This group insisted that Gómez keep faith, or there would be no Cuban republic. The revolution, he asserted, had not been serious because though the number of revolutionists was large, they were poorly armed and avoided a fight. Their method was that of "guerrilla warfare, with the torch, looting, and the violation of defenseless white women and children." The development of the Negroes' discontent and the assertion of their demands had forced Gómez into a corner with either intervention or the recognition of the Negro party, "thereby turning Cuba into a black republic." The author called for American intervention without annexation "to stop the colossal fraud, called government. . . . Cuba may need us, but we do not need the Cubans. They, as a mass, are a degenerate race lacking in all the instincts of civic pride or honor and utterly disregarding all moral obligations to themselves."[94]

Some years later Sydney Brooks, an English observer, compared the American situation in Cuba to the British in the Transvaal. He suggested that even though the Americans had invested heavily in Cuba, few Americans were "within a mile of understanding the Cuban people." The lack of real sympathy and comprehension came from "profound divergencies of social structure and mental habit." The situation became acute because "most of the money and prac-

[93] *Foreign Relations,* 1912, pp. 258–67.
[94] Walter Wigdill, "Addition Without Division = Revolution," *The Independent,* LXXII (June 13, 1912), 1352.

tically all the money-making enterprises, except politics" were in the hands of aliens, who were not loyal Cubans and who, for business and financial reasons, would prefer American rule to Cuban rule. The island republic received a "bad press" from the American newspapers, who seemed to expect "Cuba to surpass the whole world in the art of self-government."

The situation was complicated by the fact that, by burning a few mills and cane fields, a small minority of Cubans could, with the aid of American interests, precipitate intervention. In addition, the pronouncement of Secretary Root had been forgotten and intervention had become "intermeddling." As Brooks explained, "The habit grew up a few years ago of interfering with the details of Cuban Administration and of using the Platt Amendment to justify almost every kind of demand that officials at Washington might choose to make on the Cuban Executive and Congress."

The situation under the Taft administration at Washington and the Gómez administration at Havana was such that it was the "merest gallantry to speak of the Cubans as a self-governing people." Brooks alleged that they were at every turn "hampered and hauled up by the American Minister in Havana, acting under instructions from Washington," so much so that they could not tell where they were or with whom they were dealing. The Platt Amendment had been so manipulated "that it practically amounted to a system of governing Cuba from Washington without the bother and expense of formal occupation of the island."[95]

The Negro revolt in 1911 evidently destroyed the major sentiment towards annexation to the United States. The policy-makers in the United States were satisfied to control Cuba through the Platt Amendment without the concomitant dangers of annexation.

During the years of the First World War, Cuba worked closely with the United States. After the war, Cuban politics were such that some kind of intervention to insure a stable government was necessary. The method chosen was not direct intervention sanctioned by the Platt Amendment, but rather indirect intervention. Persuasion and economic pressure were applied so effectively that the formal use of the Platt Amendment was unnecessary. The Depart-

[95] Brooks, "Some Impressions of Cuba," *North American Review*, CXCIX, 743.

ment of State, through manipulation of the Cuban president and the use of pressure achieved through control of Cuban business, achieved the same result as direct intervention.

An illustration of the method of economic control is shown by the manipulations of Cuban policies under the Lever Act of August 10, 1917. Under the Lever Act, the Food Administration could control the marketing and production of food. The United States government, with the co-operation of the British government, was able to force the Cubans to accede to prices established by an International Sugar Committee headed by Earl Basbst, the president of the American Sugar Refining Company.[96]

If the island's populace became restive as a result, the Cuban government was persuaded to invite the American government to use the tropical climate of Cuba as a training ground for the United States Marines. The coincidence of United States training missions with periods of Cuban restiveness was scarcely accidental.

The United States, as a result of the early obsolescence of several specific provisions of the Platt Amendment, maintained only two of the original provisions of the Platt Amendment by 1932. The two provisions dealt with debts and the right of intervention. As shown above, the need to intervene was no longer necessary nor desirable from the American point of view. It was, therefore, an advantage to the United States to give up the final two provisions. Fitzgibbon observed:

> It is a defensible thesis . . . that probably the wisest political step the United States has yet taken toward Cuba was the action of the Roosevelt administration in abrogating the Platt Amendment. It not only redounded immeasurably toward the improvement of the atmosphere between the two countries but had the same general effect between the United States and Latin America as a whole. The phraseology of the treaty of 1934, with its implications of parity, was calculated to enhance Cuban self-respect. This concrete examplification of the "good neighbor" policy will probably do more to increase the prestige and influence of the United States than would any number of forcible interventions.[97]

[96] Robert F. Smith, *The United States and Cuba: Business and Diplomacy*, p. 20.
[97] Fitzgibbon, *Cuba and the United States*, pp. 258–59.

VI

Puerto Rico: Suspension Between Statehood and Dependency

Puerto Rico, the easternmost and smallest of the Greater Antilles, is located within the tropics east of the Dominican Republic and is separated from the island of Hispaniola by the Mona Passage. The greatest length is from east to west, a little over one hundred miles, and the island is about thirty-six miles wide.

The name *Puerto Rico*[1] is applied to a large island around which there are three smaller islands that, for political purposes, are part of Puerto Rico. Of these the most important is the island of Vieques located about thirteen miles from the eastern shore of Puerto Rico. Vieques is approximately twenty-one miles in length and has an average width of about six miles. The other islands around Puerto Rico are similar to Vieques but are not as important.

Puerto Rico proper is very compact with a mountainous interior which can be cultivated. The island is within the region of the southwest trade winds, which blow with great regularity. The temperature range is very slight, indicating a uniform climate. Altitude causes a lowering in the mean temperature in some areas, such as in the highlands of the interior.

RACIAL CHARACTERISTICS

The original inhabitants of Puerto Rico were Indians who, for the most part, either left the island or were forced into slavery by the Spaniards. They were found to be less suited to agricultural planta-

[1] The spelling *Puerto Rico* will be used throughout this work except when in direct quotations. The spelling *Puerto Rico* was approved by Congress, S. J. 36, and signed by the President on May 17, 1932.

183

tion labor than the Negro; therefore, they were replaced by the latter as a source of labor in the island.

In 1860 the total white population in Puerto Rico was 300,406 and the total colored population was 282,775. The Census of 1899 divided the Puerto Ricans into two main classes—the pure white and the non-white. According to this classification, out of a population of 953,243, the whites constituted 61.8 percent and the nonwhites 38.2 percent of the population. The proportion of white to colored had been lowest in the Census of 1820; the whites had since shown a somewhat regular tendency upward. Although the "accuracy of enumeration has varied," yet when omissions occurred, they were usually more numerous among the colored than among the white inhabitants.

The Census of 1899 reported that of the 363,817 persons listed as colored, 33.6 percent were of mixed blood. The observation was made that the "statistical evidence," reinforced by competent witnesses, would lead to the conclusion that persons of mixed blood were more numerous in Puerto Rico and Cuba than in the other West Indian islands or the United States, and more numerous in Puerto Rico than in Cuba.[2]

LOCATION AND POPULATION

Puerto Rico's location in the tropics and a population composed of a mixture of Negro, Indian, and Spanish ancestry were considered by many in the United States to be factors which rendered the island incapable of independent self-government. Some observers conceded that the Spanish and Negro mixture had a conditioning effect on each other. In a discussion of the nature of the Puerto Rican population, it was not possible to separate the Latin from the African race. The people were more closely woven together in the Spanish-Amrican areas than in Anglo-Saxon areas. According to Charles M. Pepper, "They exist together in those islands and their future is woven together inseparably. Each race has kept its own identity, yet there has been reciprocal or a mutual influence. The African has benefited by the tolerance and kindlier consideration, the less pronounced antipathy of the Spaniard as compared with the Anglo-Saxon." As in other

---

[2] *Census of Porto Rico,* War Department, Office Director of Census of Porto Rico, 1899 (Washington: United States Government Printing Office, 1900), pp. 11, 55–58.

Spanish-American areas, the previous condition of slavery did not give the Negro a badge or caste to be passed down from generation to generation. Pepper concluded that the Negro by living side by side "with the Latin race has modified the Latin temperament."[3]

In a report the Committee on Pacific Islands and Puerto Rico pointed up the difficulty of determining race on the American standard in Puerto Rico. Since the complexion of the average Puerto Rican was quite dark, it was difficult to tell the difference between white and colored persons. The committee reported that there was some color prejudice in Puerto Rico and that there was a tendency for the mulatto to deny the existence of Negro blood in his veins. Under the Spanish, this denial was not necessary or was of little consequences, for it was just as significant to have Spanish blood in one's veins. But to the Americans, the question of the presence or absence of Negro blood was the difference between being classified white or colored. Thus, one of the first fruits of American occupation was to bring to Puerto Rico a disdain for Negro blood. The development of this attitude on the part of the Puerto Ricans was noticed by the American forces, as General Davis noted when he wrote that it was "a warrantable presumption that a very considerable number of those who rate themselves, or are rated, as white are actually mulattoes and would be classed as colored in the United States."[4]

The acquisition of Puerto Rico by the United States increased her interest in the Dominican Republic and Haiti. The location of Puerto Rico could be considered one of the basic reasons why the United States desired the island, but the United States was not prepared to incorporate the island and its people into the Republic.

The Puerto Ricans had welcomed the Americans in 1898 as liberators, not as conquerors. They had believed the words of General Miles's proclamation of July 28, 1898, and thought that the United States forces had come "bringing the banner of freedom" and the "fostering arm of a nation of free people whose greatest power is in justice and humanity to all those living within its folds."[5]

Though General Miles seems to have looked upon the Puerto Ri-

[3] Charles M. Pepper, "The Spanish Population of Cuba and Porto Rico," *The Annals,* XVIII (July 1901), 163.

[4] General Davis' Report, Annual Report of the War Department, *House Document,* No. 2, 56 Cong., 2 sess., XIV, 94.

[5] *Ibid.,* pp. 19–20.

cans as human beings worthy of the freedoms traditional under the American flag, General Davis, the military governor, held a different concept. General Davis reported that the inhabitants of Puerto Rico could not be "metamorphosed" into Anglo-Saxons. "They are what they are, and must remain for a long time." He thought it would be impossible to absorb the Puerto Ricans by American immigration because the country was more densely populated than India or any state in the Union.[6]

RACE—A DETERMINANT OF CITIZENSHIP

The Treaty of Paris which terminated the Spanish-American War stated in Article II:

> Spain cedes to the United States the island of Porto Rico and other islands now under Spanish sovereignty in the West Indies.

Article IX of the treaty states:

> Spanish subjects, natives of the peninsula, residing in the territory over which Spain by the present treaty relinquishes or cedes her sovereignty, may remain in such territory or may remove therefrom, retaining in either event all their rights of property, including the right to sell or dispose of such property or of its proceeds; and they shall also have the right to carry on their industry, commerce and professions, being subject in respect thereof to such laws as are applicable to other foreigners. In case they remain in the territory they may preserve their allegiance to the Crown of Spain by making, before a court of record, within a year from the date of the exchange of ratifications of this treaty, a declaration of their decision to preserve such allegiance; in default of which declaration they shall be held to have renounced it and to have adopted the nationality of the territory in which they reside.
>
> The civil rights and political status of the native inhabitants of the territories hereby ceded to the United States shall be determined by the Congress.[7]

The question of the civil and political rights of the Puerto Ricans came up when Congress started to work out postwar trade rela-

[6] *Ibid.*, p. 36.
[7] Treaty of Peace Between the United States of America and the Kingdom of Spain, *Foreign Relations*, 1898, pp. 831–40.

tions between Puerto Rico and the United States. President McKinley suggested free trade, implying the extension of the Consitution to Puerto Rico as had been the practice in the annexation of other territories. President McKinley realized that under the Treaty of Paris the Puerto Ricans were left in a difficult position. The President was willing to help the Puerto Ricans economically, for he acknowledged in his message to Congress, December 5, 1899, that Puerto Rico had lost her free trade markets with Spain and Cuba and that "the markets of the United States should be opened to her products." It was, he insisted, "our plain duty . . . to abolish all customs tariffs between the United States and Puerto Rico and give her products free access to our markets."[8]

Tho Committee on Pacific Islands and Puerto Rico recommended in a majority report that the concept implied by the President should not prevail and that the Constitution should not be extended to Puerto Rico. The committee felt that extension of the Constitution to Puerto Rico raised very important questions concerning the power of Congress to enact such legislation. A majority of the committee was certain that Congress had the power to enact legislation which did not comply with the concept that the Constitution followed the flag. It was their conclusion that if the United States should acquire territory which was populated by

an intelligent, capable, and law-abiding people, to whom the right of self-government could be safely conceded, we might at once with propriety and certainly within the scope of our constitutional power, incorporate that territory, and people into the Union as an integral part of our territory; but if the territory should be inhabited by a people of wholly different character, illiterate, and unacquainted with our institutions, and incapable of exercising the rights and privileges guaranteed by the Constitution to the States of the Union, it would be competent for Congress to withhold from such people the operation of the Constitution and the laws of the United States, and continuing to hold the territory as a mere possession of the United States, so govern the people thereof as their situation and necessities of their case might seem to require. In other words, the Constitution and laws of the United States do not *ex proprio vigore*, extend

[8] James D. Richardson, *Messages and Papers of the Presidents, 1785–1905,* XIV, 6403–6404.

to territory acquired by the United States, but only by Congressional action.[9]

The chief law officer of the War Department supported the view of the committee. Charles E. Magoon reported that "the sovereignty of the United States 'follows the flag' wherever the flag is raised by the authority of that sovereignty, whether the raising is accomplished by a discoverer, an ambassador, or a military commander, but the territorial boundaries of the United States do not until appropriate action has been taken by Congress."[10]

In his report, Magoon answered the question on citizenship in the insular possessions conditionally. To the question, "Are the inhabitants of said islands 'citizens' of the United States?" he replied that if *citizen* meant "a member of the civil state entitled to all privileges," the question should be answered in the negative; for even in the treaty it was provided that "the civil rights and political status of the native inhabitants . . . shall be determined by the Congress." At the time of the discussion of the bill to provide temporary civil government for Puerto Rico, Congress had not made a determination as to the status and rights of the Puerto Ricans. It was found by the chief law officer that the Puerto Ricans did not fulfill the requirements of the Fourteenth Amendment to the Constitution. Even though they were subject to the jurisdiction of the United States, they were not "persons born or naturalized in the United States." However, if *citizen* meant one who owes allegiance to the United States government in return for the protection which the government affords him, then the inhabitants of Puerto Rico were citizens of the United States.[11]

Many congressmen and publicists contended that Article IX of the Treaty of Paris was a departure from the traditional way in which inhabitants of annexed territory had been treated. They disagreed with the views expressed by the majority of the committee and by the chief law officer—that the Constitution did not follow the flag. It was pointed out that Article III of the Treaty of 1803, by which Louisiana became a part of the United States, provided "that the in-

[9] Temporary Civil Government for Porto Rico, *Senate Report*, No. 249, 56 Cong., 1 sess., pp. 8–9.
[10] *Senate Document*, No. 234, 56 Cong., 1 sess., p. 17.
[11] *Ibid.*, p. 23.

habitants of the ceded territory shall be incorporated in the Union of the United States, and admitted as soon as possible, according to the principles of the Federal Constitution, to the enjoyment of all rights, advantages, and immunities of the citizens of the United States. . . ." They were entitled to the protection of the federal government in the enjoyment of their liberty, their property, and their religion until they were incorporated into the Union. Similarly, in the Treaty of 1819, by which Florida became a part of the United States, Article VII had the same kind of legal impact. The treaties by which New Mexico, Utah, and California were acquired in 1848 contained provisions in Articles VIII and IX which were carried forward in the Treaty of 1853 by Article V, which gave the inhabitants of the areas acquired the assurances that they would be incorporated into the Union.

The only qualified exception to the rule was in the case of Alaska. In the Treaty of 1867, by which Alaska was acquired, there was no provision for the incorporation of the territory into the Union as a state or states. The citizens of Russia could return to Russia within three years if they so desired. Those who did not return to Russia, if civilized, would be "admitted to enjoyment of all the rights, advantages, and immunities of citizens of the United States and shall be maintained and protected in the free enjoyments of their liberty, property, and religion." As to the uncivilized tribes, they were left to "such regulation as the United States may, from time to time, adopt in regard to aboriginal tribes."[12] In the case of Alaska a distinction was made between civilized and uncivilized inhabitants. The Puerto Ricans were considered civilized by most Americans; exception was made to them on some other basis.

Some congressmen were unwilling to accede to the new principles which threatened to erode the Constitution. Representative Charles E. Littlefield of Maine asserted that the blood of the "chattel," Crispus Attucks, demanded that the United States should not try to govern people in her possessions without giving them constitutional rights, "without which liberty and freedom are nothing but a name."[13]

Senator Joseph L. Rawlings of Utah endeavored to show the logic of the contention that the Constitution followed the flag. He believed

[12] *Congressional Record*, 56 Cong., 1 sess., XXXIII, pt. 2: 1057 (January 23, 1900).
[13] *Ibid.*, pt. 8: 64 (February 23, 1900).

it was impossible for Congress to legislate for an area which did not come under the Constitution. "If we are legislating in respect to Puerto Rico," he argued, "or propose to legislate by virtue of the Constitution . . . it must be because to the extent that we extend the Constitution, the Constitution confers power, is operative, and extends the arms of Congress to that island. If that be true, does it not necessarily follow that Congress legislates under the limitations upon its power of legislation including the right to veto of the President, in respect to these islands, which is derived also from the Constitution?"[14]

Others held that the Constitution was not undergoing a different interpretation, but that it was the duty of Congress to keep out undesirable people in order to protect Americans. This view was held by Senator F. W. Mondell of Wyoming, who suggested that an interpretation of the Constitution which did not classify the Puerto Ricans as citizens of the United States served notice on "all concerned that the Union of States as a sovereign power can protect its citizens from the admission of undesirable citizenship and the competition of cheap labor even from its own territory," that Congress, unrestrained by the Constitution and without representatives from Puerto Rico, could be depended upon "to deal fairly, even liberally, with the people who inhabit annexed territory."[15]

The cause of the problem, according to Senator J. D. Richardson of Tennessee, was the change from democratic expansion into sparsely settled lands to the acquisition of areas like Puerto Rico, in which people were acquired without land sufficient for the migration of large numbers of Americans.[16]

The passage of the so-called Foraker Act on April 12, 1900, and subsequent Supreme Court decisions, left the Puerto Ricans in a position of political suspension. Former President Harrison pointed out that the perplexing question was related to the status of the new possessions "and to the rights of their civilized inhabitants who have elected to renounce their allegiance to the Spanish Crown, and either by choice or operation of law have become American—somethings— what? Subject or citizen? There is no other status since they are not

[14] *Ibid.*, pt. 3: 2476 (March 2, 1900).
[15] *Ibid.*, p. 2277 (February 26, 1900).
[16] *Ibid.*, pt. 2: 1947 (February 19, 1900).

aliens any longer, unless a newspaper heading that recently attracted my attention offers another. It ran thus: 'Porto Ricans not citizens of the United States *proper*.' Are they citizens of the United States *improper*, or improper citizens of the United States?"[17]

The Supreme Court in the Insular Cases decided that the Philippines and Puerto Rico were neither foreign nor domestic territory. These "decisions left the inhabitants of the islands in an unfortunate situation, being neither 'fish, flesh nor devil'; they were literally 'men without a country' in the large sense." They were citizens of Puerto Rico, but not citizens of the United States. Under the organic acts no provision was made by Congress "for the naturalization of alien residents in insular territory, as citizens of such territory, although such relief has been frequently sought. . . . In the endeavor made by insular inhabitants to obtain Federal citizenship, it was found impossible to comply with the Federal requirement of renouncing the allegiance, because the only allegiance they owe is to the United States. . . ."[18]

Harrison saw in the Puerto Rican bill also a departure from the customary methods of levying tariff, in that it was the first time that Congress had laid tariff duties on the exports of an American territorial possession. "The necessity for this radical departure from the established practice of the government seems to have been to find a safe basis for the holding and governing of regions . . . the admission of whose people to citizenship might imply statehood—or at least the right of migration and settlement in the States of an undesirable population." He pointed up the inconsistency in denying the islanders the protection of civil rights under the Constitution while holding them to strict allegiance, and at the same time protecting the mainlanders against the "insidious under-wear of greed and ambition," of which it was "safe to say that no such interpretation of the Constitution, or of the rights of the people of a territory, will ever be offered to men of American descent."[19] By implication, Harrison charged that the Constitution had been manipulated and interpreted to the dis-

---

[17] Benjamin Harrison, "The Status of Annexed Territory, and Its Free Civilized Inhabitants," *North American Review*, CLXXII (January 1901), 4.

[18] Charelton, "Naturalization and Citizenship," *The Annals*, XXX (July 1907), 108.

[19] Harrison, "Status of Annexed Territory," *op. cit.*, pp. 15–17.

advantage of the people of Puerto Rico, and that it would not have been so interpreted if the inhabitants of the islands had been white men.

Darius H. Pingrey observed that in the Dred Scott case the Supreme Court found that there was no power under the Constitution by which colonies could be established and maintained by the United States. The decision further affirmed that the organization and maintenance of colonies "would be unconstitutional and inconsistent with our republican form of government." That doctrine was an anachronism because the Court's decisions in the Insular Cases, according to Pingrey,

affirmed the doctrine for which Lord North contended during the Revolution which separated the Thirteen Colonies from the British Empire. Lord North's doctrine was that Parliament had plenary power to govern the colonies. The Supreme Court has now affirmed the possession by Congress of the same unlimited power over the dependencies of the United States. Lord North contended that though the American colonies were not represented in Parliament, they might, nevertheless, be taxed, and duties might be imposed upon their commerce. In the Insular Cases the Supreme Court has decided that the people of the "Crown Colony" of Porto Rico may be compelled to pay such import and export duties as Congress may see proper. This was Lord North's view in 1764, when the question of taxing the American colonies was being discussed. Accordingly, the doctrine of Lord North was wrong in the eighteenth century, as the Revolution demonstrated, but it is right in the beginning of the twentieth century, as the Supreme Court has so decided.[20]

Racial fears were a factor in the opposition to giving Puerto Rico free trade with the United States. The question was "Is Puerto Rico to be regarded as territory of the United States in the sense in which that term applies to Arizona, or is the island a colony under our sovereignty, but not under the Constitution? . . ." The Republicans had "adopted the colonial theory; while the Democrats, repudiating 'imperialism,' . . . regarded the annexation of Puerto Rico as the same as the earlier acquisitions of contiguous territory on the mainland." The Republicans wished to avoid awkward precedents.

[20] Darius H. Pingrey, "The Decadence of Our Constitution," *Forum*, XXXII (October 1901), 228.

They were looking at the implications of a policy of free trade on relations with Cuba and the Philippines.[21]

President Theodore Roosevelt pleaded for United States citizenship for Puerto Ricans. In his fifth annual message to Congress he said, "I earnestly advocate the adoption of legislation which will explicitly confer American Citizenship on all citizens of Porto Rico. There is, in my judgment, no excuse for failure to do this."[22]

In 1906 some modification of the conditions of suspended citizenship was made by Congress, which was somewhat less than the extension of the privilege desired by the insular inhabitants. This disappointment was due to the fact that requisite jurisdiction was not conferred upon courts outside the continental United States. However, there was an enlargement of political privileges, and a wise restriction upon its extension to peoples whose ability for self-government was still in the experimental stage.[23] Section 3 of the law provided that exclusive jurisdiction to naturalize aliens be conferred upon specified courts:

United States Circuit and District Courts now existing, or which may hereafter be established by Congress in any State, United States Courts for the Indian Territory; also all courts of record in any State or Territory now existing, or which may hereafter be created. . . .

That the naturalization jurisdiction of all courts herein specified, State, Territorial, and Federal shall extend only to aliens resident within the respective judicial districts of such courts.[24]

Laws affecting the Puerto Rican's civil and political rights were cautiously made because the Puerto Ricans, as a people, were of doubtful quality. The caution is aptly illustrated by President Taft's message to Congress on "Fiscal, Judicial, Military and Insular Affairs" in which he considered the failure to grant American citizenship to the Puerto Ricans their only grounds for dissatisfaction. "The bill conferring such citizenship," he reported, had passed the House of Representatives and was awaiting action in the Senate. In giving his support to the bill, he contended that "the demand for citizenship

[21] "Porto Rico and the Tariff," *Review of Reviews*, XXI (March 1900), 273.
[22] *Foreign Relations*, 1905, LIX.
[23] U. S., *Statutes at Large*, XXXIV, pt. 1: 596.
[24] *Ibid.*

is just, and that it is amply earned by sustained loyalty on the part
of the inhabitants of the island." The President was willing to give
his support to the cause of citizenship without the concomitant hope
of statehood. "It should be remembered," he urged, "that the demand must be, and in the minds of most Puerto Ricans is, entirely
disassociated from any thought of statehood. . . . No substantial approved public opinion in the United States or in Puerto Rico con-
templates statehood for the island as the ultimate form of relation
between us." He believed that "the aim to be striven for" was "the
fullest possible allowance of legal and fiscal self-government, with
American citizenship as the bond between" Puerto Rico and the
United States.[25]

DEMOCRATS AND PUERTO RICAN CITIZENSHIP

During fourteen years of Republican administration, American
citizenship for the Puerto Ricans was denied. When the Democrats
gained control of the House in 1912, they immediately started to act
on various proposals to give American citizenship to the Puerto
Ricans. A report on a bill to provide citizenship for the Puerto Ricans pointed out that under the Foraker Act of 1900 it was sometimes
argued that Puerto Ricans were citizens of the United States. The
basis of this argument was Section 1891 of the Revised Statutes which
declares that "the Constitution and all laws of the United States
which are not locally inapplicable shall have the same force and
effect within all the organized territories and in every territory hereafter organized or elsewhere within the United States." Some Americans, however, contended that in the meaning of Section 1891 the
Puerto Ricans were not citizens and "that the extension of the Constitution and laws over the island would not of itself have the effect
of constituting the inhabitants thereof citizens of the United States."
Many inhabitants of the states under the Constitution were not citizens, "as for instance Chinese, Indians, and others." Although the
argument in favor of Puerto Rican citizenship had been presented,
the Supreme Court had refused to "hold either that the Constitution
of the United States extends over the island of Puerto Rico in all respects and for all purposes, or that the inhabitants thereof are citizens

25 *House Document*, No. 1067, 62 Cong., 3 sess., p. 11.

of the United States." It was the purpose of the proposed bill to confer American citizenship upon the Puerto Ricans collectively, "subject only to the condition that each take the oath of allegiance and receive a certificate." Those who did not wish American citizenship would not be forced to become citizens.[26]

The debates in the House of Representatives on the question of American citizenship for the Puerto Ricans revolved around the racial questions. "Considering all the conditions with Haiti, Santo Domingo, Central America and elsewhere," Representative Joseph G. Cannon did not believe that the Puerto Ricans were competent for self-government. The United States already had her hands full in taking care of all the aforementioned countries. The Illinois congressman felt that the Puerto Ricans did not "understand, as we understand it, government of the people, and by the people," because they had a different language. He contended that "75 or 80 per cent of those people are mixed blood in part and are not the equal to the full-blooded Spaniard and not equal, in my judgment, to the unmixed African, and yet they were to be made citizens of the United States."

Representative James L. Slayden of Texas opposed the bill on grounds similar to those expressed by Representative Cannon. He took exception to the view that the hybrid, a cross between the blacks and whites or between the browns and whites, was "less well fitted for self-government than the full-blooded African Negro." According to his observations, the Negro had not shown any moderate success in government "hybrid or thoroughbred." Haiti was used as an example of an almost completely black country not able to govern itself successfully. Cuba and the Dominican Republic were cited as countries of hybrids unable to sustain republican forms of government. Slayden believed that the problem was not in language but in color, and that Representative Cannon would certainly have been more accurate if he had said that "as a whole, they have a different color." That would better have explained what he conceived to be their incapacity, for "color in this matter is more important than language." The representative declared that the climate and geography of Puerto Rico were not conducive to Anglo-Saxon government because "the Tropics seem to heat the blood while enervating the

[26] *Senate Report*, No. 920, 61 Cong., 3 sess., I, 1–3.

people who inhabit them." According to Slayden, the United States was already in "an awkward situation with reference to . . . Porto Rico . . . and every member of the House" knew it. They were charging the United States "with inconsistency and worse . . . they prove it." He continued, "They know that we tax them without permitting representation in our Congress, something that was a crime when done by the British Parliament, but which does not appear so wicked when we play the role of King George and his Parliamentarians." Representative Slayden concluded by saying that "many people in this country who want to sever the tie that binds us to tropical and alien people take that position, because they see in it danger for us." They agreed that people inhabiting lands within 20 degrees of the equator could "neither comprehend nor support representative government constructed on the Anglo-Saxon plan."

Representative James Mann of Illinois observed that if the Puerto Ricans were made citizens, they could "demand admission into the Union with greater force and with better logic." To admit into the Union as a state with the "deciding power in the Senate if not in the House" a people who were "somewhat . . . strange" to the internal problems of the United States and its civilization was not to be desired.[27]

Outside Congress influential persons expressed similar views to those expressed on the floor of the House. The former governor of Puerto Rico, R. H. Post, said, "The granting of citizenship to all of the inhabitants of Porto Rico, although but a step in the direction of complete assimilation, is still a step, and would tend to commit us to eventual statehood for Porto Rico, and might be construed as indicating that it was the policy of the United States that extraneous territory occupied by foreign races falling under the influence of the United States will eventually be admitted as sovereign States of the Union."[28]

Outlook in its editorial policy agreed that the Puerto Ricans had legitimate grievances but asserted, "Statehood would not be of advantage to the United States and of doubtful advantage to Porto

[27] *Congressional Record*, 62 Cong., 2 sess., XLVIII, pt. 3: 2796–98 (March 4, 1912).

[28] R. H. Post and W. H. Ward, "Porto Rico and the United States: Citizenship for the Porto Ricans," *Outlook*, XCIII (December 18, 1909), 860.

Rico."[29] It was opposed to blanket naturalization because "it puts Porto Rico in the line to become first an organized territory and eventually a State in the Union, and raises hope of this ultimate statehood . . . a consummation very undesirable both for them and for us. . . ."[30]

William Hayes Ward, editor of the *Independent*, wrote that he could not sympathize with a nation "which demands a special racial," intellectual, or educational "standard for citizenship or the ballot." The doctrine was aristocratic, and full democracy was "safer than aristocracy" since democracy always had the future. "Give the ballot to the ignorant and you will educate them, for you will have to. The ballot to the negro in the South gave the South the public school system, and so justified all the risk we took in the act." Ward supported unconditional statehood for Puerto Rico.[31]

Supporters of the bill, such as Representative Henry A. Cooper of Wisconsin, believed that the people of Puerto Rico were civilized and entitled to citizenship in the United States. As evidence of their civilization, Cooper pointed to the fact that they voluntarily freed their slaves, taxing themselves $30,000,000 to compensate the owners. They were entitled to citizenship because under the Constitution the United States could not hold people in subjection to its laws for an indefinite period unless they were citizens. Since the United States was committed to hold Puerto Rico forever because of the Panama Canal, citizenship was the only logical status for the inhabitants of the island.

Representative Elmer A. Morse, also of Wisconsin, noted that the Negro population was not much larger, if any, "in Puerto Rico than in the great State of South Carolina." It was his belief that "while the quality of citizenship" was not as high as it should be, the people should be given the privilege of American citizenship.[32]

The Senate failed to act on this bill in 1912. In 1913 Resident Commissioner Louis Munoz Rivera observed, "My countrymen, having waited since 1898 for a measure of absolute and ample self-government, do expect today more than ever before that their hopes

[29] "Porto Rico's Grievance," *Outlook*, XCIX (November 8, 1911), 643–44.
[30] "Blanket Naturalization for Porto Rico," *Outlook*, XCV (June 11, 1910), 273.
[31] Post and Ward, "Porto Rico and the United States," *op. cit.*, p. 862.
[32] *Congressional Record*, 62 Cong., 2 sess., XLVIII, pt. 3: 2796–99 (March 4, 1912).

will soon be realized, Congress granting them American citizenship together with a law creating two elective houses, and investing them, through their representatives in both chambers, with power to make their laws and to regulate all their local matters."[33]

It was with a degree of renewed hope that the Puerto Ricans welcomed the success of the Democrats at the polls in 1912. Democratic control of Congress and the Executive Department suggested that the concept of democratic expansion, long advocated by the party, would be applied to Puerto Rico.

President-elect Woodrow Wilson, seemed to agree with the resident commissioner when he said, "No doubt we shall successfully enough bind Porto Rico . . . to ourselves by ties of justice and interest and affection. . . . We can satisfy the obligation of generous justice toward the people of Porto Rico by giving them ample and familiar rights and privileges accorded our own citizens in our own territories. . . ."[34]

The Congress has never been noted for haste in its actions on civil and political rights, and Puerto Rican citizenship was no exception. When Congress took up the question of civil government for Puerto Rico, it was acting to replace a fourteen-year-old "Act Temporarily to Provide Revenue and Civil Government for Porto Rico and for Other Purposes."[35] Serious debate on the bill, however, was not begun until 1916. Resident Commissioner Rivera, speaking in support of the citizenship bill before the House of Representatives, observed that the Republican party by decreeing independence for Cuba had gained glory for itself. The Democratic party was bound by the "principles written into its platforms and by recorded speeches of its leaders to decree liberty for Porto Rico." The bill under consideration could not "meet the earnest aspirations" of Puerto Ricans because it was "not a measure of self-government ample enough to solve definitely" the basic political problems or to match the national reputation of the United States—a reputation which had been established by "successful championship for liberty and justice throughout the world." From this viewpoint, the Puerto Ricans were willing to accept statehood as a step in the right direction and as "a reform

[33] *Ibid.*, 62 Cong., 3 sess., XLIX, pt. 5: 4662 (March 3, 1913).
[34] *Foreign Relations*, 1913, pp. xiii–xiv.
[35] *House Report*, No. 461, 63 Cong., 2 sess., pp. 1–2.

paving the way for others more acceptable and satisfactory," which should come later provided the Puerto Ricans could demonstrate the capacity to govern themselves. To that capacity it was his "pleasant duty to assure Congress that the Porto Ricans" would "endeavor to prove their intelligence, their patriotism and their full preparation to enjoy and exercise a democratic regime."

The commissioner supported the measure only because he felt that it was the best that could be hoped for at that time. It was his opinion that Puerto Rico deserved better treatment. He pointed out that the behavior of the Puerto Ricans in the past was a testimony in favor of good behavior in the future. In spite of the Latin blood that predominated, there had never been a revolution or "an attack against the majesty of law." There was not sufficient reason to justify "American statesmen in denying self-government" to Puerto Rico and thereby compromise the basic American principle of popular sovereignty:

> ... My countrymen ... refuse to accept a citizenship of an inferior order, a citizenship of the second class, which does not permit them to dispose of their own resources nor to live their own lives nor to send to this Capital their proportional representation. . . . Give us statehood and your glorious citizenship will be welcome to us and to our children. If you deny us statehood, we decline your citizenship, frankly, proudly, as befits a people who can be deprived of their civil liberties, but who, although deprived of their civil liberties, will preserve their conception of honor. . . .

Commissioner Rivera observed that the bill "authorized those who do not accept American citizenship to so declare before a court of justice, and thus retain Porto Rican citizenship." The bill further provided that "no person shall be allowed to register as a voter in Porto Rico who is not a citizen of the United States." Rivera objected to this provision:

> My compatriots are generously permitted to be citizens of the only country they possess, but they are eliminated from the body politic; the exercise of political rights is forbidden them; by a single stroke of the pen they are converted into pariahs and there is established in America on American soil, protected by the Monroe Doctrine, a division into castes like the Brahamans and Sudras of India. The Democratic platform of Kansas City declared 14 years ago, "A nation can not long endure half empire and half republic, and imperialism abroad will lead rapidly and irreparably to

despotism at home." These are not Porto Rican phrases reflecting our Latin impressionability; they are American phrases, reflecting the Anglo-Saxon spirit, calm in its attitude and jealous—very jealous—of its privileges.

Inquiring into some of the probable reasons why Puerto Rico had not been given self-government, he found it could not be the fact that two races coexised on the island of Puerto Rico because "in America more than ten states had a higher percentage of Negroes in their population than Porto Rico." It was not the lack of adequate numbers, for Puerto Rico was more populous than eighteen other states. After examining the probable reasons, he concluded that the reason behind the denial of self-government was based on the desire of office seekers "determined to report to their superiors that the Porto Ricans were unprepared for self-government."[36]

The resident commissioner could not conceive of a people being denied the rights of self-government on purely racial grounds. His efforts to compare the racial situation in Puerto Rico with the situation in several of the Southern states was not a valid comparison. In Puerto Rico there had been considerable racial interbreeding while in the United States this practice was kept at a minimum, and in many areas by law. The incorporation of a large population of mixed races was potentially dangerous to existing racial patterns in the United States.

The importance of these racial implications was pointed up by Representative Joseph Cannon, who felt that

when you talk about a people competent for self-government, certain things are to be taken into consideration. One is the racial question. . . .
Porto Rico is populated by a mixed race. About 30 per cent pure African. I was informed by the army officers when I was down there that when the census was taken every man that was a pure African was listed and counted as such, but that there was 75 to 80 per cent of the population that was pure African or had an African strain in their blood. . . . Will anybody say that I am abusing the African. I am not any more than I am abusing the Filipino or the Moros; and I am certainly not abusing the African in the United States. . . . But the Commissioner from Porto Rico said that this

[36] *Congressional Record,* 64 Cong., 1 sess., LIII, pt. 8: 7470–73 (May 5, 1916).

bill is not as liberal as he wanted it, and he hoped more and more would be given, and as I listened to his remarks I thought he was referring to Statehood. God forbid that in his time or my time, there should be statehood for Porto Rico as one of the United States.[37]

Cannon hoped that Puerto Rico would not be admitted to statehood within the next three generations because the "people of Porto Rico did not have the slightest conception of self-government." He would vote against the pending bill because in the two hundred or three hundred years that the British had been in Jamaica, where there was also a large percentage of African blood, they had not been able to prepare the natives for self-government. In the United States the situation was reversed, for there were "10,000,000 people lately enslaved, who have made very great progress, but they were in contact with 90,000,000 of people who have proved their competency for self-government of the Caucasian race. . . ."[38]

Commissioner Rivera replied that Puerto Rico

deprived of its national sovereignty depends upon the generosity and chivalry of the American lawmakers. . . . It is very unfortunate that a Porto Rican is obliged to hear on this floor remarks offensive to the dignity of his native land. . . . It is not our fault that we are compelled to come here and ask for the enactment of legislation, of a constitution, which, should be our undeniable right to make, according to American principles ourselves. I must conclude, declaring emphatically that I am as proud to be Porto Rican as the gentleman from Illinois is proud of being an Illinoisan, and as every gentleman on this floor is proud to be an American.[39]

Representative Simeon D. Fess of Ohio saw in the Puerto Rican bill an attempt to do for Puerto Rico something that had not been done previously by Anglo-Saxons for non-Anglo-Saxons—giving them "the best form of local government" that the United States could outline for them and at the same time giving them United States citizenship.

The literacy test requirement in this bill would have disfranchised

---

[37] *Ibid.*, pt. 14: 1036 (May 5, 1916).
[38] *Ibid.*, pt. 9: 8458 (May 22, 1916).
[39] *Ibid.*, pt. 8: 7484 (May 5, 1916).

70 percent of the men in Puerto Rico over twenty-one years of age. (Under the Spanish the island had enjoyed universal manhood suffrage.) The measure was proposed by the Democrats, but also met with the approval of the Republicans. Representative Clarence B. Miller of Minnesota in alluding to its provisions observed that "for once the Democrats and Republicans of the House unite in looking facts in the face and acting intelligently in reference to them."[40]

In the Senate, John F. Shaforth of Colorado, who was charged with the bill, implied that the voting rights of the Puerto Ricans were conditioned by race. Puerto Rico had a total population of 1,118,012. The white population was 732,555. The mulatto population was 335,192 and the black population was 50,245. He stated that, in view of the provisions which had been adopted in the bill concerning those who could vote, "it may be pertinent . . . that 79.9 per cent of the population of Porto Rico live on farms or are a rural population, and of this number nearly 80 per cent are white." Through the literacy test and property qualifications (another requirement the Spanish had never imposed) incorporated into the bill, whites were at an advantage in getting the franchise in Puerto Rico.

"So far as I am personally concerned," Senator Vardaman stated, "I really think it is a misfortune for the United States to take that class of people into the body politic. They will never, no, not in a thousand years, understand the genius of our government or share our ideals of government. . . . I really had rather they would not become citizens of the United States. I think we have enough of that element in the body politic already to menace the nation with mongrelization. . . ." The senator from Mississippi was aware that some Puerto Ricans preferred independence to second-class citizenship. He affirmed that while the Puerto Ricans pleaded for independence they recognized "the fact, which any well-informed man who understands the Anglo-Saxon disposition in dealing with subject provinces will recognize, that independence is impossible, and since independence is not going to be given them, the majority of them expressed a desire to come in under the terms of this bill." Under these circumstances the bill passed, imposing on the Puerto Ricans a system

[40] Ibid., p. 7474 (May 5, 1916). See House Report, No. 461, 63 Cong., 2 sess., p. 2.

of government less democratic than the government previously allowed by autocratic Spain.[41]

In 1928 hearings were held before the Committee on Insular Affairs on a bill to provide for the popular election of the governor of Puerto Rico and for other purposes. The governor of Puerto Rico, R. H. Post, assumed this was a step toward statehood and opposed the bill more as a citizen of New York than as a friend of Puerto Rico. He considered it unwise to admit eight or ten congressmen and two senators to participate in the government of the United States "until such time as the Porto Ricans have demonstrated a real affection" for the United States. Statehood should depend also upon a real knowledge and appreciation of American institutions. It was "absurd to say that a people are unfit to govern themselves and yet invite them to come and govern us." Since the Puerto Ricans were more concerned about their own little island than about the United States, it would not be wise to give them statehood. "We have seen in recent years situations in the United States Senate where the welfare, almost the very existence, of this country depended upon the vote of one or two members, and we are not in a position to admit into that body two senators whose primary allegiance would be to their island and whose sympathies and prejudices are not our own."

Governor Post could not believe that the Puerto Ricans who were outside the continent could be Americanized, inasmuch as individual foreigners who "enter into American communities and mingle into everyday life with the American population" had failed in that achievement. It would be too much to expect "an alien people, speaking a foreign tongue, separated by geographical, traditional, and racial bariers from the American continent to succeed where the foreign colonies of New York, Boston, and Chicago have failed."[42] The persistence of this concept is shown by a 1963 syndicated article by Walter Lippman, entitled "Free Associated State." The columnist writes:

[41] *Congressional Record*, 64 Cong., 2 sess., LIV, pt. 2: 1325 (January 13, 1917); pt. 3: 2250–51 (January 30, 1917).
[42] *Hearings*, Committee on Insular Affairs, House, 70 Cong., 1 sess., H. R. 12173 and H. R. 6047, a bill to amend the Organic Act of Porto Rico. Approved March 2, 1917.

. . . But the fact of the matter is that the prospects of the United States Congress admitting Puerto Rico as a state are virtually nil.

For one thing, Puerto Rico as a state would be entitled to two senators and six representatives, which would give it more voting power in the House of Representatives than 23 of the existing states. . . .

It is hard to imagine what consideration would induce the Congress to give such political power inside the United States to what is in fact a foreign people speaking a foreign language and living under quite different social institutions. . . .[43]

Americans in positions to influence or to establish policy were not very generous in giving to the Puerto Ricans rights usually given to Americans. For the first third of the twentieth century they rationalized the inconsistency of their treatment of the Puerto Ricans on the basis of cultural differences. In the final analysis, race emerged as the determining factor in establishing policy. That policy assumed that the Puerto Ricans were radically different from the Anglo-Saxons and were unassimilable into the American body politic. To the Puerto Ricans, the frustrations caused by this policy created a reciprocal dislike for Americans who gave out their culture and democracy in "a most patronizing manner."[44] America's treatment of Puerto Rico was observed in Latin America and had some effect on attitudes toward the United States. According to one observer, the American treatment of Puerto Rico resulted from the concept of harmonious racial interbreeding brought by the Spanish to their American colonies, a concept completely alien to Anglo-Saxons. The term *Latin America* connoted cultural fraternity, and this did not serve to weaken the wall separating the United Sates from Latin America in general and Puerto Rico in particular. The difference in concepts added new buttresses to the wall in the form of factors unassimilable for the United States and recalcitrant to all absorption.[45]

PUERTO RICO AND THE NEW DEAL

In 1932 the Democrats were returned to power in Congress and

[43] *Durham Morning Herald,* June 21, 1963.
[44] Mary Weld Coates, "What's the Matter in Puerto Rico?" *Current History,* XVI (April 1922), 114.
[45] Manuel Ugarte, "Dangers Latent in Our Latin American Policy," *Current History,* XXVI (September 1927), 897.

the executive branch of the government. Four years later Senator
Millard B. Tydings of Maryland began to campaign to do something
about Puerto Rico. He proposed a bill, "introduced with the support
of the administration," which would "give the people of Puerto Rico
the option of becoming independent as a result of a national referen-
dum in the island on the question whether they would rather continue under the American flag or have independence." There were
many reasons behind the bill's introduction according to the senator. It was in line with "present day American policy, Pan American
policy, the repeal of the Platt Amendment, Filipino independence,
and a wider measure of cooperation and democracy to people who
were associated with the United States and those who were also
under the American flag."[46]

The New Deal philosophy seemed to manifest a desire to qualify
the traditional policy in regard to the Caribbean possessions. The
role of race in this changed attitude was illustrated in hearings before the Senate Committee on Insular Affairs. Senator Tydings noted
that, in cases where people of differing linguistic and national deri-
vation settled in one spot without any intermingling of Anglo-
Saxons, there was, "even in spite of man's desire to be fair and just, a
natural reluctant to incorporate a new nationalistic or linguistic element into the community." In the case of the Puerto Ricans, the
United States was not willing to do the one thing they wanted, and
that was to "grant statehood." Tydings stated, "I am satisfied the
people of Puerto Rico would all be for statehood because it would
be so much better than what they have got, but Congress, in my
judgment, isn't going to be for statehood, so that question is out. You
are either going to stay like you are . . . or you are going to be independent. . . ."[47] The Maryland senator realized that in population and
territory, Puerto Rico was as large as some of the forty-eight states
on the mainland; he also realized that it was natural for the people of
Puerto Rico to "want to be made a state and have . . . Senators and

[46] *Congressional Record*, 74 Cong., 2 sess., LXXX, pt. 6: 5925 (April 23,
1936).
[47] *Hearings*, Committee on Territories and Insular Affairs, United States Senate, 78 Cong., 1 sess., S. 952. A bill to provide for the withdrawal of sovereignty
of the United States over the island of Puerto Rico and for the recognition of its
independence and so forth, pp. 76–137.

Congressmen . . . in the Federal Government." The senator did not
consider the desire on the part of the Puerto Ricans for these things
wrong, but observed, "I am just saying that I don't see, human nature
being what it is and conditions being what they are, where that is
going to happen." He asked Puerto Rican representatives before the
committee, "Do you want to keep on in this territorial status, knowing you won't get statehood in all probability? . . ."

Senator Tydings further acknowledged the effects of racism on the
United States policy toward Puerto Rico. "I know if we tell the truth
that the probability of Puerto Rico achieving a destiny which is
worthy of her background and her tradition and leadership at the
hands of a country whose basic ethnological, linguistic and racial ex-
plorations have often come into conflict with other culture is very
remote. . . ." Clarence Senior concurred, saying, "The different cultural background and language makes it inadvisable to allow the
Puerto Ricans equality with 'Anglo-Saxon' Americans. It is discouraging to find professed liberals using the racist arguments of Hitler
and the Ku Klux Klan. . . ."[48]

Thus, Puerto Rico remained an imperial possession throughout
the New Deal period.

On August 5, 1947, the Organic Act of Puerto Rico was amended
to allow the election of the governor of Puerto Rico by Puerto Ricans
who were citizens of the United States. The amended section read:

At the general election in 1948 and each such election quadrennially
thereafter the Governor of Puerto Rico shall be elected by the qualified
voters of Puerto Rico and shall hold office for a term of four years com-
mencing on the 2d day of January following the date of election and until
his successor is elected and qualified. No person shall be eligible to election as Governor unless at the time of election he is a citizen of the United
States, is at least thirty years of age, is able to read and write the English
language, and has been a bona fide resident of Puerto Rico during the
immediate preceding two years.[49]

In the fall of 1952 Congress approved the Constitution of the
Commonwealth of Puerto Rico,[50] which had been adopted by the peo-

[48] Clarence Senior, *Self-Determination for Puerto Rico*, pp. 19–20.
[49] U. S., *Statutes at Large*, LXI, pt. 1: 770–71.
[50] *Ibid.*, LXVI, 327.

ple of Puerto Rico on March 3, 1952. In this way, the assumption that Puerto Ricans were not competent to participate in the governing of Anglo-Saxons led to a relationship which avoided statehood and the concomitant admission of Puerto Rican representatives to the United States Congress.

VII

United States
Imperial Relations to Hispaniola

The island of Hispaniola[1] is located between Cuba and Puerto Rico. The western portion is occupied by the Republic of Haiti and guards the Windward Passage into the Caribbean Sea. The eastern two-thirds of the island is occupied by the Dominican Republic, which guards the Mona Passage into the Caribbean Sea. The geographical location of the island made it important in the American canal policy which began to manifest itself during the last third of the nineteenth century.

Historically, Hispaniola has played an important part in the political and economic history of the United States. Coupled with the other foreign islands of the West Indies, it figured in the colonial trade triangle and was one of the many causes leading up to the American Revolution.

Following the successful continental revolution, Haiti succeeded in gaining her independence from France in 1804. The relations of the United States with Hispaniola were conditioned from the first by the character of the population that inhabited and controlled the island after 1804, resulting in the United States withholding recognition of the Haitian republic until 1862. The existence of Haiti and the participation of representatives of the same racial characterics as those in Haiti at the Panama Congress in 1826 influenced America's attitude toward that congress.

Senator John McPherson Berrien of Georgia, in explaining why the United States should not be represented at the congress, con-

---

[1] Hispaniola is the name that will be used to refer to the island that includes the Republic of Haiti and the Dominican Republic.

tended that the Haitian government advocated a principle of universal emancipation. This was a danger to the islands of Cuba and Puerto Rico which the Republic could not tolerate. The United States, "with due regard to the safety of the Southern States," could not afford to see the islands pass into the hands of buccaneers, drunk with their newborn liberty. Berrien referred to the revolted slaves of Hispaniola "who, although years have passed away since they broke their fetters, have recently afforded the most decisive evidence of their incapacity for freedom." He saw in the Pan American Congress the danger that areas under the government of revolted slaves would define the relationship to exist between the United States and those countries. Since the officers of Haiti were Negroes and officers of many of the other Latin-American republics were mulattoes, very little support was given to the idea of sending delegates to the congress in Panama.[2]

During the years prior to the American Civil War, the Haitians were afraid of relations with the United States or any other country that had a white population. After 1844, when the Dominican Republic gained its independence, there ensued a period in which the mixed-blood, Spanish-speaking Dominicans feared conquest by the black, French-speaking Haitians. The Dominicans soon found that they could not command any more respect from the United States than the Haitian republic. The Dominicans could not ask for protection from the United States for fear that they would be annexed and slavery reintroduced. Nor could they stand alone for fear of reconquest by black Haiti. This situation led the Dominicans to seek protection from some European country, resulting in the annexation of the Dominican Republic to Spain in 1861. The annexation lasted until 1865, when the Dominicans again gained their independence. The annexation to Spain had been occasioned to prevent dominance by Haiti. In the following year, 1862, the United States recognized Haiti. The South was not in the Union to oppose the action.[3]

[2] Register of Debates in Congress, 1825–1826, Part I, Co., 285.
[3] Rayford W. Logan, The Diplomatic Relations of the United States with Haiti, 1776–1891 (Chapel Hill: University of North Carolina Press, 1941), p. 303. See also Bemis, A Diplomatic History of the United States, p. 395.

A treaty negotiated October 5, 1854, between the United States and the Dominican Republic was not ratified by the Dominican congress because of Article III, which reads as follows:

> The citizens of the contracting parties shall be permitted to enter, sojourn, domiciliate and reside in all parts whatsoever of the said territories, and to have and occupy warehouses provided they submit to the laws, as well general as special, relative to the rights of residing and traveling. . . .[4]

The Dominican congress alleged that this provision made Dominicans submit

> to the special laws which are in force in the several States of the Union, and these laws being so much at variance in different States, it is necessary, in order that there may be perfect reciprocity, that said article should be conceived in these terms, that all Dominicans, without any distinction of race or color, shall enjoy in all States of the American Union, the same equal rights and prerogatives, that citizens of those States enjoy in the Dominican Republic.[5]

The reason given for insisting on the above amendment was that there were states in the Union where all men were not equal before the law, "but where there is a race and branches of the same, which are entirely excepted." The Pierce administration refused to accept these conditions, and the revised treaty was never submitted to the Senate for ratification.

Following the Civil War, President Andrew Johnson saw in Hispaniola an opportunity for America to foster republican ideas as opposed to the monarchical principles practiced in Europe. Johnson decried the fact that the United States had not given support to her republican neighbors. With the idea of promoting these principles, he entered into negotiations for the purchase of the Danish Islands. It was his belief that national policy sanctioned the acquisition and annexation of adjacent insular communities, and that the United States would ultimately have to lend some help in solving the social and political problems of Hispaniola. President Johnson was satisfied

[4] *Diplomatic Correspondence of the United States, Inter-American Affairs, 1831–1860*, Doc. 2264, VI, 133.
[5] *Ibid.*, p. 152n.

that the time had arrived "when even so direct a proceeding as a proposition for the annexation of the two republics of the island of Santo Domingo would not only receive the consent of the people interested, but would also give satisfaction to all foreign nations."[6]

President Grant tried to carry into effect the principle of annexation outlined by Johnson but failed because of opposition in the Senate led by Charles Sumner of Massachusetts. "The acquisition of [Hispaniola]," Grant stated, "is desirable because of its geographical position. It commands the entrance to the Caribbean Sea and the Isthmus transit of commerce."He saw in the acquisition a cure for many of the hemispheric ills, ranging from supporting the Monroe Doctrine to making "slavery insupportable in Cuba and Porto Rico at once and ultimately so in Brazil." The acquisition would settle the conditions in Cuba and put an end to the conflict there. It was his belief that additional population from the United States could be introduced into the island, since it was sparsely populated and could support an additional population of at least 10,000,000 people.[7]

In 1871 President Grant sent a commission of inquiry to the Dominican Republic, which reported that there were possibly 207,000 inhabitants in that nation. According to the report, however, a figure of 150,000 would have been a more accurate figure. There were some colored migrants from the United States in the population. The remainder was made up of native Dominicans and a few European traders. The report stated that the Negro blood was preponderant in Haiti, but the African type was not common even there. White blood was preponderant in the Dominican Republic, "but pure whites in the popular sense of the word" were not numerous. The majority were a mixed race "much nearer white than black."[8]

This commission echoed the view of President Grant in its appeal to use the Dominican Republic as an example of liberty which would "by the inevitable laws of trade . . . make slave labor in the neighbor-

[6] James D. Richardson, *Messages and Papers of the Presidents, 1785–1905,* VI, 688–89.

[7] *Ibid.,* VII, 61–63.

[8] *Report of the United States Commission of Inquiry to Santo Domingo,* p. 14. It is interesting to note that this commission in explaining the decline of the white population in the Dominican Republic relative to the Negro population, did not use the concept of the "survival of the fittest" as it was subsequently used in the 1890s and early 1900s to explain the decrease in native populations relative to white in Cuba and Hawaii.

ing islands unprofitable and by the spread of its ideas render the whole slave and caste system odious."[9]

The history of Hispaniola has been one of turmoil and conflict since its earliest days. At the beginning of the twentieth century the Dominican Republic, plagued by financial difficulty and revolution, sought American protection.[10] In 1904 revolutions caused the government to submit to United States assistance in meeting its obligations to foreign creditors. The United States did so through an agreement between the Dominican government and the President of the United States. Not until 1907 was a formal treaty signed sanctioning the appointment of a receiver general of customs by the United States. The receiver general was to handle a sinking fund for the gradual paying off of the Dominican debt.[11]

The policy of aid to governments of the Caribbean area incapable of maintaining stable governments, the "Roosevelt Corollary to the Monroe Doctrine," among other things gave the United States an excuse to control strategic Caribbean areas without the danger of annexation.

The policy was developed through Roosevelt's experiences in Cuba and was expressed in his annual messages of 1904 and 1905. In these messages the President declared, "Any country whose people conduct themselves well can count upon our friendliness. If a nation shows it knows how to act with decency in industrial and political matters; if it keeps order and pays its obligations, it need fear no interference from the United States." However, wrongdoing or incapacity to maintain government according to "civilized society" would finally require "intervention by some civilized nation," and in the Western Hemisphere the United States could "not ignore its duty."[12]

In a letter to the Senate, Roosevelt showed his aversion to any plan which might lead to the annexation of Hispaniola. "Our position," he said, "is explicitly and unreservedly that under no circumstances do we intend to acquire territory in or possession of either

[9] *Ibid.*, p. 33.

[10] Bemis, *Latin American Policy of the United States*, p. 154.

[11] *Report of the Secretary of the Navy, 1920.* Report of Rear Admiral Snowden, military governor, pp. 331–32. Congress was concerned about the method used by the Executive Department to effect, without "the advice and consent of the Senate," an agreement that amounted to a treaty.

[12] Commager, *Documents of American History*, pp. 213–14.

Haiti or Santo Domingo . . . even if the two republics desired to become a part of the United States, the United Sates would certainly refuse its assent."[13]

Senator Francis G. Newlands, writing on the Dominican question in 1905, stated that he had substantially agreed with the view of President Roosevelt in 1896. It was his desire to let the Pan American Union bring about the desired stability, but to use unilateral intervention as a last resort. By the time of the Dominican crisis, he had changed his views. America's experiences in "Cuba, the Philippines and Panama had convinced" him that "however beneficent our purpose might be in the beginning, we were likely to be drifted, either by circumstances, self-interest or desire for military glory, into a policy which we would have repudiated at the start."

Newlands used the seizure of Panama as an illustration of what could occur in the situation in the Dominican Republic. He showed that what had started as aid to Cuba had ended with the subjugation of the Philippines. The contract for a railroad right of way in Panama led to Colombia's being "raped of her territory." These occurrences "might make the most ardent advocate of the moral duty of the United States hesitate regarding the innocent possession of the Dominican Custom-houses as a means of enabling San Domingo to settle with her creditors."

He referred to the undesirability of the population in Cuba, Hispaniola, and Puerto Rico. Without population, they would be exceedingly desirable because of their climate and soil. Hispaniola, he contended, was controlled by two so-called republics, Haiti and the Dominican Republic. Puerto Rico belonged to the United States, and Cuba was under a United States protectorate. Haiti was in a condition of unrest, and if the Dominican Republic drifted into the hands of the United States, she would likely follow. Such a development would add "over a million blacks" to the population of the United States, complicating an already difficult race problem. The Dominican Republic was, therefore, "undesirable; and we should be cautious in entering upon a policy which will ultimately make her a part of this country." However, Senator Newlands was not adverse to a protectorate over the whole island because of its location.

Reason for control could be found through consent or if domestic

[13] Richardson, *Messages and Papers*, X, 859.

revolutions made it necessary for "the United States in self-interest to intervene." Newlands advocated the use of the whole island of Hispaniola to solve the race problem in the United States. He believed "it might be possible . . . to adjust the race question in this country by providing for the gradual colonization of the blacks in the United States on these islands, under conditions as to individual proprietorship of land and industrial development. . . ." This proposal, if not a new approach, was an improvement on the old effort to colonize the Negro in Africa. It was his belief that the African experiment had failed because of distance and hardship. Hispaniola was "of unsurpassed fertility of soil and richness of resources, admirably adapted to the black race."

The senator from Nevada, pointing to the rapid increase of the Negro to a figure of 12,000,000 in a population of 80,000,000, feared that with increased education and a decrease in the death rate among Negroes, the race question would soon become a greater problem. He believed that if "the colonization of the negro is possible, it could not be accomplished under more favorable conditions, and . . . a policy could be inaugurated which would preserve this country for all time for the white race."[14]

AMERICAN ASSUMPTIONS

T. Lothrop Stoddard asserted that the bulk of the population of the Dominican Republic was mulatto, "a weak and degenerate stock." The people created from this Spanish-Negro cross lacked ambition and endurance "both physically and mentally." Only among the pure whites or pure blacks were good physical types found.[15]

Admiral Knapp explained the characteristics of the Haitian population as being "practically one of the Negro race," the overwhelming part of the population consisting of blacks, the descendants of slaves. The mulattoes were to be found in the ascendant class "which the ignorant black peasant distrusts and fears." The language of the masses was "creole patois, bastard French," and the culture was of a very

[14] Francis G. Newlands, "The San Domingo Question," *North American Review*, CLXXX (June 1905), 885–99.
[15] T. Lothrop Stoddard, "Santo Domingo: Our Unruly Ward," *Review of Reviews*, XLIX (June 1914), 731.

low type, which in remote places was "little removed from savagery." The ethical standards of the population of Haiti, according to the admiral, were "naturally low." There were many manifestations of these standards, one being the difficulty of arriving at the truth in any investigations concerning the Haitians. Even "in courts of law" witnesses could not be depended upon to tell the truth, reflecting the low standards of ethics. He observed that "men of known general probity will . . . show utter inability to appreciate the impropriety of acts regarding which an Anglo-Saxon would entertain no doubts. Men high in government places will agree to do one thing and then do the opposite." According to this report, the people were nominally Roman Catholic, but the Catholic faith was mixed with the religion brought from Africa, voodooism. This prevalent religion was essentially snake worship, which "in its extreme rites" required the "sacrifice of human beings and the drinking of their blood, and the eating of their flesh." Information received from Haitians themselves estimated that 95 percent of the population believed in voodooism to a greater or lesser extent.[16]

INTERVENTION IN THE DOMINICAN REPUBLIC

After 1908 unsettled conditions and a financial crisis in the Dominican Republic caused the government to appeal to the United States for help. The result was the sending of a commission to the Dominican Republic, which worked out a solution reconciling the factions. Bordas Valdes was elected president and had only served one year when revolutions again threatened, resulting in another call to Washington and reconciliation in the election of Juan Isidro Jiminez as president. A revolt of the minister of war resulted in the landing of United States Marines. Once order was restored, Dr. Francisco Henriquez y Carvajal was elected provisional president for six months. The United States stipulated as a condition for recognition of Dr. Henriquez's government the signing of a new treaty which would guarantee the continuance of peace and provide for the payment of Dominican obligations. Dr. Henriquez refused to submit to these terms. After over three months of resistance, the United States decided on November 29, 1916, to establish a military government to

[16] *Report of the Secretary of the Navy, 1920*, p. 222.

"carry out the terms of the existing treaty for the payment of public debt and for the establishment of peace throughout the Republic."[17]

The events leading up to the occupation of Haiti were similar to those in the Dominican Republic. According to W. P. Livingstone, the Haitians' fear of white domination may have saved Haiti from earlier control by the United States. He writes that the United States had broken the chain of foreign-held islands in the approach to South America by controlling Cuba and Puerto Rico. However, between the two was Hispaniola, which more than any other island in the area was the key to the Caribbean. The island from the social and political point of view was "practically derelict." Haiti's attitude toward foreigners was one of fear and hostility, causing the Haitians to "cut themselves off from the rest of mankind; they are careful not to give occasion to any power to interfere in their internal affairs, and they keep clear of foreign loans and other entanglements which might menace their autonomy." A Haitian president was quoted as having said that the Haitians would do nothing to bring the white man to Haiti because they knew that once he was there, their independence would be lost.[18]

In the case of the Dominican Republic, foreigners were invited into the country to help develop the country's resources. The Americans had taken advantage of this and consequently were the greatest single influence on the island. This influence led to the control of Dominican customs by the United States.

Livingstone conceded that there was a natural reluctance among the responsible classes of Americans "to bring a further batch of the colored race into a commonwealth already dominated and overshadowed by the Negro problem." A plan short of annexation was seen as the most satisfactory solution. Livingstone advanced the "sense of mission" concept to cover the ulterior desire to control the whole island. "The aim should be to place the country under the tutelage of a nation which, while refraining from exploiting it, would bring to bear upon the natives the outside influences that seem to be necessary to lead them into a higher existence." This ar-

[17] *Ibid.*, pp. 321–22.
[18] W. P. Livingstone, "A Caribbean Derelict," *North American Review*, CXCV (February 1912), 260–65.

rangement was similar to the use of the Platt Amendment in Cuba.[19] Charles F. Dole showed the closeness between Roosevelt's approach to the Dominican Republic and Wilson's approach to Haiti. Both Presidents used methods that were high-handed and undemocratic without debate and with an implied "contempt for colored people,"[20] a viewpoint supported by United States diplomatic correspondence with Haiti.[21]

AMERICAN RULE IN HAITI

An article which appeared in August, 1915, quoted Rear Admiral Caperton as explaining that the military occupation of Port-au-Prince was instigated "to re-establish peace and order. It has nothing to do with any diplomatic negotiations of the past or the future." Yet even a casual examination of the diplomatic correspondence prior to the intervention shows that the United States had tried to establish the kind of protectorate over Haiti as had already been established over the Dominican Republic. Haiti had refused; therefore, the latest revolution was used as a pretext to accomplish the desired goal. The article, quoting the Brooklyn Eagle, said that if President Gillaume Sam had asked for a protectorate, his term of office would have been longer. The most popular candidate among the Haitians, Dr. Ronsolvo Bobo, was not acceptable because of his opposition to American control.[22]

The Wilson administration seemed to be determined to teach the Haitians respect for the Anglo-Saxon's wishes, for once the entry was made, little in the way of respect for constitutional rights was accorded the Haitians. The administration's "short and abrupt" manner toward the Republic of Haiti suggested an attitude of "strict discipline for Haiti or perhaps corporal punishment." The United States submitted to General Sudre Dartiguenave and his council, the hand-picked puppets of the American occupation, a convention which left Haiti without sovereignty and gave the American employees

19 Ibid.
20 Charles F. Dole, "Letter on Haitian Occupation," Nation, CI (October 14, 1915), 462.
21 Foreign Relations for 1913 through 1915.
22 "Our Call to Duty in Haiti," Literary Digest, LI (August 14, 1915), 288.

the first claim on Haitian revenues. The provisions of the convention stipulated:

1. Haitian receivership of customs would be established under the control of Americans. This would include an American administrator-general of customs and an American collector in charge of the custom-house at each port.
2. A native Haitian rural and civic constabulary would be established under the control of marine corps officers.
3. The United States would be solely responsible for all expenditures of public monies, to the extent necessary to prevent speculation and safeguard the interest of the American people.
4. Haiti could not cede land to any nation other than the United States.
5. The revolutionary forces would be disarmed.
6. The convention would run for a period of ten years.

The United States also demanded that revenues collected by Americans temporarily in charge be distributed in the following order of precedence: to pay American employees, to settle Haitian bonds, and to defray expenditures for which appropriations were made under the budget.[23]

Despite the claim that the United States had only one purpose, "that is to help the Haitian people and prevent them from being exploited by irresponsible revolutionists," the United States had created a situation which allowed the exploitation and the subjugation of the Haitians by more experienced Americans. It should be noted that these arrangements were made in violation of the Haitian constitution.

The position to which the Haitians were forced to subscribe can be appreciated only by considering the fact that the secretary of the navy, Josephus Daniels, who was in charge of the occupation, had little respect for the dignity and worth of colored peoples. In addition, the navy and marine corps were staffed for the most part by

[23] "Strait-jacketing Haiti," *Literary Digest,* LI (September 4, 1915), 456. See also Commager, *Documents of American History,* p. 292.

Southerners, who were not noted for their love and respect for persons of color and who were subjecting Haiti to naval control without the consent of the Haitian people.

Perhaps there was a sense of resentment that there were black people who did not care for contact with the vaunted blessing of American control, manifested by Haiti's refusal to accept offers of help. Whatever the reason, the Wilson administration indicated that might was right and that even in his own country the black man had no rights which the Anglo-Saxon was bound to respect.

The Wilson administration's contempt for the Haitians was evident in the methods employed in extending American control over the black republic. "This method of negotiation," Secretary of State Robert Lansing wrote Wilson, "with our marines policing the Haytien capital, is high handed. It does not meet my sense of a nation's sovereign rights and is more or less an exercise of force and an invasion of Haytien independence. From a practical standpoint, however, I cannot but feel that it is the only thing to do if we are to cure the anarchy and disorder which prevails in that Republic."[24]

Evidently the election of Woodrow Wilson in 1912 had presaged Southern racism's ascension to the presidency. The assertion of the secretary of the navy, Josephus Daniels, that the South would not be satisfied until its position on race became the national position seemed to be valid.

Wilson implied that he was in complete accord with the Southern point of view at the University of North Carolina. "It is all very well to talk of detachment of view and of the effort to be national in spirit and in purpose, but a boy never gets over his boyhood, and never changes those subtle influences which have become a part of him, that were bred in him when he was a child. So I am obligated to say again and again, that the only place in the country, the only place in the world, where nothing has to be explained to me is in the South. . . . With all the old memories I know the region to which I naturally belong."[25]

Oswald Garrison Villard charged Wilson with carrying the color line into domestic and international politics. Villard said of Wilson,

[24] The Lansing Papers, Foreign Relations (1914–1920), II, 526.
[25] Josephus Daniels, The Wilson Era: Years of War and After, p. 609.

"Nowhere do we find any indication that his democracy is not strictly limited by the sex line and the color line."[26]

In drafting the treaty concerning Haiti's finances, economic development, and tranquility, the Haitians were asked to put their faith and trust in the good intentions of the United States. Here the failure of Americans to establish empathy with non-Anglo-Saxons was illustrated. The United States, a nation which had refused to give diplomatic recognition to Haiti for over half a century, now asked that nation to put its trust in its autocratic rule. Even the hand-picked puppets suspected and protested the conditions which the United States sought, for the treaty provisions robbed Haiti of her sovereignty and sanctioned a violation of the Haitian constitution. It was somewhat ironic that the United States, the great champion of constitutional government and self-determination for all peoples, should in the 140th year of her independence, crush the constitutional life out of this 111-year-old black republic.

Booker T. Washington saw the problem that would result from the occupation of Haiti and pleaded for patience on the part of the United States. He asked that the government institute a system of education for the people of the island republic. Seeing the difficulties that military control would bring, he urged that the class of white men sent to Haiti be carefully selected. "Here is the first experience American white people have had to live and work in a black man's country with black people." The American officials should know in advance that "every Haitian would rather be swept from the face of the earth than give up the independence won by their fathers." They should also know that the Haitians did not want to be dominated by the white man. They were a proud people; and "neither the average American white man, army officer, navy officer, white soldier, nor white marine is fitted to work with them." The racial lines drawn in the United States and other countries would not be tolerated in Haiti. Therefore, "the white men sent must be able to be white men in a black man's country if their work is to be fundamental."[27]

From the outset the Haitians attempted to receive the Americans as friends, but "the troops apparently treated the Haitians as ene-

[26] Jay D. Humes, *Oswald Garrison Villard, Liberal of the 1920's,* p. 82.
[27] Booker T. Washington, "Haiti and the United States," *Outlook,* CXI (November 17, 1915), 681.

mies." The islanders desired American protection through a treaty of friendship and commerce and an agreement for aid if needed.[28] Of course, they assumed that the United States would be willing to deal on equal basis with a republic consisting of blacks and mulattoes. If conditions in black Haiti were bad, the situation in the mulatto Dominican Republic was not much better. A letter from the Dominican Republic, dated October 27, 1916, a month before Admiral H. S. Knapp declared the island under military government, asserts that "for three months Americans have not paid the teachers nor the government employees, in accordance with the budget of the country." The United States was using a financial squeeze to force the Dominicans to accept the kind of conditions successfully concluded with its own representatives in Haiti. The writer appealed to the sense of fair play and conscience in asking whether Americans could not "say something in the [American] press" concerning conditions in the Dominican Republic, or bring to the attention of President Wilson the reality that the Dominicans were "a noble people and not a country of savages," as was believed in the United States.[29]

In an editorial, the *Nation* traced the whole Caribbean policy as stemming from Theodore Roosevelt's idea that "the United States should act as the Big Policeman of this hemisphere." Roosevelt liked to point to the Dominican Republic as an example of what could be done if his logic were applied. He held that the revolutions were caused by various interests trying to get control of the customs receipts. If the customs receipts were taken away, the causes of revolution would be removed. The *Nation* pointed out that in the case of the Dominican Republic the logic did not work, and the Wilson administration faced the problem of revolutions in that country.

The *Nation* cautioned the Wilson administration that it should not give real focus "to the protest of prominent Dominicans . . . that the United States has taken advantage of the ignorance of some of the members of the Dominican cabinet and of treachery of others to prepare a treaty nominally for the purpose of aiding the republic while in reality it in no way favors Santo Domingo, is in every respect beneficial to the United States and is a mask to the sinister design of

[28] "Editorial," *Outlook*, CXI, 648–49.
[29] "Santo Domingo on Our Hands," *Literary Digest*, LIII (December 23, 1916), 1646.

the American administration upon the national integrity of the Dominican Republic."[30]

THE RIGHTS OF SMALL, COLORED NATIONS

President Wilson stated at the meeting of peace delegates in Washington:

We believe these fundamental things: First, that every people has a right to choose the sovereignty under which they shall live. . . . Second, that small States of the world have a right to enjoy the same respect for their sovereignty and for their territorial integrity that great and powerful nations expect and insist upon. And third, that the world has a right to be free from every disturbance of its peace that has its origin in aggression and disregard of the rights of peoples and nations.

So sincerely do we believe in these things that I am sure that I speak the mind and wish of the people of America when I say that the United States is willing to become a partner in any feasible association of nations formed in order to realize these objects and make them secure against violation.[31]

President Wilson's pronouncements and actions at that time were in conflict. At this time Hispaniola was under the control of the United States. Were Wilson's principles of democracy limited by color?

The President dominated the sessions of the Peace Conference at Paris, where, despite being busy in "his efforts to make the world safe for democracy, he always found time to hear appeals for justice from oppressed nationalities in Europe." The President, though very sympathetic "to the interest of small European nationalities," apparently had no desire to do anything for oppressed colored people "near at home." It was observed that when the *de jure* president of the Dominican Republic went to Paris "expressly to present his country's case to Mr. Wilson, in expectation that the League of Nations might extend its benevolent supervision to the Western Hemisphere, Mr. Wilson could not find time to see him."[32]

[30] "Again the Big Policeman," *Nation*, XCIX (July 23, 1914), 91–92.
[31] *Congressional Record*, 64 Cong., 1 sess., LIII, pt. 14: 1069–70 (May 29, 1916).
[32] Kincheloe Robbins, "What Santo Domingo Wants," *Nation*, CX (March 6, 1920), 312–13.

Information concerning the American occupation of Hispaniola was difficult to obtain during the war years because of American preoccupation with the larger problems of saving Europe for democracy. Therefore, few articles on Haiti and the Dominican Republic appeared in leading publications during 1916 and 1917. The American Academy of Political and Social Science at its meeting in 1917 discussed the occupation of Hispaniola and was given adequate coverage by the press.

The discussions revealed that pacifism and militarism came to grips in several instances. Oswald Garrison Villard led the peace legions and was countered at every point by Theodore Marbury, former minister to Belgium. Villard openly attacked the diplomacy of the United States and called American intervention in Hispaniola a policy of conquest. "American authority as represented by Captain Harry S. Knapp of the United States Navy suppressed free speech and free press in the 'black republic'," he declared. "Any newspaper that dared to report the truth of the situation or opposed the Government under the occupation, was put out of business."[33]

The scarcity of news concerning the occupation was pointed up in October, 1919, when the *New York Times* wrote that during the war the American people had almost forgotten the existence of Haiti, even though American marines were keeping order in the "black republic," United States treasury officers were collecting Haitian revenues, and the people of Haiti were supposedly advancing towards self-government "under an American protectorate."[34]

After the initial period of excitement caused by the occupation of Haiti in 1915 and the establishment of military government in the Dominican Republic in 1916, most materials presented a favorable picture of the American occupation of the island.[35] In the fall of 1919, however, press releases and editorial comment became more critical of the occupation when it was learned that up to that time the occupation had been conducted under strict military censorship and that

[33] *New York Times*, April 22, 1917. See Oswald Garrison Villard, "The Rights of Small Nations in America: The Republics of the Caribbean," *The Annals*, LXXII (July 1917), 165–71.

[34] *New York Times*, October 26, 1919.

[35] "Wards of the United States: Notes on What Our Country Is Doing for Santo Domingo, Nicaragua, and Haiti," *National Geographic*, XXX (August 1916), 143.

the American press had not portrayed actual conditions in the island. The record of the United States in Hispaniola came under attack from Otto Schoenrich of New York, the former secretary to the minister of finance of the Dominican Republic. "The record made in Santo Domingo," he said, "must bring us deep disappointment, while the mess in Haiti must awaken feelings of resentment and shame." The chief fault was that the federal government had no regard for the inhabitants of this island. He alleged that in Haiti there were three governments: that of the Haitians, that of the American treaty officials, and that of the military occupation, adding that the "first was imprudent, the second inefficient, and the third indifferent. The *New York Times* took editorial exception to these charges.[36]

The presidential campaign of 1920 brought to light the situation in Hispaniola. Senator Warren G. Harding, the Republican candidate from Ohio, asserted that the Democratic vice-presidential candidate had admitted, even boasted, that he was associated with misdeeds in Haiti. Franklin D. Roosevelt was quoted as having said, "I have had something to do with running of a couple of little republics. The fact is, that I wrote Hayti's constitution myself, and if I do say it, I think it is a pretty good constitution." Harding considered this an official admission by the Democratic administration "of the rape of Santo Domingo."[37]

Later, in an effort to place blame for the situation in Haiti, Josephus Daniels gave some idea of the lack of respect held for the Haitians by the Wilson administration.

When the Navy was charged with the duty of keeping Haiti and Santo Domingo out of German hands and helping those nearby nations to get on their feet, Roosevelt spent some time in each country with the navy and marine officers charged with important duties there. He took so much interest in the road building and other improvements that for a long time the papers persisted in quoting Roosevelt as having said, "I wrote the Constitution of Haiti." Even President Harding quoted it, and then Franklin felt the time had come to deny that he had penned the imperialistic document. However, I think it was written in the State Department, which insisted on dominating Haiti after I had advised withdrawing the marines and letting Haitians govern themselves. The story of how General Smed-

[36] *New York Times*, May 21, 1920.
[37] *Ibid.*, September 18, 1920.

ley Butler, by a virtual shotgun party—which he didn't relish but—"orders is orders"—secured the adoption of the constitution and the putting in office of the hand-picked president at the direction of the State Department, smacked of imperialism. Butler said: "I won't say we put him in. The State Department might object. Anyway he was put in. . . ."[38]

Perhaps the attitude of the United States in regard to Hispaniola can be compared to the practice of congressmen from states where Negroes are denied the right to vote—congressmen who declare, and may even believe, that they represent all the people of their districts, but in reality, as their votes show, represent only the white people of those districts. Evidently Wilson's self-determination and democracy was meant "for whites only."

The *Nation* quoted Franklin D. Roosevelt as saying that the voting strength of the United States in the League of Nations was not one vote, but about twelve. The vice-presidential candidate was reported to have said in Butte, Montana, that President Wilson had "put one over" on the British prime minister because the United States had "the votes of Haiti, and Santo Domingo, Panama, Cuba, and Central American countries. . . . I had two of them myself, and now Secretary Daniels has them." The *Nation*, alluding to "the rape of Santo Domingo," noted that Wilson had "certainly succeeded in putting over the most complete sabotage of our ideals and traditions that this republic has suffered in one hundred and forty-four years of its national existence."[39] Harding's apology to Roosevelt did not minimize the interest that had been created in the American relations to the island.[40]

Dr. Francois Dalencour, a citizen of Haiti, discussing the efforts of Haitian journalists to discuss questions on misconduct in Haiti, said:

. . . Journalists striving to discuss these questions were put in prison. Faithful to his promise to protect the existing administration, Rear Admiral Caperton took no measures to maintain the freedom of the press. Confronted with many protests and much opposition, the Haitian Government then took the decision to dissolve the Parliament. This was done on April

[38] Daniels, *The Wilson Era*, p. 254.
[39] "Editorial," *Nation*, CXI (August 28, 1920), 231.
[40] *New York Times*, September 22, 1920. Harding apologized to Roosevelt for the attack made on Roosevelt and the Wilson administration on September 18, 1920.

4, 1916. Rear Admiral Caperton gave his consent to this disloyal and criminal proceeding. And this marked the beginning of Haitian hostility to America. How can a democratic country, white or negro, live without a Parliament in which the vital problems of a people are discussed?

This Haitian questioned the ratification of the new Haitian constitution in 1918 by a yes and no vote of the population. "How can public acts be ratified in a lump of people who have no power to discuss and examine them?" Haiti was in a state of anarchy, he declared, with the approval of American officials, "anarchy of legislation, anarchy of administration, with no parliament to discuss the living interest of its people, with no freedom of thought, of speech, of act, and deprived of justice and legality."[41]

His allegations were discredited in the fashion usually practiced in Southern areas of the United States, the testimony of a white witness refuting that of a Negro witness. *Current History Magazine* followed Dr. Dalencour's article with one by Major W. W. Buckly of the marine corps, who contended, "Before Admiral Caperton landed marines at Port-au-Prince in July, 1915, it was not safe for white men of any nationality to go into the interior, and even in coast towns it was well to be in touch with a legation. Now white men are seldom attacked even by bandits. The treaty with the United States does not please all parties, but the people are prospering under the American 'protectorate'."

News of the action of the marines brought charges of cruelty, and Harry A. Franck reported, "American marines largely made up of and officered by Southerners, opened fire with machine guns from airplanes upon defenseless Haitian villages, killing men, women and children in the open market places, for sport." According to this reporter, the casualty figures of three thousand blacks killed to only twelve marines were due to the difference in equipment, "rather than the boasted marksmanship of the marines." The reporter blamed Secretary Daniels and President Wilson for failing either to control the situation in the black republic or to take steps to change the prevailing low value placed on the lives of the natives by the forces of occupation.

[41] Dr. Francois Dalencour, "Haiti and the American Occupation," *Current History*, XI (October 1919), 547.

By 1920 the American people realized that they were not being informed of the actual conditions in Haiti. The *New York Times* suggested that a searching inquiry, exposing the true conditions in Haiti and fixing responsibility for military inefficiency and official mismanagement of government policy, was in order.[42]

The parallel situation in the Dominican Republic was being presented to the American people. The *Nation* published an article by the former Dominican minister plenipotentiary, who charged the American military government with ruling through "censorship and justice administered by officers of the army of occupation as a means of prevention and punishment." The function of the executive in the Dominican Republic was carried out by a rear admiral of the United States Navy. There were no constitutional restrictions on his actions. The legislative powers which were granted to the secretary of state under the Dominican constitution were exercised by seven navy and marine corps officers in conjunction with the rear admiral. This form of government was instituted without the consent of the Dominican people. Existing laws were amended, "new laws were promulgated which affected the moral and traditional culture of the country," and new taxes were created by this nonrepresentative body. The rigid censorship covered many injustices, including incompetence in office by Americans "with no technical knowledge" and sometimes with no greater capability than Dominicans. American soldiers were accused of burning women and children in homes that they had set afire, of hunting men through the streets like wild animals, and of using the water cure to get information. When the censorship was finally removed by military order on January 15, 1920, the Dominicans could not protest. For the "Catch-22" in that that order forbade any utterances against the United States.

The regulations for the censorship December 28, 1919, forbade the following publications: articles hostile to the government of the United States, its policies, and its functionaries, or that criticized them in such a way as to excite public unrest, disorder, or revolutions; publications that by their nature were hostile to the military government, its policies, and its functionaries, whether civilians or military, or that criticized them in such a way as to incite the masses to unrest,

[42] *New York Times*, October 15, 1920.

disorders, or revolutions; articles defaming, discrediting, or ridiculing the conduct of the government of the United States, or of the military government or its functionaries in such a way that its publication might cause disorders or revolt in the republic; articles pointing out actual conditions in the Dominican Republic in a way deemed manifestly unfair and untrue, and in terms that might provoke disorders among the masses.[43]

The foregoing indictment of the United States occupation was substantiated by Samuel Guy Inman, the executive secretary of the American section of the Committee on Cooperation in Latin America. Inman alleged that the Dominican Republic had been wholly under American rule since November 29, 1916. "The Government of Santo Domingo has been absolutely in the hands of the military forces of the United States," he wrote. "How absolutely one is not prepared to appreciate until one goes to the country. A Rear Admiral of the United States Navy is the President of the republic, and his cabinet is made up of officers of the United States Marine Corps. There is no semblance of a Dominican legislative body."

While publication of this information was denied in the United States until 1920, the facts were being circulated in the foreign press and could hardly be beneficial "to the high Pan-American interests to whose solidarity the Dominican Republic subscribed." Inman called for an investigation hoping that the exposure of the truth and the "punishment of the guilty would prove that the equitable spirit of the institutions of the United States has not been weakened in different climes to which the enterprises of that so often glorious flag have carried them, to cooperate with afflicted peoples, and not to cover miserable criminals with its glorious folds."[44]

The *Nation* believed that the opportunity was at hand for the "altruistic and constructive statesmen assembled in Washington to give some thought to Caribbean affairs" and suggested that they might "take up in a serious way the island of Haiti-Santo Domingo, where the right of the smaller peoples to self-determination has been

[43] Tulio M. Cestero, "American Rule in Santo Domingo," *Nation*, CXI (July 17, 1920), 81.
[44] Samuel Guy Inman, "American Occupation of Santo Domingo," *Current History*, XIII (December 1920), 501–506.

worked out according to the best American ideas by the Honorable Josephus Daniels, who is Czar of Haiti and Lord Protector of Santo Domingo, by virtue of his office as Secretary of the Navy." The article charged that "among those rights usually enjoyed by American citizens which do not follow the flag into the Caribbean are civil government, trial by duly constituted civil courts, freedom of the press, of speech, and of assemblage." In his capacity as American ruler over the whole island, Secretary Daniels "decided that those American constitutional privileges would only be abused by the dwellers on his Caribbean estates unless modified to suit the tropical environment. . . ." It was conceded that neither country was menaced by the German navy. Neither country was held as American territory "or occupied by the consent of the inhabitants." Neither country had been completely pacified by the United States Marine Corps.

According to the article, martial law in Hispaniola was not the best means of educating the citizens to the "responsibilities of representative government." How could the United States make the world safe for democracy while the secretary of the navy ruled "with absolute power and without consent of the governed"? Martial law had been proclaimed in Hispaniola and continued in force even though the courts of both countries were still intact. Under martial law a marine in Haiti could do no wrong to a native Haitian, and the same condition prevailed in the Dominican Republic.[45]

American lawmakers were concerned about Ireland and the rights of the Irish but showed little concern for their own Ireland. In a letter to the *Nation*, E. M. Agnew held that justice at home was as important as justice abroad, and, in referring to a telegram concerning Ireland sent to Lloyd George by eighty-eight congressmen, pointed out that of special note was the statement of profound conviction that further warlike acts should be avoided. These same congressmen did not enter a protest on behalf of the oppressed peoples of Hispaniola.[46] To have upheld "the spirit of American freedom" in this quarter would have been more appropriate.

The difficulty of getting the situation before an American public

[45] "America's Ireland: Haiti–Santo Domingo," *Nation*, CX (February 21, 1920), 231–33.
[46] *Nation*, CX (June 5, 1920), 765.

which, though not empathic to the situation of "inferior peoples," was quite concerned over dangerous precedents that might endanger their freedom, is illustrated by a Haitian editor, quoted by Samuel Guy Inman. "We want a civil government so that we can approach the men who govern us. You go to one of the military authorities; you know he is a very fine man, but he has a guard at the door who unceremoniously tells you to get out, and do it quick! Is it any wonder that the bandit situation does not improve under such treatment, or that the American soldier acts as he does under conditions described, when he has never had any training for administrative or democratizing work?"

Inman compared the situation in Haiti to the conditions which Taft had found in the Philippines. When Governor Taft talked about "our little brown brother," it took strong measures to repress the sarcasm of the soldiers who sang, "He may be a brother of William H. T. but he ain't no kin to me." The marines under Secretary Daniels and President Wilson had no one to tell them that the mulattoes of the Dominican Republic and the blacks of Haiti were their brothers. Daniels had said that they were neighbors, but he had never treated Negroes as neighbors in North Carolina. If the marines did not take him seriously, it was not to be wondered why. Inman believed that while the American people "are willing to pay no attention to our relations with small countries—naïvely supposing that because we are Americans our actions will always be altruistic and the world will recognize the fact—the world is continually talking about these things. It has taken a Presidential campaign to get a few columns into the newspapers about Santo Domingo and Haiti. . . ."[47]

According to L. S. Gannett, the Dominican Republic was conquered territory and had "less independence and fewer rights than had a Belgian under German occupation." The Dominican had no one to crusade for his rights because the great crusader for the rights of small nations was the oppressor of his country.

Some Americans may salve their colored consciences by the thought that Haitians are black, and that what we do to Haitians must therefore be

[47] Inman, "Hard Problem in Haiti," *Current History*, XIII (November 1920), 338–42.

discounted. [But since Dominicans are white,] we have not even the invalid excuse of color. We, the United States of America, who prate of democracy and republicanism and small nations and rights have driven out the lawful officials of the Dominican republic, dissolved the Congress, forbidden elections, ruled by martial law, and sanctioned atrocities—and with an ironic honesty unequaled even in Prussian annals we solemnly declare that we will continue to rule "in accordance with the Constitution and laws of the Republic of Santo Domingo in so far as these are not modified by military government."

Disregard for the rights of the Dominicans was shown in the reply of Admiral Snowden to the Dominican Consulting Board when he stated that "Santo Domingo would have a Congress," but he, the admiral, would be that congress.[48]

Charges of American misrule in the Dominican Republic were made by Archbishop Novel, head of the Church and at one time President of the Dominican Republic. His position and station was analagous to that "of Cardinal Mercier of Belgium, who complained with pathetic but heroic vehemence against the conduct and actions of Germans." Cardinal Mercier's plea was heard around the world, but little or nothing was "known about a similar plea made by the chief Prelate of Santo Domingo." Therefore, the State Department could affirm that "ninety per cent of the people of Santo Domingo favor the American occupation," and only a few politicians would take issue with their pronouncement.[49]

Felix Frankfurter wrote that the American occupation of Haiti was the same old story of temporary intervention to restore order "ripening by steady stages into effectual annexation; it was the story of Great Britain, France, Italy, Belgium, and Portugal in Africa, of American enterprise in Panama, Santo Domingo, Nicaragua and Haiti." It was also an "exploitation of and brutality towards the 'inferior race' and degradation of the 'superior race'."[50]

[48] L. S. Gannett, "The Conquest of Santo Domingo," Nation, CXI (July 17, 1920), 64–65.
[49] William E. Pulliam, "Troubles of a Benevolent Despot," Oulook, CXXVI (December 29, 1920), 758–59.
[50] Felix Frankfurter, "Haiti and Intervention," New Republic, XXV (December 15, 1920), 72.

In response to press disclosures about conditions in the black republics, Secretary Daniels ordered Admiral Knapp to make a complete report. The report contained stereotype concepts of the Negro at home and abroad and absolved the occupation forces of all wrongdoing. The Haitians were predictably described as savages, liars, voodoo worshipers, and cannibals. Admiral Knapp, who was personally acquainted with the marine corps officers in charge of the occupation, said, "From intimate personal acquaintance with the senior officers . . . I know that they have done their duty with earnest and prime desire of furthering the well-being of the Haitian people, and that none more greater regrets mistakes or more heartily condemns the few cases of improper conduct on the part of juniors than these same high-minded American officers and gentlemen."

The main excuse offered for mistakes made by occupation forces concerning the life, liberty, and property of men of color was that the soldiers' duty was trying in itself, performed under trying conditions "in a backward country among backward people." Notwithstanding their mistakes, the occupational forces had performed "with a cheerfulness and altruistic spirit that deserved the highest praise."

In his report Admiral Knapp openly admitted that Haiti was run by a puppet government and that the United States for two years prior to the intervention had tried, without success, to negotiate a treaty with the Haitian government similar to the one with the Dominican Republic, giving the United States the control of the customs. However, with the puppet government, success had been achieved. Knapp's report supported the contention of some observers that the occupation was naked, unrestrained power. In referring to the length of time it took to secure ratification of the treaty, the admiral stated that in the meantime "the forces of occupation were not idle. . . . Customs duties were collected under the direction of naval officers of the Pay Corps." The first steps were taken to organize the native constabulary and to "officer it from the Marine Corps." He might have added, "all without the consent of the Haitian people or even the approval of the United States puppets in Haiti." Just as Tillman had said, the black man had no rights worthy of respect by the Anglo-Saxon even in his own country. This section of the report concluded, "The receivership general was, in principle, a going concern when the treaty went into effect."

The occupation of Haiti according to Admiral Knapp was "a great experiment" which was a "matter of national importance to the United States, and so far as the naval service is concerned, of service pride." Almost as an afterthought, he added, "It is, of course, a further matter of doing the greatest possible good for Haiti."

In a statement to the press, the secretary of the navy reported that he had also ordered reports from Major General John A. Lejeune and General George Barnett, both marine corps officers, who would have reported any abuse of the natives by Americans. Therefore, it was logical to assume that they found no abuse.

In General Lejeune's report, Colonel John H. Russell, the officer in charge of the marines in Haiti, was praised as an able, just, and humane officer. Not only had he handled the bandit situation in a masterly manner, but he had issued "the most comprehensive instructions requiring a kindly treatment of the inhabitants by our men, and . . . the subordinate officers were enforcing his instructions in a legal and conscientious manner."[51] The general found that "there existed throughout Haiti a strong sentiment of gratitude to the marines for the work that they were doing for the welfare of the industrious, peaceful, and law-abiding Haitian people. . . ."

This logic did not take into consideration the fact that marine officers could not be expected to bring back an indictment of their own conduct. It is worthy of note that the orders to make the reports were not put in writing. General Lejeune refers to his "verbal orders," while General Barnett refers to his "oral orders."[52]

Admiral Snowden followed the same kind of logic in his report on the conditions in the Dominican Republic by asserting that the only opposition to the occupation was from bandits and that "95 per cent of the people are gratefully availing themselves of the peaceful opportunities to pursue their calling." The rest were revolutionary and grafting politicians incapable of any fruitful work. The military government changed the local government in the island republic so that the "semi-independent governors" were reduced to the "status of civil governors with very limited governmental functions. Those

[51] *Report of the Secretary of the Navy, Miscellaneous Reports, 1920*, pp. 222–42.

[52] See reports of Major-General John A. Lejeune and Brigadier General George Barnett, *ibid.*, pp. 241, 245.

loyal to the occupation were retained in office, and prominent public-spirited citizens were appointed to posts made vacant by the dismissal of unworthy ones."[53]

In 1920 H. J. Seligman wrote that after five years of violence in Haiti, "without sanction of international law or any law other than force," a period ensued in which "the military authorities [were] attempting to hush up what had been done. . . . The history of the American invasion of Haiti is only additional evidence that the United States is among those powers in whose international dealings democracy and freedom are mere words, and human lives negligible in the face of racial snobbery. . . . The five years of American occupation have served as a commentary upon the white civilization which still burns black men and women at the stake. . . .

"The prevailing attitude of mind among the men sent to assist Haiti has been such determined contempt for men of dark skins that decency has been almost out of the question. The American disease of color prejudice has raged virulently. . . ."

Seligman charged the United States with not being selective in sending officers to Haiti. Some officers were sent there with records of brutality gained at the expense of the natives in the Philippines. All that the United States had to show for its "indefensible invasion of a helpless country, after the professions of solicitude and good will which accompanied the crime" were military roads, a civil hospital in Port-au-Prince, and the Haitian Gendarmerie. No beginning had been made to educate the Haitian people or to send "civil doctors or even military doctors to minister to the needs of diseased Haitians in the interior." Seligman asserted, "These sins of commission and omission are attributable less to the men confronted with overwork and the difficulties . . . in Haiti than to an administration, and especially a State Department ready to countenance armed invasion without plan and to undertake, by a nation which has signally failed in administering its own color problem, the government of a black republic."[54]

The truth behind Seligman's arguments was amply illustrated by the lynching of three Negroes in Duluth, Minnesota. The *Nation*

[53] Report of Rear Admiral Thomas Snowden, U.S.N., *ibid.*, pp. 321–22.

[54] H. J. Seligman, "The Conquest of Haiti," *Nation*, CXI (July 10, 1920), 35–36.

stated that this established the furthest point north that race hatred had penetrated.

The lynchings presented no unusual circumstances. "There was the customary deliberateness which refutes the extenuation of a citizenry 'blinded by passion'." Citizens were recruited with the help of an automobile which paraded through the main streets for two hours. The attack on the police station was followed by a "trial" by the "infuriated" mob. There was the usual "inadequacy of police who, though outnumbered, could have checked the crowd but for specific instructions not to use revolvers: Finally, there was the customary innocence of at least one, if not all of the victims." The *Nation* concluded that it was not only Duluth, but "our entire country which continues to besmirch itself with atrocities that would shame the Turk. . . . It has become a compelling duty for all Americans—especially to be commended to those who are agitating in behalf of oppressed nationalities in other parts of the world—to end our own infamy."[55]

Supporting the contention that race hatred was a national problem, the *Literary Digest*[56] showed that as a result of race riots in 1917 at East St. Louis, Illinois, a Northern city, 125 persons were killed. In Washington, D. C., seven were killed and scores injured in July, 1919; beginning July 26, 1919, in Chicago thirty-eight persons were killed and five hundred wounded. On October 2, 1919, thirty persons were killed and one hundred were wounded in street fighting in Omaha, Nebraska. All of the cities named were outside of the South.

The Tulsa riot of 1921 resulted in more than twenty Negro and ten white deaths. More than two hundred of both races were injured, and five thousand Negroes were burned out of their homes by a white mob. The "crime" committed by the Negroes is described in the *Black Dispatch* of Oklahoma City: "Whatever the issue, the fact remains undisputed that in Tulsa, in a white man's country, the negroes were attempting to uphold the law and white men were attempting to destroy it." A *New York World* editorial alleged that "in vast sections of the country, government has a habit of ceasing to exist where the legal rights of the negro are concerned."

[55] "Editorial," *Nation*, CX (June 26, 1920), 841.

[56] "Mob Fury and Race Hatred as a National Danger," *Literary Digest*, LXIX (June 18, 1921), 8–9.

If these were the prevailing conditions at home under the Constitution, where civil law prevailed, what rights could a black man expect in an insular possession, under military law and without the Constitution?

The National Association for the Advancement of Colored People endeavored to correct the situation at home and abroad. In questioning the candidates for the presidency in 1920, it asked, among other things, would the candidates "favor the enactment of laws making lynching a federal offense?" What were their attitudes "towards the the disfranchisement of Americans of Negro descent?" Would they advocate that Congress enforce the Fourteenth Amendment and "reduce the representation of states which disfranchise their citizens?" Would they work to "bring about the abolition of 'Jim Crow' cars in interstate traffic" and "withdraw armed or other interference with the independence of Haiti?" If the prospective candidates' responses were any indication of their respect for the Negro voter—then that respect was nugatory, for none of the candidates made any commitments.[57]

The *Nation* seems to have been the forum which the NAACP used to call attention to the injustices of the occupation of Hispaniola. In a series of articles published in the *Nation*, James Weldon Johnson, on the basis of an NAACP report, accused the United States of failing to provide a system of public education in Haiti, which had been the custom in other countries where control had been established—Puerto Rico, Cuba, and the Philippines. In most instances youths selected from "these countries were taken and sent to the United States for training in order that they might return and be better teachers, and American teachers were sent to these islands in exchange." The American occupation in Haiti had not advanced public education a single step. "Not a single Haitian youth has been sent to the United States for training as a teacher, nor has a single American teacher, white or colored, been sent to Haiti."

Johnson, in referring to the Haitian national guard, alleged that the pledge to replace the officers by capable Haitians had not been

[57] W. E. B. Du Bois, "The Republicans and the Black Voter," *Nation*, CX (June 5, 1920), 757–58.

kept and had, like others, become a mere scrap of paper. It was noted that "graduates of the famous French Military Academy of St. Cyr, men who have actually qualified for commissions in the French Army, are denied the opportunity to fill even lesser commissions in the Haitian Gendarmerie, although such men, in addition to their pre-eminent qualifications of training, would because of their understanding of local conditions and their complete familiarity with the ways of their own country make ideal guardians of the peace."

Johnson found that the most serious aspect of American brutality in Haiti was not to be found in individual cases of cruelty, numerous and inexcusable though they were, but in the American attitude which was illustrated by the American officer who said, "The trouble with this whole business is that these people with a little money and education think they are as good as we are." Herein was the keynote to the problem; American racism was being exported to Haiti, planting a feeling of caste and color prejudice where it had never existed before.[58]

Johnson saw Haiti as a "spoilsman's paradise," where several hundred American civilian "placeholders" could find the "veritable promised land of 'jobs for deserving Democrats'." The majority of these were Southerners. The head of the customs service had formerly held a job as clerk of one of the parishes of Louisiana, and his second in command had served as deputy collector of customs at Pascagoula, Mississippi, a city with a population of 3,379. Many of the officers of the marine corps were of the same caliber as the civilian "placeholders." They usually took their wives and families to Haiti. Those at Port-au-Prince lived in beautiful villas. Marine and civilian families who were unable to have servants in the United States had "half a dozen servants" in Haiti. All the heads of departments in Haiti had automobiles "furnished at the expense of the Haitian government." Members of the Haitian cabinet, "who are theoretically above them," had no such luxury.[59]

The *Nation's* editorial recitation of the known facts in the occupation of Hispaniola constituted a damning indictment. "Every prin-

[58] James Weldon Johnson, "Self-Determining Haiti" (four articles reprinted from the *Nation* embodying a report of an investigation made for the NAACP), pp. 16–18.

[59] Johnson, "Self-Determining Haiti," *Nation*, CXI (August 28, 1920), 236–38.

ciple painstakingly established by the makers of our history, which has given us a just pride and thrill to be called American, has after especial elaboration and sublimation by President Wilson himself been scrapped, making American pretensions and good faith a mockery throughout the world. . . ."

This was an issue that the opposition could use in the campaign, though the *Nation* wondered if the Republicans had sufficiently clean skirts to pose as the champions of liberty and freedom in the Caribbean. "Certainly there could be no more effective way of showing up the hollow sham embodied in the Wilson League—with its false promises of peace, self-determination, disarmament, universal justice —than by contrasting Wilsonian words about the promised world with Wilsonian deeds in a small section of it. . . ."[60]

The criticism of conditions in Hispaniola ultimately led to the passage of a resolution introduced by Senator Hiram W. Johnson of California, which authorized the Senate Committee on Foreign Relations "to investigate all circumstances attending the participation of Americans, either civilians or members of the military or naval establishments, in the governmental affairs of the Republics of Haiti and Santo Domingo."[61]

SENATORIAL INVESTIGATION

The initial information furnished by the campaign of 1920 and the American press focused interest upon the American occupation of Hispaniola. Many articles both favorable and unfavorable to the continued occupation appeared in leading journals and newspapers. Articles favorable to a continuation of the occupation generally alluded to the unselfish motives, the sense of mission and uplift that the marines were taking to the island. The dangers inherent in leaving the island to its inhabitants were also pointed up. These writers usually commended the navy and marines for their splendid work under difficult circumstances.[62]

Articles such as the *National Geographic's* were prejudiced against the Haitians, portraying only the benevolence of altruistic Americans.

60 "Editorial," *Nation*, CXI (August 28, 1920), 231.
61 *Congressional Record*, 66 Cong., 3 sess., LX, pt. 3: 1658 (January 19, 1921).
62 "Our Imperialist Propaganda—*The National Geographic's* Anti-Haitian Campaign," *Nation*, CXII (April 6, 1921), 508.

This type of propaganda persuaded Americans to think that whatever they did to "inferiors" was done with the highest motives in mind, though many times the facts showed just the opposite. This belief was a concept manifested in the Western European idea of extraterritoriality. In Hispaniola it led to the allegation that those who opposed the occupation were trying to destroy the good name of the navy and marine corps and that the natives were incapable of telling the truth; they were credited with telling the truth only when they said they wanted the occupation to continue.

The Haitian Patriotic Union charged that the revolution of July 28, 1915, "merely furnished a long-sought pretext for intervention," for the United States' interests were in no way imperiled. The union attributed the rise of "coco-ism"[63] to the brutalities inflicted upon the Haitian population by the marines. "Coco-ism" was not a crime but rather a revolt against an alien invasion. The union also charged that mismanagement of finances did not begin until the Americans took over the finances.

The *Nation* said that if the union's charges did not arouse the American people, "then its conscience is indeed dead." The editors could not believe that "all the professions of good faith, decency, fair play, all our great and honorable traditions upheld for nearly a century and a half" could be tossed aside so lightly. The Republic of Haiti was a small and inoffensive country, the second oldest in the hemisphere, which had abolished slavery fifty years ahead of the United States. Haiti had contributed to the cause of freedom for other Latin-American countries through aid to Bolívar while the United States stood aloof. The *Nation* held that "the facts could not be whitewashed . . . or lied away. . . ." The acid test was what action would be taken on behalf of the Haitians.[64]

Twenty-four American lawyers, representing both political parties, stated that the continued presence of United States military forces in Haiti after the disturbances of July, 1915, had quieted down was "violative of well-recognized American principles. The United States had violated principles of international law when the marines in 1915 seized the Haitian national funds." They concluded that the "impo-

[63] *Coco-ism*: Haitian banditry.
[64] "Haiti Speaks," *Nation*, CXII (May 18, 1921), 708.

sition and enforcement of martial law without a declaration of war by Congress and the actions of Admiral Caperton before the treaty was accepted by the Haitians" constituted a clear violation of international law and the Constitution. The method employed in Haiti to achieve the ratification and acceptance of a treaty formed in the United States, namely, "the direct use of military, financial, and political pressure, violates every command of fair and equal dealing between independent sovereign nations and of American professions of international good faith." The continuance of military forces in Haiti or the control of treaty officials "under cover of the treaty of September, 1915," was considered a "conscious and intentional participation in the original agression and coercion." Inasmuch as the existing government of Haiti was a puppet of the United States, unsupported by any elected Haitian representative since 1917, and since it was at the end of its term of office, "no negotiations should take place with such government which involve the future of Haiti" or which could in any material way affect Haiti's future.

Duties of a department of colonies assumed by the navy and conferred on it by executive action, according to these lawyers, were "unauthorized by Congress or by other sanction of law, and should be condemned as essentially illegal and as a usurpation of power." The group declared that the honor and good name of the United States, the sovereignty and liberty of Haiti, as well as the assurance of future amicable relations with Latin America required:

(a) The immediate abrogation by the United States of the treaty of 1915, unconditionally and with no qualifications.
(b) The holding of elections of representatives to the legislative bodies of Haiti and of a president by the free will of the people at an early date.
(c) The negotiation of a new treaty with a new Haitian administration for friendly cooperation between the United States and Haiti upon such terms as shall be mutually satisfactory to both countries and by methods that obtain between independent states.[65]

The charges made by native Haitians and substantiated by the twenty-four American lawyers had very little influence on the federal government.

[65] *Congressional Record,* 67 Cong., 2 sess., LXII, pt. 9: 8949 (June 19, 1922).

The *Literary Digest*, showing that disregard for the rights of the Haitians was a nonpartisan matter, reported that the Haitian delegates who charged the United States with misrule, according to the Indianapolis *Star* and the Nashville *Banner*, were "misled into believing that the new administration would welcome an opportunity to discredit the old one."[66]

The new secretary of the navy seemed to be of the opinion that nothing was to be done on behalf of the Haitians and Dominicans that would bring discredit to the occupying forces. He reassured Americans that conditions in Haiti were continuing to improve and that the natives were "returning to a peaceful and contented status." There was no serious bandit activity in Hispaniola according to his report. Secretary Edwin Denby's disbelief of the charges made by the Haitians was illustrated by the statement that he was "sick of having this thing recur, be disproved and recur again." His visit to Haiti had convinced him that "the presence of American marines in the country was still indispensable."[67]

The Senate committee investigating American naval administration in Hispaniola returned on December 21, 1921. A preliminary report to President Harding advised him to keep the United States Marines in the two republics for the present and exonerated the marines from charges of committing atrocities. Senator Medill McCormick of the committee urged a definite policy, "making it clear that annexation is not intended." There was no analysis of the charges of "brutality by the marines." Showing the nonpartisan nature of the committee, Senator Atlee Pomerene of Ohio, a Democrat, was quoted as saying that reports of atrocities were largely exaggerated. The Haitian–Santo Domingo Independence Society in New York, on learning of the report, stated that "the Committee had done irrevocable damage to the good name of the United States, especially in Latin America."[68]

Senator William King, Democrat of Utah, said that the President's

---

[66] "Haiti Charges Us with Misrule," *Literary Digest*, LXIX (June 18, 1921), 12.

[67] "Haiti's Indictment of Uncle Sam," *The Independent*, CV (May 21, 1921), 543.

[68] "Haiti," *Current History*, XV (February 1922), 868.

appointment of a high commissioner to Haiti[69] was not authorized because no such position existed, and the President could not create such a position without the consent of the Senate. He, therefore, introduced a resolution requesting the Committee on the Judiciary "to investigate the question as to the power of the President under the Constitution to appoint an Ambassador extraordinary to Haiti, without the advice and consent of the Senate in that behalf, and report their findings and opinion to the Senate."[70]

A formal reply was never received from the Judiciary Committee, but some members claimed that since General Russell was a personal representative of the President, the Senate had no authority to advise. Senator King disagreed. "The administration seems quite unconcerned about the wrong which has been done to the people of the helpless nations. Our Republican friends criticized the former administration—but only during the campaign—and they are now silent and apparently endorse the course of the last administration, and seem prepared to continue the wrongful and unlawful occupation of the two republics."[71]

When news of the appointment of General Russell as high commissioner was published, it brought an immediate reaction from the Haiti-Santo Domingo Independence Society. The society protested, as had Senator King, the executive creation of the office without the advice and consent of the Senate. It objected to the unusual powers which were given to the high commissioner, amounting to the complete control of Haiti. The society also pointed out that the appointment had been made before the report of the committee to investigate conditions in Hispaniola was complete and made to the Senate.

It was under General Russell that many of the abuses to the Haitian people had occurred. He was the only one of the commanding generals in Haiti that had not been called to testify before the Select Senate Committee. The Haiti–Santo Domingo Independence Society charged his administration with ten counts of unconstitutional and

---

[69] For the appointment of Brigadier General John H. Russell as high commissioner by President Harding, and subsequent directions of Haitian affairs through the State Department, see *Foreign Relations*, 1922, II, 461–560.

[70] *Congressional Record*, 67 Cong., 2 sess., LXII, pt. 4: 3943 (March 16, 1922).

[71] *Ibid.*, pt. 9: 8954 (June 19, 1922).

illegal conduct, among which was the "imposition upon the Haitian people by military force . . . the Constitution of 1918 by means of an illegal plebiscite, fraudulently carried out by the marines under his command."[72]

In addition, there were three provisions to which the Haitian people were unalterably opposed, and General Russell was the officer who had blocked their efforts to explain their real meaning to the State Department prior to their enforced adoption by the illegal "plebiscite." These three provisions were (1) the article granting to foreigners the same rights as Haitians in the courts; (2) the article granting to foreigners the right to own land; and (3) the special article ratifying and legalizing all the acts of the occupation and making it impossible for the government or people, collectively or individually, to secure reparation for injury or loss as a result of the invasion and occupation of Haiti, which was written into the Haitian constitution under the duress of marines under the command of General John H. Russell. This article reads as follows:

All the acts of the United States during its military occupation of Haiti are ratified and legalized.

No Haitian may be liable for civil or criminal suits for any act committed by virtue of the orders of the occupation or under its authority.

The acts of the court-martial of the occupation without in any way affecting the right of pardon will not be subject to revision. (The right of pardon was later taken over by the occupation.)

The acts of the Executive power (the President) up to the promulgation of the present Constitution are equally ratified and legalized.

As a result of his part in conducting the "plebiscite" under these conditions, and of the fact that he participated, as chief of the occupation, in the attempted coercion of the President of Haiti to secure special financial privileges for the National City Bank in 1920, Russell stood convicted, according to the testimony before the Special Senate Committee, of participation in acts of "International Brigandage."[73]

It seemed as though the general was being rewarded for having done a good job of disregarding the rights of the Haitians. The conduct of United States officials in Hispaniola showed their lack of re-

[72] *Ibid.*, pt. 4: 3467 (March 7, 1922).
[73] *Ibid.*

spect for peoples of color. Ernest H. Gruening, managing editor of the *Nation*, in summing up the indictment of the American activity in the island, argued that the cases of Haiti and the Dominican Republic were analogous:

> . . . In both instances the United States clearly desired to gain control of these republics. In both instances, when attempts to secure this by peaceable means failed, advantage was taken of internal disorder to land forces. Then what could not be obtained by peaceable means was sought by military pressure. In Haiti the United States was able to force through a treaty and today this treaty is held up as the sanction for all America's acts in that republic since. In Santo Domingo the treaty could not be forced through, and a ruthless destruction of all forms of Dominican self-government followed. These acts are indisputably proved by the record. They violate the Constitution of the United States. They violate every treaty involved. . . . While we were preparing to enter the struggle against Germany to oppose ruthless military conquest we were secretly practicing it. . . .[74]

The Select Senate Committee's final report on navy and marine activities in Hispaniola countered the above-mentioned charges by asserting that "the diplomatic representatives and naval forces of the United States made it possible for the Haitian Assembly to sit in security." The committee found that the pressure exerted by American representatives in the selection of the President of Haiti and in the ratification of the Constitution of 1915 was similar to pressure used on the Cuban government to secure the adoption of the Platt Amendment into the Cuban constitution.

The committee observed that there was little criticism of "the custom collections under American supervision, or of the American Receiver General." It was conceded that the financial adviser was the object of bitter attack, but this was due to personal relations with Haitian officials.

Senator George W. Norris of Nebraska speaking of Financial Adviser McLlhenny asserted that he "was an aristocrat . . . and the last man in the world to send . . . to Haiti to try to do business with the poor Haitians. It was about as bad as sending Elihu Root over to Russia to try to do business with the Socialists." The financial adviser

[74] Ernest H. Gruening, "Conquest of Haiti and Santo Domingo," *Current History*, XV (March 1922), 895–96.

did not allow civil service employees to ride at the same time on the elevator with him. He had also been criticized for withholding "under instructions from the Secretary of State" salaries of principal Haitian officials "as a measure of coercion." Senator Norris asked, "Does anyone think that kind of man is a pretty good fellow to deal with the ignorant Haitians?"[75]

To the charge of military oppression, the committee found that there were few complaints from 1915 to 1917 and only a few complaints in 1919. The complaints coincided with organized banditry, which became serious in 1918 but was almost completely suppressed in 1919. There was an estimate of 1,500 casualties, including some noncombatants. The killing of noncombatant bystanders was often unavoidable due to the necessity of attacking the bandits instantly when encountered. The committee found that in illegal executions, those who were killed had been caught bearing arms and had previously been imprisoned. It was decided to let the matter rest, for of the three Americans who could be held responsible "if the facts were judicially established, one was insane, one dead and the other had been discharged from the service."

In summarizing its findings, the committee found the accusations of military abuses "limited in point of time to a few months." Very few of the many Americans who served were accused. The others had restored order and had "generally won the confidence of the inhabitants." Only two cases of execution without trial were judicially determined. Eight other cases were not established clearly enough "to allow them to be regarded without much doubt as having occurred." The executions were, however, contrary to the policy of the brigade commanders. The implication in these findings was that responsibility could not be established. This was an exportation of the attitude which regarded lynching as illegal and contrary to Anglo-Saxon justice; but when practiced against Negroes, the guilty were seldom, if ever, brought to trial. Though the committee consisted of two Republicans and two Democrats, there was no dissenting view in the report. They found that charges of torture of Haitians by Americans were not substantiated. If it did exist, it was done by natives to natives without the knowledge of the American officers. The

[75] *Congressional Record,* 67 Cong., 2 sess., LXII, pt. 9: 8968–69 (June 19, 1922).

report affirmed that "mutilations have not been practiced by Americans." And any killing of civilians was "unavoidable, accidental, and not intentional." There was no undue severity or reckless treatment of natives. The committee was of the opinion that the investigations by naval authorities of the charges against members of the navy and marine corps displayed no desire to "shield any individual, but on the contrary, an intention to get the facts."

According to the report, the testimony of native witnesses was highly unreliable and their accusations were politically inspired. There was no fear in Haiti of repression, and since the Haitians had delayed in bringing the charges, the veracity of the charges was questionable. The committee concluded its investigation by expressing confidence in the ability of the Navy Department to conduct its own investigations.

Haitians and fair-minded Americans were not long in attacking the report. Professor Pierre Hudicourt, in "Haiti's Appeal to America," protested "with all the emphasis of which I am capable, in the name of your own immortal principles, against the decision rendered . . . by a Senatorial Commission which went to Haiti supposedly to investigate conditions there." He observed that the commission spent weeks in the United States listening to the testimony of marine officers and bankers interested in Haiti, but "when it came to hear the Haitian side . . . it spent . . . only five days on the island, of which but one and one-half was devoted to taking testimony. The rest of the time was spent in the company of the marine corps and of American investors." The committee's report recommended that "the marines stay in Haiti; that there be no abrogation of the convention; that a High Commissioner, who would be a virtual dictator, should coordinate the various civil and military functions"; and that a loan should be put through at once. "If this is 'establishment of a firm and stable government by the Haitian people'; I leave it to your sober judgment. . . . If the United States desires to annex Haiti, to make it an American colony, of which America's every single act affords convincing evidence, why not say so? Why continue the show and the hypocrisy of pretending against the will of the entire Haitian people, that you are there for philanthropic reasons. . . ."[76]

[76] *Ibid.*, pt. 7: 7222–24 (May 19, 1922).

In "Senator McCormick Sees It Through," the *Nation* said, "The Select Committee of the Senate which . . . has been investigating the American occupation of Haiti for a year has made its final report. It is the expected whitewash with trimmings." The racism displayed in the report "reveals the investigator's bias. Emphasis is placed on the unreliability of Haitian witnesses."[77]

The committee did not report on the Dominican Republic because the United States was preparing to withdraw from that republic. However, in the several days of hearings in the city of Santo Domingo, Helen Leschorn charged:

At one stage . . . Chairman McCormick, showing rare judgment and caution, indicated to the counsel of the Dominicans that it would be just as well if no more of that accusing evidence were given. Already an alarming effect of the at times unlistenable testimony of maimed natives on the Dominican auditors was noticeable. . . . The committee ended the hearings with astounding suddenness and left . . . three days earlier than the time that had been announced. . . . The evidence already in the record of this case puts Uncle Sam . . . on the defensive in a matter of our international relations and involving our integrity, and apparently the four members of the Senatorial committee realized that this investigation was developing in such a way that our country's honor was at stake.

Horace G. Knowles, formerly United States minister to the Dominican Republic, and counsel for the deposed government before the committee, "issued a statement denouncing the report, the very use for which was a plea made by the Navy Department in attempted defense of its actions."[78]

Senator Tasker L. Oddie of Ohio, trying to stem the criticism of the occupation, inserted in the *Record* an indoctrination report of the marine corps brigade commander of the marines in the Dominican Republic which was supposed to reflect the consideration of Americans for all classes of Dominicans. In reality, the report, "Indoctrination Anent Proper Attitude of Forces of Occupation Toward Dominican Government and People," showed the concepts of racial superiority which were indoctrinated into the marines. In part, it conceded that

[77] *Nation*, CXV (July 12, 1922), 32.
[78] Helen Leschorn, an American who for six years was private secretary to the attorney general of Porto Rico, "American Atrocities in the Dominican Republic," *Current History*, XV (April 1922), 881.

some of the criticism of the occupation came from "Dominican citizens of high standing who, although they [know] the United States is their friend, feel that their independency and sovereignty is so dear to them that they want to govern themselves, even though they cannot do it as well as we can." The marines were asked not to fight the Dominicans because they (the marines) should pride themselves on their superior intelligence.

Senator George W. Norris was greatly impressed with the still unrefuted charges and felt that "our government was engaged from the beginning in a program of deception. Instead of taking possession of the country, for which there might be some argument advanced, to develop it for the benefit of the people who were there . . . representatives of our Government engaged in little political tricks that would disgrace the worst political machine in America. It has been disclosed here that official telegrams from the Secretary of the Navy, advising the Admiral what to do, and coercion was used to compel the people of Haiti to adopt a certain course. . . ."[79]

The American people had established at home a relationship with peoples they considered inferior, a relationship which paralyzed their sensibilities as to justice and constitutional government. In dealing with similar peoples abroad, they practiced deception without the majority realizing that the Republic was approaching the nadir of national integrity. This degradation was manifestly shown in America's relations to Hispaniola.

"There can be no defense," Norris contended, "for that kind of conduct. It is no defense to say these people are barbarous, not fit for self-government, and, therefore, we must take charge of them. If for the sake of argument we admit that to be true, we at least ought to be fair enough to say to the world in truth what we are going to do instead of practicing deceptions at every step of the way that properly merits the criticism and condemnation of civilization."

An address to the secretary of state by the National Popular Government League of Washington, D.C., related the occupation of Hispaniola to the domestic race problem. "The race question," the address pointed out, "is sufficiently acute in the United States as to cause our Government to hesitate at any act which will accentuate it.

[79] *Congressional Record*, 67 Cong., 2 sess., LXII, pt. 9: 8956 (June 19, 1922).

Yet it is undeniable that the colored people throughout the United States are fully aware of what has happened in Haiti and resent it. . . ."[80]

Senator Borah commented, "It was said we went to Haiti for the purpose of restoring law and order." However, the things the United States had done since being in Haiti made it appear that the occupation would last forever. The Haitians had committed no offense against American citizens or American property. After eight years of American occupation, the self-proclaimed masters of self-government had failed to give the Haitians any form better than a military government, the "most arbitrary and cruel form of government that can be placed over a dependent people." It was only after the American occupation that the provision in the Haitian constitution which forbade the ownership of land by foreigners was forcibly changed. The new constitution adopted by the Haitians was forced upon them by 110,000,000 people with a great army and navy against 3,000,000 people without an army or navy."

To the argument that lives were in danger in Haiti, Senator Borah replied:

We talk . . . about the sacredness of life and the security of property in Haiti. Property was just as secure and life just as sacred in Haiti when we entered as it is in some parts of this country. . . . They were not as efficient and capable of self-government as we claim to be, and yet I venture to say that, compared in population, the sacredness of human life was just as thoroughly observed in that island . . . as it has been for months and months in some of the great cities of the United States. When you examine the record of robberies and murders in great cities, the lynchings and burnings in this country, and compare them with lawlessness in Haiti, you will find little excuse for our going to Haiti.[81]

Finding that appeals to decency, to fair play, to the Constitution, and to international law had little or no effect on his fellow senators, Utah's William King decided to try to awaken the American conscience by showing that imperialism in Hispaniola cost the American people great expenditures in taxes. His proviso to the naval appro-

[80] *Ibid.*, pp. 8969–70.
[81] *Ibid.*, p. 8942.

priation bill stated that "no part of the said amount shall be used for the purpose of maintaining or employing marines, either officers or enlisted men, in the Republic of Haiti or the Dominican Republic after June 30, 1923."[82]

The senator took a view consistent with basic American constitutional principles and considerate of the rights and privileges of men regardless of race. "The people of San Domingo and the people of Haiti," he maintained, "have the right to determine their own form of government. It is not our island. It is not under the American flag. It is inhabited by people of a different race, who have lived under different conditions from those prevailing in the United States. They did not invite us there. They do not want us there. It is their island, and the true government on the island ought to be controlled by the people themselves. . . ." If self-determination had any justification in "morals or in fact," now was time to apply it. The United States "with all its power, notwithstanding its altruism and its benevolent intentions, ought not to subject an alien people such as these to the control of the Government of the United States."[83]

EXPANSION IN THE CARIBBEAN

American treatment of the island inhabitants illustrated the difference between imperialism and expansion. In differentiating between the two concepts, William Bourke Cockran noted:

Expansion has always signified the extension of our institutions through enlargement of our frontiers. Imperialism is not the diffusion of American Constitutionalism over new lands, but the establishment in conquered territory by this government of another government, radically irreconcilable to the spirit of our own constitution and essentially hostile to it. Expansion, then, may be defined as the peaceful development of our political system through an increase in the area of the United States, and imperialism as the forcible exercise by our government in other countries of power denied to it at home. . . .[84]

---

[82] *Ibid.*, 67 Cong., 4 sess., LXIV, pt. 2: 1117 (December 30, 1922).
[83] *Ibid.*, p. 1131.
[84] William Bourke Cockran, *In the Name of Liberty*, p. 43.

The relationship between the United States and Hispaniola met every consideration in the foregoing definition of imperialism.

In 1926 a committee of six Americans representing several American organizations visited Haiti to study conditions in the Negro republic. The group drew conclusions and made recommendations. They alleged that the situation in Haiti was "what one would expect under existing conditions: a black people and white Americans; moreover, a black people, the more powerful group of whom are educated, cultured, ambitious, proud; the white Americans of the group particularly noted for its caste system—the military—and of the division of that group that prides itself on absolute exclusion of the black American...."[85]

One recommendation suggested that "United States officials in Haiti be scrupulous in showing a full official courtesy and respect to Haitians as would be shown under the same circumstances to people of the white race. ... Above all, in the selection of persons to be sent to Haiti ... an effort should be made" to send only those who, together with their families, would refuse to "draw the color line." It was "obviously impossible to have normal relations or fruitful co-operation with a population which is treated as of an inferior caste."[86]

Debate on Haiti continued throughout the 1920s. On October 31, 1929, a student strike in Haiti awakened the Executive Department to the fact that all was not well there. In a message to Congress on December 7, 1929, President Hoover explained that he was very much disturbed over the condition of internal affairs in the Republic of Haiti. He asked for authority to appoint a special commission to go there and study conditions. The President felt that the magnitude

[85] Emily Green Balch, *Occupied Haiti*, p. 116. The committee consisted of Charlotte Atwood, English teacher at Dunbar High School, Washington, D.C.; Tonia Barber, formerly a professor of geography at the University of Chicago; Emily Green Balch, member and vice president of the United States section of the International Executive Committee of the Women's International League for Peace and Freedom; Paul H. Douglas, professor of industrial relations at the University of Chicago, representing the Foreign Service Committee of the Society of Friends (Quakers); Mrs. Addie Hunton, president of the International Council of Women of the Darker Races; Mrs. J. Harold Watson, vice president of the National Association of Colored Women, representing the Fellowship of Reconciliation.
[86] *Ibid.*, p. 153.

of the disorders required that the commission be sent to Haiti without delay. He, therefore, requested Congress to authorize the immediate "sending of such a Commission and to appropriate for this purpose $50,000."[87]

In a letter to Secretary of State Henry L. Stimson, the President, in speaking of the proposed investigation of conditions in Haiti, stated that he thought that there would be a large "amount of Congressional attack and detailed complaint . . . coming forward during the next few months," and he was doubtful whether his administration "wants to pledge itself to undertake to take on the indefinite policies of the last administration in connection with this island."[88]

Senator Henrik Shipstead of Minnesota supported Hoover's request and accused the newspapers of carrying scare headlines about the terrible conditions. He expressed his desire to see the commission produce something other than the usual whitewash of "what has been going on in Haiti."[89]

Representative George Huddleston of Alabama observed that since additional marines were being sent to Haiti, and since the Americans had disarmed the Haitians, there would never be a battle between the marines and Haitians. There would only be a "massacre" limited by the ability of the Haitians to get out of the reach of the marines. Huddleston believed that the recent outbreak in Haiti was not a congressional problem. Congress "did not authorize that the adventure be entered upon. Congress has not sanctioned it. The American people have not been consulted. It is purely and wholly the adventure of the executive branch of our Government."

While not blaming the President for a situation he inherited, the Alabama representative charged Hoover with the "responsibility for any changes which may have occurred since the 4th of March. I charge him with the heavy responsibility of having done nothing . . . to prevent the calamities which are now occurring." According to his view, the President did not need a commission because he would not find out anything he did not already know. The military rulers of

[87] *Congressional Record,* 71 Cong., 2 sess., LXXII, pt. 1: 286 (December 9, 1929). See also "Haiti,"*Foreign Relations,* 1929, III, 207–208.

[88] *Foreign Relations,* 1929, III, 205. Secretary Stimson blamed former President Wilson for American difficulties in Haiti.

[89] *Congressional Record,* 71 Cong., 2 sess., LXXII, pt. 1: 286 (December 9, 1929).

Haiti were the President's agents, as was the President of Haiti. Representative Huddleston would have liked to see a real committee of Congress, "a fearless, honest, and patriotic committee, investigate the connections we have had with Haiti . . . even though it would cover us with humiliation before the nations of the world, because it would enlighten the people of the United States, the real sovereigns and rulers of this country. . . ."

The congressman was "not especially interested in the Haitians." If it had been only their interest, he would not have spoken, even though his heart beat for them. It was true that Huddleston recognized "toward them the responsibilities of one human being to others," and that he would be "glad to see them enjoy the same blessings of liberty and rights of self-government which we claim for ourselves." However, these considerations would not have caused him to "raise [his] voice upon this occasion." As he said, "I am interested most in this question from the standpoint of my own country." He further observed:

> Men say of the Haitians, "Oh, they are just a lot of monkeys; they are a lot of savages, a lot of cannibals; they are unfit to govern themselves. They are a lot of fetish worshipers and believers in voodooism," . . . . There may be some truth in that. . . . I do not suppose they are fit to govern themselves. Maybe they are not; I am willing to concede that they are not; but I dare assert . . . that God has not given to us the right to rule over them because of their own incapacity. We have no right under natural laws or moral laws, and none under laws that govern between nations.

Representative Huddleston exploded the myth that the occupation of Haiti was necessary for the defense of the Panama Canal, charging that the canal was supposed to be used for America's defense but that it had become a liability which had to be defended. The United States had to do things that decent nations would not do because of the Panama Canal. While he would regret seeing Haiti become a protectorate of some other nation, there were many worse things that could happen. The representative pointed out that there were other nations with territory much nearer to the Panama Canal than Haiti. The greatest nation in the world "has possessions nearer and much more convenient for attack on the Canal than Haiti, and we have a thousand occasions for conflict with that nation for one we might have with any other nation that might go to Haiti." Also France "has possessions in the Caribbean closer to Panama than Haiti. . . ." There were more statesmanlike solutions to the problem of Haiti than the alternative policies of robbing the Haitians ourselves or allowing somebody else to do so.

It was Huddleston's contention that a nation practicing imperialism abroad could not retain democracy at home. He saw American policy toward Latin America in general as imperialism—pure and simple. The United States neither treated with the Latin countries as equals, nor respected their rights, nor "accorded to them the same principles under international law that we claim for ourselves."[90] In concluding his speech, he maintained:

> No man loves liberty for himself that does not love it as much for others. If ever the time comes when American people are so servile and undemocratic in their ideals that they are willing to abandon the basic principles of the Declaration, and by the strong arm deprive other peoples of their civil rights, then we may be sure that we cannot hold on to our own rights.
>
> It is an amazing American who can excuse conduct in Haiti. It is an amazing American who can balance off material advantage against human liberty. I leave you to your choice.[91]

Congress voted the necessary funds to finance the investigation. President Hoover appointed a commission headed by W. Cameron Forbes, as chairman.[92] The purpose of the special commission as set forth by the President was to recommend when and how the United States was to withdraw from Haiti. The second question to be answered centered around the treaty of 1915 which was to expire in 1936. There was no mandate to continue the relationship after that date. But since the United States had an obligation to the people of Haiti, some plans should be made for discharging that obligation. President Hoover, in his instructions, pointed out the "need to know . . . what subsequent steps should be taken in cooperation with the Haitian people to bring about this result." He added that he had

[90] *Ibid.*, pp. 316–18.
[91] *Ibid.*, p. 678.
[92] *Foreign Relations*, 1929, III, 208. The other members of the commission were Henry P. Fletcher, Elie Vezina, James Kerney, and William Allen White.

no desire for representation of the "American Government abroad through our military force."[93]

In speaking of the President's action in establishing this commission, the *Nation* stated that "exposure rather than investigation" was needed. "It would be a disgrace if the commission sent to Haiti feels that patriotism 'requires it to whitewash' General Russell and his associates in Haiti." Taking into consideration the appeal to racism and charges of incapacity of the Haitians to govern themselves, the *Nation* pointed out some of the glaring examples of bad government in some of the large cities of the United States. The Haitians had maintained their independence for more than a century "until Admiral Caperton landed the marines, with the quaint ambition . . . to ensure, establish, and help maintain Haitian independence." It was true that Haiti had been subjected to revolutions, but so had the United States. However, none of Haiti's revolutions had been as destructive of life and property as the American Civil War. Haiti in her period of independence had lost exactly the same number of presidents as the United States by assassination, despite propaganda to the contrary. There was voodooism in Haiti as there was hexing in Pennsylvania. The upper-class portion of the Haitian population dominated that country, perhaps more efficiently than the upper-class oligarchy dominated in Mississippi and Arkansas.[94]

THE COMMISSION REPORT

The Forbes Commission found that the attitude of the treaty officials was based upon "the assumption that the occupation would continue indefinitely." The commission report expressed disappointment upon finding that "the preparation for the political and administrative training of Haitians for the responsibility of government had been inadequate."

The commission found the criticisms leveled at the occupation during the 1920 campaign to be generally true, even though some ten years had passed since the charges were first made. The McCormick

[93] *Report of the President's Commission for the Study and Review of Conditions in the Republic of Haiti*, p. 1.
[94] "Failure in Haiti," *Nation*, CXXIX (December 18, 1929), 739.

Report had not brought about any appreciable change in conditions. To support this contention, the Forbes Commission noted that the Haitian Garde had not been turned over to the Haitians as stipulated in the treaty.

The commission recommended to President Hoover nine sequential steps to be followed in the withdrawal of the United States from Haiti. One of the most significant of the suggested steps laid down a principle which, if it had been adhered to in the earlier relations with Hispaniola, would have softened the imperial burden of the black man, namely, that "in retaining officers now in the Haitian service or selecting new Americans for employment therein, the utmost care be taken that only those free from strong racial antipathies should be preferred."[95]

The "good neighbor" policy was put into practice in Hispaniola soon after the election of Franklin D. Roosevelt in 1932. An executive agreement of 1933 provided for the evacuation of Haiti and stipulated that any controversy "that might arise in the future over the continuing receivership and service bonds . . . which could not be settled by diplomacy, was to be referred to arbitration. . . ." The marines were withdrawn from Haiti in 1934, and the treaty giving the United States the right to enforce the customs receivership in Haiti expired on May 3, 1936, without renewal.

The treaty of 1924 establishing a protectorate over the Dominican Republic was abrogated by a treaty signed at Washington in 1940, ending the protectorate and providing for the "arbitration if necessary of any dispute arising over service of the bonds. . . ."[96] This act ended, for all practical purposes, the imperial era in the relations between the United States and the black republics of Hispaniola.

95 *Report of the President's Commission,* pp. 8–21.
96 Bemis, *Latin American Policy of the United States,* p. 293.

VIII

Conclusion

I n 1943 Samuel Flagg Bemis suggested that American imperialism was "an imperialism against imperialism." In discussing the American withdrawal from the imperial adventure, Bemis contended that imperialism "was never deep-rooted in the character of the people."[1] The lack of tenacity on the part of Americans for imperialism was in sharp contrast with the earlier practice of Americans in the acquisition of territory. Historically, contiguous territory once acquired was never given up, for in the words of the devotees of imperialism, What we have we hold! was the motto of Anglo-Saxon blood.

Overseas expansion involved noncontiguous territory—territory already populated, which could not accommodate, for the most part, large numbers of American whites. Hawaii, Cuba, and the Dominican Republic could accommodate larger populations; but the Philippines, Puerto Rico, and Haiti already had large populations. None of the races of these insular possessions were considered equal to Americans of Anglo-Saxon extraction. Their existence modified the Anglo-Saxon motto. Similarly, the existence of so-called inferior races of these areas limited the extension of the principles of republican government.

Twenty years later, in 1963, Frederick Merk suggested an answer to the lack of deep-rooted commitment on the part of Americans for insular imperialism. Merk points out that efforts to acquire all of Mexico in the period 1846–48 raised overwhelming racial objections to having the Mexicans brought into the Union. Though the Mexicans were a neighboring people known to the people of the United States for generations, they were unacceptable to Americans as a

---

[1] Bemis, *Latin American Policy of the United States*, p. 385.

part of the body politic. In the light of the Mexican experience, one had reason to question whether Americans would be anxious to rule Filipinos, Hawaiians, Cubans, Dominicans, or Haitians—peoples assumed to be in the same or lesser state of development as the Mexicans. The influence of racism on the American imperial adventure is suggested in Merk's question, "Is it not likely that racism prior to the war with Spain was a deterrent to imperialism rather than a stimulant of it?"[2]

According to Merk, a fundamental principle in the Manifest Destiny of the 1840s, which was overthrown in the imperialism of the 1890s, was that "a people not capable of rising to statehood should never be annexed."[3] My own thesis is that American racism provided one of the most influential forces for her imperial adventure and at the same time formed the basis for the ambivalent character of American imperialism.

The fundamental principle which Merk says governed the expansion of the 1840s was never really overthrown. Stated in slightly different terms, it was retained in the handling of the overseas acquisitions. Convinced that people who were not capable of self-government should not participate in the governing of Anglo-Saxons, the late nineteenth-century imperialists used racism to compromise the American constitutional principle that all citizens of a republic ought to enjoy an equality of rights. The imperialist compromise was to allow the flag to advance *but to deny that the Constitution followed the flag.*

The anti-imperialists and the imperialists argued from the same premise, both sides believing that the peoples of the newly acquired insular possessions were not capable of self-government. In the expansion which took place between 1898 and 1916, all of the noncontiguous territory acquired was inhabited by races considered by Americans to be inferior.

As a result of contacts during the economic and social development of the Republic, the American people developed an attitude of racial superiority.[4] This was a contradiction of the American principles of

[2] Frederick Merk, *Manifest Destiny and Mission in American History: A Reinterpretation*, p. 247.
[3] *Ibid.*, pp. 256–57.
[4] Hofstadter, *Social Darwinism in American Thought*, pp. 170–200.

equality of rights and opportunity. Although in conflict with American principles, racial superiority was an attitude which naturally accompanied America's sense of mission. This attitude grew from contact with the Indian, the Chinese, the Japanese, and the Negro. In addition to the dissimilarities between the cultures of these races and that of the Anglo-Saxon, there were commutable characteristics of the ethnic groups named. These minority groups lacked political, economic, or military power. The absence of power made these groups a negative force at the mercy of and subject to the prerogatives of the Anglo-Saxon majority group.

The Indian exerted positive power as long as he was a military force. The existence of that force contributed to the national unity of the majority group. When the Indian ceased to exist as a military force, he became a negative force which contributed to the attitude that Americans held toward peoples on a lower scale in their political and social development. The relations of the Anglo-Saxon with the Indian were something less than a relationship of equals. The Anglo-Saxon perpetrated injustices upon the Indian without fear of punishment. These injustices were rationalized by the feeling that the Indian blocked the advance of civilization and was thus expendable. Pursued to its ultimate conclusion, the policy became in the popular mind a slogan—The only good Indian is a dead Indian.

The Chinese spurred the development of the attitude, on the part of white Americans, of racial superiority. As members of an alien race, they were outside of the provisions of the American Constitution, but not outside of the American principles of equality of rights under law and human equality. Nonetheless, they were subjected to ill treatment by Americans who had no fear of reprisals because of the absence of power among these people. The solution to the problem of maltreatment of people of Chinese extraction was to remove the victims from the path of the Anglo-Saxon. The Chinese exclusion acts were the result, with the chance of a Chinaman becoming synonymous with no chance at all.

Agitation on the West Coast against the presence of the Japanese resulted in the "gentleman's agreement" of 1907 and the Immigration Act of 1924. Again, the pattern was to get rid of the victim of injustices rather than to correct the abuse.

The Negro had been the subject of the great debate over the institution of slavery. The arguments which had been used to justify this institution served to intensify the Anglo-Saxon's feeling of racial superiority despite the loud voices of the abolitionists. If the Civil War represented the breakdown of the principle of compromise essential to the democratic process, the Negro was the irritant that rendered compromise difficult. The power possessed by the Negro after the Civil War was maintained by federal bayonets—a situation which did not endear the Negro to his former masters. The last quarter of the nineteenth century witnessed the curtailment of the Negro's political power. Like the Indian, the Chinese, and the Japanese, he was also subjected to injustices inflicted at the hands of the Anglo-Saxon. Unlike the other races, however, he was protected by the Constitution, which entitled him to the equal protection of the laws. Nevertheless, in practice, where the Negro was concerned the equal protection of the laws did not apply. The method of dealing with the injustices inflicted upon the Negro was to remove the victim from the protection of the Constitution. This development, translated to the popular mind, brought about the conviction that the Negro had no rights that a white man was bound to respect.

In three instances a policy was pursued which assumed that "inferior" people who became the object of injustices should be removed. In the fourth instance, the so-called inferiors who were victims of injustices were citizens of the United States and entitled to the protection of the Constitution. In this case, equal protection under that document did not apply.

By the last decade of the nineteenth century, Americans had adopted attitudes which compromised basic constitutional principles. These attitudes gave birth to the racism which influenced the United States in its professed mission of Christianizing and civilizing its non-white insular possessions. It became expedient to "camp outside the letter and spirit of the Constitution."

Racism became the common denominator of imperial policy. The philosophy of the Democratic party and the anti-imperialists was that the colored peoples who inhabited the islands could not be completely incorporated into the United States without degrading the citizenship of the Republic. Nor could these peoples be governed by the United States as subjects without eroding the nation's basic constitutional principles. Democrats and anti-imperialists argued that either constitutional rights had to be granted the inhabitants of the insular possessions or the inhabitants would have to be given independence. Independence was by far preferable to granting these "inferiors" constitutional privileges equal to those of the American whites. Throughout the debates on each of the insular possessions the abhorrence to the inclusion of dissimilar people in the body politic was evident. Both parties held that people assumed to be incapable of self-government should not participate in the governing of Anglo-Saxons.

The Republican party and the leading advocates of imperialism agreed that the peoples of the insular possessions were not capable of self-government and were not entitled to constitutional rights. However, the Christianizing-civilizing mission required that methods be found whereby they could be taught self-government without giving them full citizenship in the Republic. The Constitution could be interpreted as allowing the United States to maintain colonies. In the ensuing debate the Republican philosophy temporarily prevailed. Methods which temporarily compromised basic constitutional principles were used in dealing with possessions inhabited by dissimilar peoples thought to be incapable of self-government. Racism, developed as a result of domestic contacts with "inferior" peoples, fixed the pattern for dealing with similar peoples in the insular possessions. The Republicans employed the Democratic party's methods of dealing with the Negro in Southern states in order to control the inhabitants of insular possessions.

Paradoxically, it was the Americans from the Southern states who most vociferously attacked the policy of imperialism, not out of a sense of equality of human rights, but rather on the grounds of racial inequality. They feared that once annexed, the peoples of the insular possessions would be accorded constitutional rights and eventually participate in the governing of Anglo-Saxons.

Racism was used to keep Hawaii in a territorial status throughout this period. The arguments used to keep Hawaii out of the Union were in turn used to secure independence for the Philippine Islands. Thus, in the expansion of the United States into the region of the Pacific, racial assumptions influenced the relationship between the insular possessions and the Republic.

In the Caribbean area, the assumption that the Cubans were incapable of governing themselves prevented the recognition of a truly independent Cuba and led to the Platt Amendment and to subsequent interventions in Cuban affairs. Annexation of the island was avoided due to an aversion to the incorporation of a population with a large percentage of colored people.

Arguments used to keep Puerto Rico in a state of dependency centered around racial and cultural differences between the Puerto Ricans and the American majority of Anglo-Saxon extraction. The dissimilarities, according to these arguments, made it impossible for the Puerto Ricans to understand the Anglo-Saxons' concept of self-government. Since the Puerto Ricans were a mixed race with a large percentage of colored peoples in the population, they were destined to remain an imperial possession after 1946.

The United States intervention in Hispaniola was in part motivated by the belief that the inhabitants were incapable of governing themselves. There was no desire on the part of the American people to annex either Haiti or the Dominican Republic because of the nature of their populations.

In the acquisition of these possessions, the United States rendered the inhabitants politically and militarily impotent. They found themselves to be at the mercy of the representatives of the United States. However, the inhabitants of these islands did possess a negative power as a result of their impotency. Anti-imperialists used the actions of Americans in relation to these people to illustrate the inconsistency between America's professed principles of human equality and constitutionalism and the practice of superiority and autocracy in the insular possessions. The policies based on Anglo-Saxon racism led to injustices which questioned the honor and character of the United States.

In less than a quarter of a century, the United States began a retreat from imperialism. The seeds for retreat were sown as early as the debates on the Treaty of Paris. The subsequent investigations and hearings on affairs in the Philippines, Cuba, Hawaii, Puerto Rico, Haiti, and the Dominican Republic pointed out the inconsistencies between America's avowed principles and actual practices. Although some of the investigations endeavored to whitewash these activities, as in the case of the 1921 investigation of affairs in Hispaniola, enough evidence was recorded to indicate that American policy-makers were

not ready to accord to peoples of color the same rights and considerations they readily accorded to Anglo-Saxons.

By 1934 direct imperialism was in full retreat, as manifested by
the abrogation of the Platt Amendment in a treaty with Cuba. Another sign of this movement was the act granting independence to
the Philippine Islands. The withdrawal of marines from Haiti and
the termination of the protectorate over the Dominican Republic
completed the retreat. The "good neighbor" policy seemed to grant
to the insular possessions the right, as John Sharp Williams stated,
"not to be Race-Ruled" by Anglo-Saxons.[5]

Tho influence of racism in the final policies affecting the relations
between the United States and her insular possessions can be seen in
Senator Millard B. Tydings' avowal that Puerto Rico had but two
alternatives in relations to the United States—to stay like it was (dependent) or to become independent.[6] In presenting a bill designed
to give the Puerto Ricans the option of either becoming independent
or remaining an imperial possession, Tydings said that the policy was
"in line with present-day American policy, Pan-American policy, the
repeal of the Platt Amendment, Filipino independence, and a wider
measure of cooperation and democracy to the people who are associated with us and those who are under our flag as well."[7]

The senator's outlining of the New Deal program in relation to
insular possessions was reiterated by President Roosevelt in an address at Chautauqua, New York, August 14, 1936, in which he said,
"On the 4th of March, 1933, I made the following declaration: In the
field of world policy I would dedicate this nation to the policy of the
good neighbor—the neighbor who respects his obligations and respects the sanctity of his agreements in and with a world neighbor. . . .
But [this declaration] represents more than a purpose, for it stands
for a practice. To a measurable degree it has succeeded."[8] He held
that the United States was definitely opposed to any armed intervention and pointed out that the United States had negotiated a Pan-
American convention embodying the principle of nonintervention.
Roosevelt further commented, "We have abandoned the Platt Amend-

[5] See Chapter IV, p. 117.
[6] See Chapter VI, p. 205.
[7] *Congressional Record*, 74 Cong., 2 sess., LXXX, pt. 6: 5925 (April 23, 1936).
[8] *Ibid.*

ment, which gave us the right to intervene in the internal affairs of the
Republic of Cuba. We have withdrawn American marines from Haiti.
. . . We seek to dominate no other nation. We ask no territorial expansion. We oppose imperialism. . . . We believe in democracy; we
believe in freedom. . . ."[9]

The President's support enabled legislators to acquiesce to a program which, among other things, avoided statehood for territories
with non-Anglo-Saxon populations. The partial fulfillment of the
policy became a reality on July 4, 1946, by the proclamation of the
independence of the Philippine Republic. However, at the time of
Philippine independence, two other insular possessions maintained
an imperial relation with the United States—Hawaii and Puerto
Rico. The implications drawn from the practices of Americans with
domestic race problems was that the Filipinos, like the Japanese
and Chinese, were to be removed. Cuba and Hispaniola were not
annexed because of race. Hawaiians and Puerto Ricans were in the
same class as the Negro—without constitutional guarantees of equal
protection of the laws. Despite racism Hawaii was eventually granted
statehood, but for Puerto Rico this step was never seriously proposed.

The attitude persisted through 1946 that Puerto Rico was not sufficiently "Americanized" to warrant statehood. Other considerations
exerted some influence on Puerto Rico's continued subordinate relationship to the United States, but Anglo-Saxon racism seemingly
outweighed all other factors, causing Puerto Rico to be retained as a
commonwealth subordinate to the United States.

[9] Ruhl T. Bartlett, *The Record of American Diplomacy,* p. 551.

Bibliography

I. PRIMARY SOURCES

A. *Official Documents*

Congressional Record, XXV–XCII, 1893–1946.

Diplomatic Correspondence of the United States, Inter-American Affairs (1831–60), VI.

Duty of Americans in the Philippines, The, *Senate Document*, No. 191, 58 Cong., 2 sess. Address of the Honorable William H. Taft.

Foreign Relations of the United States (1893–1945). Washington: United States Government Printing Office.

Gazetter of the Philippines, *Senate Document*, No. 280, 57 Cong., 1 sess.

Hearings, Affairs in the Philippines, *Senate Document*, No. 331, 57 Cong., 1 sess.

Hearings, Committee on Insular Affairs, House, 70 Cong., H. R. 12173, and H. R. 6047.
A bill to amend the Organic Act of Porto Rico.

Hearings, Sub-Committee, Committee on Territories, House, 74 Cong., 1 sess., Statehood for Hawaii, H. R. 3034. Washington: United States Government Printing Office, 1936.

Hearings, Committee on Territories and Insular Affairs, United States Senate, 78 Cong., 1 sess., S. 952.
A bill to provide for the withdrawal of sovereignty of the United States over the island of Puerto Rico and for the recognition of its independence, and so forth. Washington: United States Government Printing Office.

Hearings, Committee on Territories, House of Representatives, 79 Cong., 1 sess., H. R. 3643, Statehood for Hawaii. Washington: United States Government Printing Office, 1946.

House Document, No. 405, 55 Cong., 2 sess.
Report on Affairs in Cuba.

House Document, No. 1, 56 Cong., 2 sess.
Annual Report of the War Department. Report of Major-General John R. Brooke.

House Document, No. 2, 56 Cong., 2 sess.
Annual Report of the War Department.

House Document, No. 2, 57 Cong., 1 sess.
Annual Report of the War Department.

House Document, No. 1, 58 Cong., 3 sess.
Papers Relating to Foreign Affairs.

House Document, No. 2, Vol. 1, 58 Cong., 2 sess.
Report of the War Department. Report of William H. Taft, Secretary of War, and Robert Bacon, Assistant Secretary of State, of what was done under the instructions of the President in restoring peace in Cuba.

House Document, No. 1067, 62 Cong., 3 sess.
Message of the President on Fiscal, Judicial, Military and Insular Affairs, December 6, 1912.

House Document, No. 155, 60 Cong., 1 sess.
Annual Report of Charles E. Magoon, Chief Law Officer.

House Report, No. 1355, 55 Cong., 2 sess.
Report of House Committee on Foreign Affairs, Majority and Minority Views on Annexation of Hawaii.

House Report, No. 1808, 55 Cong., 3 sess.
Civil Government for the Territory of Hawaii. Majority and Minority Views.

House Report, No. 1276, 57 Cong., 1 sess.
Reciprocity with Cuba.

House Report, No. 461, 63 Cong., 2 sess.
Report on a bill to change the political status of the inhabitants of Porto Rico from citizens of Porto Rico to citizens of the United States.

House Report, No. 499, 64 Cong., 1 sess.
Independence for the Philippines.

House Report, No. 350, 68 Cong., 1 sess.
Report on Restrictions on Japanese Immigration.

Lansing Papers, The, *Foreign Relations* (1914–1920).

Register of Debates in Congress, 1825–1826.

Report of the Philippine Commission, The Civil Governor and Heads of Executive Departments of the Civil Government of the Philippine Islands, 1900–1903. Bureau of Insular Affairs, War Department, Washington: United States Government Printing Office, 1904.

Report of the President's Commission for the Study and Review of Conditions in the Republic of Haiti. Washington: United States Government Printing Office, 1930.

Report of the Secretary of the Navy, 1920.

Report of the Secretary of the Navy, Miscellaneous Reports, 1920.

Report of the United States Commission of Inquiry to Santo Domingo. Washington: United States Government Printing Office, 1871.

Report on the Census of Cuba, 1899. United States War Department Office, Director, Census of Cuba; Washington: United States Government Printing Office, 1900.

Richardson, James D. *Messages and Papers of the Presidents, 1785–1905.* Washington: Bureau of National Literature and Art, VII–XI, 1907.

Senate Document, No. 16, 55 Cong., 3 sess.
Hawaiian Commission Report. Contains treaties and laws of Hawaii.

Senate Document, No. 138, 56 Cong., 1 sess.
Schurman Report on the Philippines.

Senate Document, No. 234, 56 Cong., 3 sess.
Report on the Legal Status of the Territory and Inhabitants of Islands acquired by the United States during the War with Spain. Charles E. Magoon, Chief Law Officer.

Senate Document, No. 205, 57 Cong., 1 sess.
Charges of cruelties to the Filipinos.

Senate Document, No. 277, 59 Cong., 1 sess.
Hearings, Revenue for the Philippine Islands.

Senate Document, No. 151, 75 Cong., 3 sess.
Hearings, Statehood for Hawaii.

Senate Report, No. 227, 53 Cong., 2 sess.
Conditions in Hawaii.

Senate Report, No. 681, 55 Cong., 2 sess.
Annexation of Hawaii. Contains treaties and background information to 1898.

Senate Report, No. 885, 55 Cong., 2 sess.
Affairs in Cuba.

Senate Report, No. 249, 56 Cong., 1 sess.
Temporary Civil Government for Porto Rico.

Senate Report, No. 920, 61 Cong., 3 sess.
Citizenship for the Porto Ricans.

Treaty of Peace between the United States of American and the Kingdom of Spain, *Senate Document*, No. 62, 55 Cong., 3 sess.

United States Statutes at Large.

B. *Primary Materials*

Bartlett, Ruhl T. *The Record of American Diplomacy*, Second Edition. New York: Knopf, 1950.

Commager, Henry Steele. *Documents of American History*, Fourth Edition. New York: Crofts, 1948. An excellent collection of source materials pertaining to American history.

Lodge, Henry Cabot. *Letters of Theodore Roosevelt and Henry Cabot Lodge*, Two Volumes. New York: Scribners, 1925. Very good for views of two individuals instrumental in establishing policy during an important part of the period 1893–1946.

The Works of Theodore Roosevelt (Memorial Edition) 20 Volumes. New York: Scribner's, 1926. Unexcelled for views of Theodore Roosevelt.

C. *Newspapers*

Durham Morning Herald, June 23, 1963.

New York Times, 1917–1920.

Washington Post, December 27, 1900.

D. *Special Monograph*

Taft, William Howard. *The South and the National Government.*

Address delivered at the dinner of the North Carolina Society of New York, Hotel Astor, December 7, 1908.

E. *Contemporary Books of Controversy*

Balch, Emily Green. *Occupied Haiti.* New York: Writers Publishing, 1927. A report on conditions in Haiti with suggestions for improving American relations with the Haitians.

Cockran, William Bourke. *In the Name of Liberty.* New York: Putnam's, 1925. Essays on concepts of liberty.

Daniels, Josephus. *The Wilson Era: Years of War and After.* Chapel Hill: University of North Carolina Press, 1946. A good work covering the Wilson years, especially the postwar period. Written from the point of view of a cabinet official.

Jordan, David Starr. *Imperial Democracy.* New York: Appelton, 1901. A protest by an anti-imperialist to expansion on grounds of racial dissimilarity.

Kalaw, Maxime M. *The Case for the Filipinos.* New York: Century, 1916. Subjective from the point of view of one dedicated to independence of the Philippines.

Kidd, Benjamin. *The Control of the Tropics.* New York: MacMillan, 1898. Important for the development of the idea that Anglo-Saxons could not live in the tropics.

Lodge, Henry Cabot. *The War with Spain.* New York: Harper, 1899. Furnishes information on the war from the point of view of one of the individuals who was greatly interested in the expansion of the United States into the Caribbean.

Schultz, Alfred P. *Race or Mongrel.* Boston: L. C. Page, 1908. A good example of the kind of literature supporting the doctrine of racial superiority.

Schurman, Jacob Gould. *The Philippine Affair: A Retrospect and Outlook.* New York: Scribner's, 1902. Important for the expressed views which became the basis of subsequent Philippine policy.

Stoddard, T. Lothrop. *The Rising Tide of Color.* New York: Scribner's, 1922. Good example of literature that played a part in conditioning Americans to prejudice against the Orientals.

Storey, Moorfield. *The Conquest of the Philippines.* New York:

Putnam's, 1926. A good work by an American sympathetic to the cause of Philippine independence.

Strong, Joshiah. *Our Country: Its Possible Future and Its Present Crisis.* New York: Baker and Taylor, 1885. Considered one of the important works in spreading the ideas of the superiority of the Anglo-Saxon to other peoples.

Wilson, Woodrow. *Constitutional Government in the United States.* New York: Columbia University Press, 1908. Good for Wilson's views on the development of constitutional government.

F. *Periodical Articles*

Agnew, Daniel. "Unconstitutionality of the Hawaiian Treaty," *Forum*, XXIV (December 1897), 467–70.

"Aguinaldo on Philippine Independence," *Current History*, XII (October 1920), 112–13.

Aldama, M. Carnillo. "The Cuban Government's Side," *The Independent*, LXI (September 20, 1906), 663.

Alder, Felix. "The Philippine War: Two Ethical Questions," *Forum*, XXXIII (June 1902), 387–99.

Alvord, T. Gold, Jr. "Is the Cuban Capable of Self-Government?" *Forum*, XXIV (September 1897), 123.

"America's Ireland: Haiti–Santo Domingo," *Nation*, CX (February 21, 1920), 231–33.

Anderson, Thomas M. "Our Role in the Philippines," *North American Review*, CLXX (February 1900), 272–83.

Bailey, Thomas A. "Japan's Protest Against the Annexation of Hawaii," *Journal of Modern History*, III (March 1931), 46–61.

———. "The United States and Hawaii During the Spanish-American War," *The American Historical Review*, XXXVI (July 1931), 552–60.

Becker, Carl L. "Law and Practice of the United States in the Acquisition and Government of Territory," *The Annals*, The American Academy of Political and Social Science, XVI (November 1900), 407–408.

Bernstein, Barton J. "Case Law in Plessy v. Ferguson," *Journal of Negro History*, XLVII (July 1962), 192–98.

Beveridge, Albert J. "Cuba and Congress," *North American Review*, CLXXII (April 1901), 548–49.

———. "The Development of a Colonial Policy for the United States," *The Annals*, The American Academy of Political and Social Science, XXX (July 1907), 3–15.

Bingham, Robert. "Sectional Misunderstandings," *North American Review*, CLXXIV (September 1904), 357–70.

Blakeslee, George H. "Hawaii: Racial Problems and Naval Bases," *Foreign Affairs*, XVII (October 1938), 90–99.

"Blanket Naturalization for Porto Rico," *Outlook*, XCV (June 11, 1910), 273.

Bowman, Sydney S. "Hawaii Knocks at the Door," *Forum*, XCV (June 1936), 350–51.

Brooks, Sydney. "Some Impressions of Cuba," *North American Review*, CXCIX (May 1914), 734–35.

Bryce, James. "The Policy of Annexation for America," *Forum*, XXIV (December 1897), 389–91.

Bullard, Robert L. "The Cuban Negro," *North American Review*, CLXXXIV (March 1907), 623–30.

"Caste Notion of Suffrage, The," *Nation*, LXXVII (September 3, 1903), 182.

Cestero, Tulio M. "American Rule in Santo Domingo," *Nation*, CXI (July 17, 1920), 78–81.

Charelton, Paul. "Naturalization and Citizenship in the Insular Possessions," *The Annals*, The American Academy of Political and Social Science, XXX (July 1907), 104–14.

Coates, Mary Weld. "What's the Matter in Puerto Rico?" *Current History*, XVI (April 1922), 108–14.

Cooley, Thomas M. "Grave Obstacles to Hawaiian Annexation," *Forum*, XV (June 1893), 389–406.

Crawford, David L. "Hawaii—Our Western Frontier," *Review of Reviews*, XCI (January 1935), 60–74.

Currier, Charles Warren. "Why Cuba Should Be Independent," *Forum*, XXX (September 1900), 139–46.

Dalencour, Francois. "Haiti and the American Occupation," *Current History*, XI (October 1919), 542–49.

Davis, Mrs. Jefferson. "The White Man's Problem," *Arena*, XXIII (January 1900), 1–41.

Dole, Charles F. "Letter on Haitian Occupation," *Nation*, CI (October 14, 1915), 462.

Du Bois, W. E. Burghart. "The Republicans and the Black Voter," *Nation*, CX (June 5, 1920), 757–58.

"Failure in Haiti," *Nation*, CXXIX (December 18, 1929), 739.

Foster, John W. "The Annexation of Cuba," *The Independent*, LXI (October 25, 1906), 965–68.

Frankfurter, Felix. "Haiti and Intervention," *New Republic*, XXV (December 15, 1920), 71–72.

Gannett, L. S. "The Conquest of Santo Domingo," *Nation*, CXI (July 17, 1920), 64–65.

Green, Elizabeth. "Race and Politics in Hawaii," *Asia*, XXXV (June 1935), 374.

Griffiths, Arthur Llewellyn. "The Philippine Insurrection, Why?" *Arena*, XXII (November 1904), 496–500.

Gruening, Ernest H. "Conquest of Haiti and Santo Domingo," *Current History*, XV (March 1922), 885–96.

"Haiti," *Current History*, XV (February 1922), 868.

"Haiti Charges Us with Misrule," *Literary Digest*, LXIX (June 18, 1921), 12.

"Haiti's Indictment of Uncle Sam," *The Independent*, CV (May 21, 1921), 543.

"Haiti Speaks," *Nation*, CXII (May 18, 1921), 708.

Harper's Weekly, XLI (January 2, 1897), 2.

Harrison, Benjamin. "The Status of Annexed Territory and Its Free Civilized Inhabitants," *North American Review*, CLXXII (January 1901), 1–22.

Hart, Albert Bushnell. "Brother Jonathan's Colonies," *Harper's*, XCVIII (January 1899), 328.

Hill, Robert T. "Cuba and Its Value as a Colony," *Forum*, XXV (June 1898), 404.

Hinton, Richard J. "Cuban Reconstruction," *North American Review*, CLXIII (January 1899), 92–102.

Independent, LXXII (January 25, 1912), 209.

Independent, LXXII(May 30, 1912), 1139.

Independent, LXXII (June 13, 1912), 1352.

Inman, Samuel Guy. "American Occupation of Santo Domingo," *Current History*, XIII (December 1920), 501–506.

————. "Hard Problem in Haiti," *Current History*, XIII (November 1920), 338–42.

Iyenaga, Troyokichi. "Japan and the Japanese California Problem," *Current History*, XIII (October 1920), 1.

"Japanese Feeling Against America," *Review of Reviews* (August 1907), 132–34.

Johnson, James Weldon. "Self-Determining Haiti." Four articles reprinted from the *Nation* embodying a report of an investigation made for the National Association for the Advancement of Colored People. In the Arthur A. Schomburg Negro Collection, New York Public Library, 135th Street Branch.

————. "Self-Determining Haiti," *Nation*, CXI (August 28, 1920), 236–38.

Judd, Lawrence M. "Hawaii States Her Case," *Current History*, LI (July 1940), 40–42.

Kennan, George. "The Regeneration of Cuba," *Outlook*, LX (June 1899), 202.

Kipling, Rudyard. "White Man's Burden," *McClure's Magazine*, XII (February 1899), 290–91.

Le Bon, Gustave. "The Influence of Race in History," *Popular Science Monthly*, XXXV (August 1889), 495–98.

Le Roy, James A. "Race Prejudice in the Philippines," *Atlantic Monthly*, XC (July 1902), 100–12.

Leschorn, Helen. "American Atrocities in the Dominican Republic," *Current History*, XV (April 1922), 875–81.

Livingstone, W. P. "A Caribbean Derelict," *North American Review*, CXCV (February 1912), 261–65.

Locan, Clarence A. "The Japanese Problem in California: Past and Present Phases of a Situation that Threatens International Complications," *Current History*, XIII (October 1920), 7–9.

Lodge, Henry Cabot. "Our Blundering Foreign Policy," *Forum*, XIV (March 1895), 8.

————. "Our Duty to Cuba," *Forum*, XXI (March 1896), 278–87.

————. "The Spanish-American War," *Harper's*, XLVIII (December 1898–May 1899), 449–64.

Mahan, Alfred T. "Hawaii and Our Future Sea Power," *Forum*, XV (March 1893), 1–11.

Martin, Harold. "Manila Censorship," *Forum*, XXXI (June 1901), 462–71.

Matheson, Walker. "Hawaii Pleads for Statehood," *North American Review*, CCXLVII (March 1939), 130–31.

"Men We Are Watching," *The Independent*, LXI (December 13, 1906), 1429.

"Mob Fury and Race Hatred as a National Danger," *Literary Digest*, LXIX (June 18, 1921), 8–9.

Morgan, John T. "The Duty of Annexing Hawaii," *Forum*, XXV (March 1898), 11–16.

————. "The Logic of Our Position in Cuba," *North American Review*, CLXIX (July 1899), 109–15.

Morgan, Thomas J. "Epaulets or Chevrons?" *The Independent*, L (June 30, 1898), 846.

Nation, LXVII (July 14, 1897), 21.

Nation, LXVII (October 27, 1898), 304–306.

Nation, LXXII (February 21, 1901), 146.

Nation, LXXII (May 2, 1901), 347.

Nation, LXXII (May 30, 1901), 423.

Nation, LXXII (June 27, 1901), 501.

Nation, LXXVII (August 13, 1903), 126.

Nation, CX (June 5, 1920), 765.

Nation, CX (June 26, 1920), 841.

Nation, CXI (August 7, 1920), 146.

Nation, CXI (August 28, 1920), 231.

Nation, CXV (July 12, 1922), 32.

Neal, Robert W. "Hawaii's Land and Labor Problem," *Current History*, XIII (December 1920), 389–97.

Newlands, Francis G. "The San Domingo Question," *North American Review*, CXXX (June 1905), 885–99.

"Oriental on the Pacific Coast, The," *The Pacific Review*, I (December 1920), 349–421.

"Our Call to Duty in Haiti," *Literary Digest*, LI (August 14, 1915), 288.

"Our Imperialist Propaganda—The *National Geographic*'s Anti-Haitian Campaign," *Nation*, CXII (April 6, 1921), 508.

Pacific Review, I (December 1920), 377.

Parker, John H. "What Shall We Do with the Philippines?" *Forum*, XXXII (February 1902), 662–70.

Pepper, Charles M. "The Spanish Population of Cuba and Porto Rico," *The Annals*, The American Academy of Political and Social Science, XVIII (July 1901), 163–78.

Phillips, J. S. "Uncle Sam and His Asiatic Wards," *Contemporary Review*, CXLIX (March 1936), 349–50.

Pingrey, Darius H. "The Decadence of Our Constitution," *Forum*, XXXII (October 1901), 226–31.

Platt, Orville H. "Cuba's Claim Upon the United States," *North American Review*, CLXXV (August 1902), 145–51.

———. "Our Relations to the People of Cuba and Porto Rico," *The Annals*, The American Academy of Political and Social Science, XVIII (July 1901), 154.

———. "Solution of the Cuban Problem," *World's Work*, II (May 1901), 729–35.

"Plea for Annexation of Cuba, A," *Forum*, XXX (September, 1900), 202–14.

"Porto Rico and the Tariff," *Review of Reviews*, XXI (March 1900), 273.

"Porto Rico's Grievance," *Outlook*, XCIX (November 18, 1911), 643–44.

Post, R. H. and W. H. Ward. "Porto Rico and the United States: Citizenship for the Porto Ricans," *Outlook*, XCIII (December 18, 1909), 860–63.

Procter, John R. "Hawaii and the Changing Front of the World," *Forum*, XXIV (September 1897), 34–35.

———. "Isolation or Imperialism," *Forum*, XXVI (September 1898), 25–26.

Pulliam, Wiliam E. "Troubles of a Benevolent Despot," *Outlook*, CXXVI (December 29, 1920), 758–60.

Reid, Gilbert. "China's View of Chinese Exclusion," *Forum*, XV (June 1893), 407–15.

Review of Reviews, XIX (February 1899), 160.

"Right of Suffrage, The," *Outlook*, LXVIII (July 27, 1901), 711–12.

Robbins, Kincheloe. "What Santo Domingo Wants," *Nation*, CX (March 6, 1920), 312–13.

Robinson, Albert G. "The Work of the Cuban Convention," *Forum*, XXI (June 1901), 401–12.

Roosevelt, Theodore. "Review of Brooks Adams, *The Law of Civilization and Decay*," *Forum*, XXII (February 1897), 575–89.

———. "Review of Benjamin Kidd, *Social Evolution*," *North American Review*, CLXI (July 1895), 94–109.

Rostow, Eugene V. "Our Worst Wartime Mistake," *Harper's*, CXCI (September 1945), 193–201.

Runcie, J. E. "American Misgovernment of Cuba," *North American Review*, CLXX (February 1900), 284–94.

"Santo Domingo on Our Hands," *Literary Digest*, LIII (December 23, 1916), 1646.

"Satisfactory Solution, A," *Review of Reviews*, XXI (April 1900), 388.

Scheiner, Seth M. "President Roosevelt and the Negro, 1901–1908," *Journal of Negro History*, XLVII (July 1962), 169–82.

Seligman, H. J. "Conquest of Haiti," *Nation*, CXI (July 10, 1920), 35–36.

Seymour, Horatio W. "Democratic Expansion," *North American Review*, CLXXIX (July 1904), 96–104.

"Shall Negro Disfranchisement Reduce Southern Representation?" *Outlook*, LXVII (January 12, 1901), 85.

Smith, Goldwin. "The Moral of the Cuban War," *Forum*, XXVI (November 1898), 284–90.

Stoddard, T. Lothrop. "Santo Domingo: Our Unruly Ward," *Review of Reviews*, XLIX (June 1914), 726–31.

"Strait-jacketing Haiti," *Literary Digest*, LI (September 4, 1915), 456–57.

Sumulong, Juan. "The Philippine Problem from a Filipino Standpoint," *North American Review*, CLXXIX (December 1904), 860–67.

Sweetland, Monroe. "Our 49th State—Hawaii," *Asia*, XLIV (September 1944), 411.

Swith, Charles J. "Practical and Legal Aspects of Annexation," *Overland Monthly*, XXV, 2d Series (January–June 1895), 586–96.

Symes, Lillian, "What About Hawaii?" *Harper's*, CLXV (October 1932), 533.

"Talk of Cuban Annexation," *World's Work*, II (October 1901), 1249.

Thacker, George A. "The Southern Problem," *Forum*, XXXII (September 1901), 116–18.

Thorpe, Francis Newton. "The Civil Service and Colonization," *Harper's*, XCVII (May 1899), 858–62.

Ugarte, Manuel. "Dangers Latent in Our Latin American Policy," *Current History*, XXVI (September 1927), 897–901.

Villard, Oswald Garrison. "The Rights of Small Nations in America: The Republics of the Caribbean," *The Annals*, The American Academy of Political and Social Science, LXXII (July 1917), 165–71.

Waldron, Webb. "A New Star in the Union? Hawaii's Bid for Statehood and Its Part in the Oriental Problem," *American Magazine*, CXXII (April 1937), 36–37.

"Wards of the United States: Notes on What Our Country Is Doing for Santo Domingo, Nicaragua, and Haiti," *National Geographic*, XXX (August 1916), 143–77.

Washington, Booker T. "Haiti and the United States," *Outlook*, CXI (November 17, 1915), 681.

Wellman, Walter. "The Cuban Republic Limited," *Review of Reviews*, XXII (December 1900), 708–12.

Wigdill, Walter. "Addition Without Division = Revolution," *The Independent*, LXXII (June 13, 1912), 1352–56.

Wilbur, Ray Lyman. "Statehood for Hawaii," *Atlantic Monthly,* CLXVI (October 1940), 494–97.

Williams, John Sharp. "Why Should a Man Vote the Democratic Ticket This Year?" *The Independent,* LVII (October 13, 1904), 964–67.

Williams, Talcott, "The Causes of Cuban Insurrection," *Outlook,* LXXXIV (September 15, 1906), 111–14.

———. "The Ethical and Political Principles of Expansion," *The Annals,* The American Academy of Political and Social Science, XVI (July 1900), 227–42.

Wood, Edmond. "Can Cubans Govern Cuba?" *Forum,* XXXII (September 1901), 66–73.

II. SECONDARY WORKS

Baldwin, Leland D. *Survey of American History.* New York: American Book Company, 1955. A good survey written from a philosophical point of view.

Bemis, Samuel Flagg. *A Diplomatic History of the United States.* Third Edition. New York: Holt, 1950. Excellent background material covering the relations of the United States with the insular interests, as well as with other countries.

———. *Latin American Policy of the United States: A Historical Interpretation.* New York: Harcourt Brace, 1943. A specialized study of the relations between the United States and Latin-American countries.

Blake, Nelson M. and Oscar Barck. *The United States in Its World Relations.* New York: McGraw-Hill, 1960. An excellent discussion of the United States in relation to the insular possessions and other countries.

Bowers, Claude G. *Beveridge and the Progressive Era.* New York: Houghton Mifflin, 1932. Perhaps the best work on Senator Albert J. Beveridge for insights on the ideas and character of the great supporter of imperialism.

Burgess, John W. *Recent Changes in American Constitutional Theory.* New York: Columbia University Press, 1923. Important for Burgess' opinion of his influence on many other individuals.

———. *Reconstruction and the Constitution, 1866–1876.* New

York: Scribner's, 1902. Especially good in the discussion of constitutional question of civil rights.

Burns, Edward McNall. *The American Idea of Mission*. New Jersey: Rutgers, 1957.

Clough, Shepard B. and Charles W. Cole. *Economic History of Europe*. Revised Edition. Boston: Heath, 1946. A good work on the development of mercantilism.

Faulkner, Harold U. *American Economic History*. New York: Harper, 1924. A good economic history of the United States.

Fitzgibbon, Russell H. *Cuba and the United States, 1900–1935*. Wisconsin: George Banta, Menasha Press, 1935. A good work covering the relations with Cuba to the abrogation of the Platt Amendment.

Forbes, W. Cameron. *The Philippine Islands*, Two Volumes. New York: Houghton Mifflin, 1928. Written from a very subjective point of view.

Franklin, John Hope. *From Slavery to Freedom*. New York: Knopf, 1949. A good survey of the Negro in United States history.

Hagedorn, Hermann. *Leonard Wood, A Biography*, Two Volumes. New York: Harper, 1931. A work very sympathetic to Governor Wood.

Handlin, Oscar. *Race and Nationality in American Life*. New York: Doubleday, 1957. Excellent for the discussion of race exploitation.

Hankins, Frank H. *The Racial Basis of Civilization*. New York: Knopf, 1926. Discusses the development of the concept of Anglo-Saxon superiority.

Hofstadter, Richard. *Social Darwinism in American Thought*, Revised Edition. Boston: Beacon Press, 1960. Excellent discussion of the development of the concept of the "survival of the fittest" as it was connected with racism and imperialism.

Humes, Jay D. *Oswald Garrison Villard, Liberal of the 1920's*. New York: Syracuse University Press, 1960. A good study of an anti-imperialist of the first quarter of the twentieth century.

Locmiller, David A. *Magoon in Cuba: A History of the Second Intervention, 1906–1909*. Chapel Hill: University of North Carolina Press, 1938. Very sympathetic to Charles E. Magoon.

Merk, Frederick. *Manifest Destiny and Mission in American His-*

tory: A Reinterpretation. New York: Knopf, 1963. Discusses the importance of race in the demise of "Manifest Destiny" and "Mission" in American history.

Moon, Parker T. *Imperialism and World Politics.* New York: Macmillan, 1926. Considered by many as the most definitive work on imperialism.

Senior, Clarence. *Self-Determination for Puerto Rico.* New York: Post War World Council, 1946. Discusses the problems of race and statehood for Puerto Rico.

Shepherd, George W. *Racial Influences on American Foreign Policy.* New York: Basic Books, 1971. A collection of essays by nine American scholars, many of whom have had "extensive diplomatic and foreign policy experience."

Simpson, George E. and J. Milton Yinger. *Racial and Cultural Minorities.* New York: Harper, 1958. An excellent analysis of prejudice and discrimination.

Smith, Robert F. *The United States and Cuba: Business and Diplomacy.* New York: Brookman Associates, 1960. A very good discussion of the relations of business to political control of Cuba.

Snyder, Louis L. *The Imperialism Reader.* Princeton, N.J.: D. Van Nostrand, 1962. A good collection of documents and readings on modern expansionism.

Wallbank, T. Walter and Alastair M. Taylor. *Civilization—Past and Present,* Single Volume Edition. New York: Scott Foresman, 1956. Good general history of Western civilization.

Woodward, C. Vann. *The Strange Career of Jim Crow.* New York: Oxford University Press, 1960. Good discussion on the methods used to relegate the Negro to a second-class status.

Index

Racism in U. S. Imperialism

COMPOSED IN LINOTYPE CALEDONIA BY HERITAGE PRINTERS
WITH SELECTED LINES OF DISPLAY IN PALATINO.
PRINTED LETTERPRESS BY HERITAGE PRINTERS
ON WARREN'S UNIVERSITY TEXT,
AN ACID FREE PAPER NOTED FOR ITS LONGEVITY.
THE PAPER WAS EXPRESSLY WATERMARKED
FOR THE UNIVERSITY OF SOUTH CAROLINA PRESS
WITH THE PRESS COLOPHON.
BINDING BY KINGSPORT PRESS IN
HOLLISTON'S NATURAL FINISH PAYKO
OVER .088 BOARDS.
DESIGNED BY ROBERT L. NANCE